Exposure Treatments
for Anxiety Disorders

Practical Clinical Guidebooks Series

Rosqvist   *Exposure Treatments for Anxiety Disorders:*
                A Practitioner's Guide to Concepts, Methods, and
                Evidence-Based Practice

Exposure Treatments for Anxiety Disorders

A Practitioner's Guide to Concepts, Methods, and Evidence-Based Practice

Johan Rosqvist

Routledge
Taylor & Francis Group

NEW YORK AND HOVE

Published in 2005 by
Routledge
Taylor & Francis Group
270 Madison Avenue
New York, NY 10016

Published in Great Britain by
Routledge
Taylor & Francis Group
27 Church Road
Hove, East Sussex BN3 2FA

Printed in the United States of America on acid-free paper
10 9 8 7 6 5 4 3 2 1

International Standard Book Number-10: 0-415-94846-0 (Hardcover) 0-415-94847-9 (Softcover)
International Standard Book Number-13: 978-0-415-94846-3 (Hardcover) 978-0-415-94847-0 (Softcover)
Library of Congress Card Number 2005004355

Library of Congress Cataloging-in-Publication Data

Rosqvist, Johan.
    Exposure treatments for anxiety disorders : a practitioner's guide to concepts, methods, and evidence-based practice / Johan Rosqvist.
        p. cm.
    Includes bibliographical references and index.
    ISBN 0-415-94846-0 (hardback) -- ISBN 0-415-94847-9 (pbk.)
    1. Anxiety--Treatment. 2. Behavior therapy. 3. Cognitive therapy. I. Title.

RC531.R67 2005
616.85'2206--dc22   2005004355

Taylor & Francis Group
is the Academic Division of T&F Informa plc.

Visit the Taylor & Francis Web site at
http://www.taylorandfrancis.com

and the Routledge Web site at
http://www.routledge-ny.com

In fond memory of
Christine
1947–2005

Contents

Preface

Once upon a time, there was a practitioner who discovered he had turned into a believer.

I used to think that if only a good therapeutic relationship could be established, then everything else would work itself out. After all, my original training was in object relations, and I had come to understand that "salvation" lay in healing connections. I was partially mistaken. Instead, I came to see that relationship was important, very important, but that it did not seem to be enough for many patients with whom I worked. They needed something else, something more. They needed symptom relief. Without it, they continued suffering. I came to believe that symptoms played a pivotal, if not central, role in the maintenance and worsening of psychopathology, and, as such, I came to see, incrementally at first, but then more and more, that symptoms alone are legitimate treatment targets. New lives can be built on the absence of symptoms, but not on their presence. While still attending closely to connection, I began specifically treating symptoms more and more and increasingly discovered that patients actually recovered, something I had not previously found.

I was astonished as this phenomenon repeated itself time and time again when I focused on reducing symptoms. To explore and better understand what I was creating, I began reading the literature of early learning theorists, and then that of more modern cognitive-behaviorists; it was almost like reading the journals of Galileo or Christopher Columbus. At first it seemed like such heresy, but with mounting successes following application of behavioral theories of learning and conditioning, I could no longer ignore or suppress what I was witnessing. I also began to feel much less like a heretic, enough so that I obtained formal training in behavior therapy. In this life, I now feel obliged to provide care that works, really works, because human suffering, especially when unnecessary, must be ameliorated. Thus these days I have to report I am a true convert, a believer, someone who has "seen the light," and with this practitioner's handbook, I hope to share with you, the reader, both theoretical and pragmatic aspects of what I now believe is an efficacious, prudent, ethical, and compassionate way of practice.

In the 14th century George Ockham suggested "keep it simple;" since that time this valuable principle has become known as Ockham's razor. Although exposure treatment may not in comparison appear "sexy," because there are many other, more interesting models for change, one irrefutable truth remains: exposure works! Although the principles of change in exposure are basic, its simple foundations have all but been forgotten in a heyday of more exciting, more complex theories of change. With this book, I aim to help practitioners rediscover exposure as the proven, yet straightforward, approach it remains for ameliorating much human suffering. I want practitioners to appreciate that although exposure, at first glance at least, might seem simple, it is not simplistic; in fact, in its simplicity, it is sophisticated enough that many practitioners have lost touch with how to properly wield this powerful method of change.

The development and necessity of *Exposure Treatments for Anxiety Disorders* arose from an increasing personal sense and clinical intuition that many in the field of psychology do not appreciate or fully comprehend the sheer power that exposure methods embody to produce profound change in various clinical phenomena. Over years of training graduate students, psychology and psychiatry residents, and consulting with colleagues on their own challenging cases, it became increasingly apparent that many professionals and paraprofessionals alike do not have a clear understanding of what the mechanisms of exposure methods are in alleviating anxiety disorders and general human suffering. Consequently, such methods had been applied without clearly knowing why and how, sometimes leading to less than desirable outcomes. Patients can fail to improve as the literature on exposure seems to suggest they should. Subsequently, practitioners become less confident in these established and proven methods, and may become conditioned to anticipate failure when using such approaches. Indeed, many do not recognize what they are doing "wrong," but some, fortunately, are at least aware that the treatments are "failing."

Naturally, then, it is understandable why these methods have been falling out of favor with the everyday practitioner. Given the lack of comprehension of mechanisms of change, I am not surprised that helping professionals of all sorts and experiences often shy away from exposure-based approaches. Additionally, the literature also points toward other competing and complementary methods of intervention, introducing even further confusion and doubt as to the appropriateness—and even the necessity—of exposure.

It was within this environment and context that I found myself providing increasing amounts of consultation, training, and supervision in how to properly use exposure methodologies. Slowly at first, it dawned on me that I was spending increasing amounts of time saying the same thing over and over again to a people who were struggling with patients in whom exposure methods were appropriate. Consequently, I began to make some demonstration and teaching tapes of both theory and application but found quickly that these improvised products almost took on a life of their own. I had an increasingly difficult time getting these training materials back to lend them to more practitioners seeking understanding, guidance, and direction. It was becoming clearer that a more comprehensive set of instructions was needed and warranted also a larger scale set of instructions. Hence, I began to conceive of this book, at first, not in its entirety, but of components that today, collectively, make up *Exposure Treatments for Anxiety Disorders*.

This book is meant to help graduate students and professionals alike bridge the gap between existing literature exploring and explaining anxiety disorders and that which specifically discusses exposure methods. Many students have asked me to recommend a book that covers these areas. Over the last few years, however, I have become all too familiar with the exasperated looks I get when I list principal articles and books I feel, collectively, provide the thorough background and instruction necessary to begin to do meaningful exposure-based work. This book gathers together the necessary background, instruction, and examples that will allow both the budding and seasoned practitioner to deliver this kind of treatment with confidence and knowledge of why, how, and when to use exposure. *Exposure Treatments for Anxiety Disorders* will allow practitioners to rediscover and reharness potent forces inherent in exposure.

This book is organized in seven major chapters, following a particular meaningful sequence. Chapter 1 describes anxiety in terms of both its normal phenomenon and when it becomes pathological. This first chapter serves as a foundation for the following chapters and should be considered first; practitioners and graduate students are advised to consider foundations before proceeding into the specifics of following chapters. Chapter 2 describes how exposure treatment attacks the main culprits of escape and avoidance behaviors and outlines multiple means of exposure. Its focus is on how safety behaviors of all sorts short-circuit ultimate mental health and well-being and how habituation and extinction are necessary to break insidious patterns established and maintained through negative reinforcement. Chapter 3 describes research bases for exposure treatments and offers models for conducting evidence-based practice. Its emphasis is on the role that research plays in informing, guiding, and facilitating optimal treatment outcomes, with an eye toward efficacy, effectiveness, and efficiency. Chapter 4 describes methods for assessment, diagnosis, case conceptualization, treatment planning, and a variety of case illustrations that my colleagues and I have personally treated using exposure methods. Although this is not a case book, *Exposure Treatments for Anxiety Disorders* offers a range of interesting and complex cases to highlight exposure's potential for success when used properly. Chapter 5 addresses many common treatment obstacles (many are not unique or exclusive) to exposure treatment and suggests solutions for managing such obstacles in ways to make treatment successful. Chapter 6 focuses on end-of-treatment considerations, from relapse prevention and booster sessions to generalization training and a mentoring program that appears especially successful in helping "graduates" of exposure therapy sustain their treatment gains. Chapter 7 closes the book by providing professional considerations for how to improve exposure's unfortunate reputation and how to generally promote dissemination of science-based treatment protocols because of their potential positive impact on human suffering. Still, if practitioners do not adopt these established methods, patients worldwide continue suffering, which seems personally, professionally, and morally unacceptable, if not repugnant.

I believe practitioners must take a chance. They must rediscover for themselves what works and what works optimally. To do so, they must play with a product that has been around for a while but that has been all but abandoned. This *rapprochement* must happen. I believe this with every ounce of my energy and soul. If this book is not enough to inspire such an exploration, I will borrow a quote from H. Jackson Browne, who once said, "Don't be afraid to go out on a limb. That's where the fruit is"—suggesting to me that much stands to be gained from taking a chance and trying out exposure treatment again when treating anxiety disorders. Not only will patients gain, but professional integrity and strength will be restored to the practice of clinical and counseling psychology. Patients and practitioners alike deserve this fruit.

Acknowledgments

Whether directly or indirectly, I am greatly indebted to many people who have made writing *Exposure Treatments for Anxiety Disorders* possible; behind it stands a substantial supporting cast. Foremost, this book would not have been plausible if it was not for countless patients who have put faith and trust in methods with which I have proposed to treat them. They have also believed in me enough to be willing to face their fears in numerous, sometimes initially unnerving, but systematic ways. In their great, commendable efforts to master what has troubled them so, they have allowed me naturally occurring moments to see, firsthand, just how these scientifically based methods work. Changes realized with evidence-based treatments are frequently astounding, if not outright profound. After finishing treatment, patients are often complimentary, using such flattering descriptors as "good guy," or such embarrassing terms as "miracle." In their significant improvements they have attributed, mostly erroneously, some part of their positive change to me *personally*. Although not denying the central importance and significant contribution of the (empirical) therapeutic relationship on optimal outcome (e.g., Ackerman & Hilsenroth, 2003; Horvath & Symonds, 1991; Norcross, 2002; Raue, Goldfried, & Barkham, 1997), I need to report that the treatment provider could have been—and can be—anyone. Indeed, there is nothing "special" or magical about me individually per se. The only aspect that perhaps makes me especially adept at this privileged work is my thorough understanding of the mechanisms of anxiety disorders and how, specifically, exposure-based treatments affect such conditions directly. However, such knowledge is nothing I solely possess, but is instead something that I can, and continuously do, share with anyone who wishes to effectively alleviate human suffering through evidence-based practice.

I am especially grateful to some of my former patients who have graciously agreed to contribute to this book by describing what exactly it is like to undergo an empirically supported treatment program. The importance and central value of this contribution cannot be underscored enough, because this is such a common question from many graduate students and therapists who are learning how to use these methods. Indeed, how empirically supported and manual-based treatments are received and experienced by patients has been the topic of ongoing, passionate debate. Unfortunately, cognitive-behavior therapy and behavior therapy methodology often have been described as cold and inhumane, calculating and irrelevant, and impersonal. I believe readers of *Exposure Treatments for Anxiety Disorders* will instead discover from patients' own accounts and descriptions, and from ample case illustrations provided, that the truth is that approaches described within are instead filled with compassion and empathy, thoughtful individual assistance, and the most ethical and prudent care for patients.

I also owe a great deal to my former and present mentors and supervisors, without whom I am not sure I would be where I am today. In their own ways, they have inspired me in important directions. For example, they encouraged greater capacity for critical thinking and provided time and space for thorough explorations of the literature about anxiety and its treatments. They also provided invaluable support and superb supervision and consultation about the clinical services I was delivering to patients, primarily guiding me toward healthy skepticism and collaborative empiricism.

In short, many have contributed to the scientist I have become. B. Steven Willis, PhD, trained me and supervised me in delivering exposure and response prevention treatment in naturalistic settings to treatment-refractory obsessive-compulsive disorder patients. His easygoing, matter-of-fact style about the theoretical underpinnings of exposure and response prevention treatment allowed me to combine theory and research firsthand into practice principles, effectively bridging the gap between science and art. In the area of obsessive-compulsive disorder, Lee Baer, PhD, William E. Minichiello, PhD, and Michael A. Jenike, MD, were all instrumental mentors and supervisors. Gail Steketee, PhD, and Sabine Wilhelm, PhD, eloquently taught me how to integrate newer cognitive therapy techniques into the treatment of obsessive-compulsive disorder, compulsive hoarding, and body dysmorphic disorder. Michel Hersen, PhD, ABPP, encouraged me to work in greater depth with anxiety disorders; in his infinite wisdom and professional insights, he has also continually persuaded me to conduct research, write, teach, consult, and supervise on the topic of anxiety treatment.

More recently, others have been greatly influential: William J. Koch, PhD, ABPP, in the treatment of posttraumatic stress disorder, generalized anxiety disorder, and hypochondriasis (health anxiety); Maureen Whittal, PhD, for specific phobias, panic disorder and agoraphobia, and bipolar depression; Lynn Alden, PhD, for social anxiety disorder and body dysmorphic disorder; Randy Paterson, PhD, and Dave Erickson, PhD, for unipolar depression, and using assertiveness and relaxation training in a host of anxiety conditions; Peter McClean, PhD, for fostering in me a greater desire for disseminating knowledge about—and teaching—empirically supported treatments; Ricks Warren, PhD, ABPP, and Robin Shallcross, PhD, ABPP, for providing outstanding, if not exceptional, postdoctoral supervision and excellent guidance around licensing and navigating managed care; and Jay C. Thomas, PhD, ABPP, for research and mentoring support. I owe a very special debt of gratitude to Linda Porzelius, PhD, for being instrumental in allowing me entry into advanced graduate training and orienting me in treating eating disorders. I am also grateful to Sandra Bates, PhD, for providing information about how exposure treatment is conducted in Scandinavia and Europe and for providing case examples for this book, and Deborah Wise, PhD, for consulting on posttraumatic stress disorder and also providing a case illustration for this book.

Surely, there are many people I have (unintentionally) left off this list who nonetheless have influenced me professionally, but because most phenomena are multidetermined, I could never give adequate justification for why and how I have come to assess, conceptualize, and treat anxiety disorders the way I do. Let it suffice to say that I am indebted to many for what I professionally do today. In not unimportant ways, even Professor Gallagher (see chapter 7) has been influential.

I am grateful beyond explanation to my wife, Julie, for her apparently endless forgiving and understanding nature. There were literally and figuratively too many nights, weekends, and "vacations" when I would somehow stew over this book. The "after this" has yet to arrive. Truly, she is my *sine qua non*, and without her this book simply could not be. Above all else, she has given us our children, Aleks, Katrine, Anneli, and Anwen. They are both my *joie de vivre* and *raison d'etre*! What else needs to be said?

Leif and GunMarie, my parents, I wish to thank in the language that is closest to my heart. Ett särskilt tack vill jag framföra till er båda två, eftersom utan er skulle inget av detta hela (inte bara denna bok) ha kunnat bli verklighet. Ni är min första inspiration i livet. Ni har båda visat mig en viss inställning till livet och människorna som gett mig en förväntan om att finna det goda i människor och situationer. Ni har fått mig att tänka djupt på vad det är som driver människor till de situationer de befinner sig i. "Tänkaren" brukade ni kalla mig. Den stilen har, som ni vet, följt mig genom livet, och den har inte bara hjälpt mig själv utan hjälper numera också de patienter jag behandlar och de doktorander jag undervisar och handleder. Genom er inspiration hjälper ni många fler människor än ni antagligen anar. Jag har aldrig kunnat visa er riktigt vilken förmån det har varit och forfarande är att vara er "första elev." Jag är mycket tacksam för den undervisning ni givit mig, och hoppas att dessa få ord kan ge er en uppfattning om vilken sorts far och mor jag känner ni har varit för mig. Den tacksamhet jag känner mot er båda är gränslös.

Finally, I wish to thank Routledge/Taylor & Francis Group for their recognition and appreciation of the inherent contribution that *Exposure Treatments for Anxiety Disorders* will make in educating graduate students, the theoretical and clinical guidance it will give to practitioners, and the many points of considerations provided for researchers and academicians. Further, it is my hope that it can also serve as a point of interaction between practitioners and an increasingly complex and demanding healthcare industry. A special thanks to Dana Bliss, who was exceptionally helpful during the entire publication process.

Johan Rosqvist

CHAPTER 1

The Anxiety Phenomenon: Nature and Disorder

Therefore, do not be anxious about tomorrow,
for tomorrow will be anxious for itself.
Let the day's own trouble be sufficient for the day.
—Matthew 6:24

DESCRIPTION OF ANXIETY AS A NORMAL PHENOMENON AND IN ANXIETY DISORDERS

Anxiety is a normal and naturally occurring universal phenomenon that plays an ongoing role in people's daily life. In foundation, it is a primitive biophysiological process meant to protect the person experiencing it during times of danger through preparing and priming the person to act in self-preserving ways. Indeed, in the face of threat, this biophysiological process *should* activate to increase pure odds of physical survival. This process works in a predictable fashion, and has, over evolution, served to protect species of all sorts, including people. In fact, people have successfully survived to procreate and have consequently furthered the human species in the face of much ecological adversity *because* of their capacity to react with anxiety. In this vein, anxiety is good and normal (e.g., Darwin, 1872/1965; Skinner, 1963).

Anxiety, in short, is adaptive in that it holds great survival value. In times of danger, anxiety can be a person's "best friend." Yet, few people who experience anxiety in modern times proclaim much fondness for the response. Anxiety, for all its greatness and utility, can be perceived and experienced as physically and emotionally quite uncomfortable and disturbing. Some people are even frightened by anxiety, especially when they do not understand what it is and why it occurs. In this sense, people might become anxious about anxiety or fearful of fear (e.g., Barlow & Craske, 2000; Craske & Barlow, 2000; Craske, Barlow, & Meadows, 2000; Otto, Jones, Craske, & Barlow, 1996; Otto, Pollack, & Barlow, 1995). Just how frightened or uncomfortable a person feels when experiencing anxiety is directly related to the presence and immediacy of threat; the closer in proximity, both in space and time, threat is, the less uncomfortable the anxiety will seem, because it then makes common sense and has an obvious source and inherent value (Barlow, 2002; Craske, 1999; McLean & Woody, 2001). When threat is further away, however, or is perhaps even theoretical or abstract, experienced discomforts are more negatively viewed as the anxiety response, which is then less useful in the immediate moment. Under such conditions, it just feels bad. Unfortunately, people are not terribly accurate about what constitutes threat or danger; in fact, so long as the person perceives or believes there to be danger (i.e., whether real, imagined, or misconstrued), his or her body will predictably react as if it is genuinely being threatened, and begins activating the self-preserving survival mode. The brain is in essence a loyal listener, but may not necessarily be an accurate judge of what is real and what is not real.

Most people experience an anxiety reaction, or the activation response, in presence of true threat. This action should work this way and is highly desirable. For instance, if a person crossing a street glances over and sees a car heading straight toward him or her, giving no signs of slowing down, there is a perceived danger of being hit by the car if some action is not taken to avoid being hit. The anxiety response then, almost instantaneously, kicks in, reacting to the estimated threat of potentially being killed or being seriously injured or maimed if he or she does not get out of the way.

This reaction of anxiety to the presence of true threat constitutes a normal type of one-way reasoning and reactivity that all people have the capacity for. Again, for purposes of survival, this is a desirable and preferred way of responding. Most people who have jumped out of the way of oncoming cars, and the like, are indeed probably thankful and happy this capacity exists. Although the circumstance could have been experienced as frightening—as almost being hit by a car can be—the activating response is probably not viewed negatively, and the person who survived the experience typically reasons he or she responded as he or she should have. Given the situation, that person responded as needed (with anxiety and fear) and survived it. Fanselow (1984) suggested that fear is a motivational system that organizes an organism's response at many different levels (e.g., overt behavior, autonomic functioning) so that the response is coordinated toward the function of protecting against environmental threats—more precisely, predation. This coordination restricts responses to a behavioral response set consistent with an evolutionary history of thwarting predation; in lab rats, for example, the dominant response is freezing, usually next to a wall, in a corner, or in a darkened area, because doing so optimizes antidetection properties of freezing. When it freezes, the lab rat exhibits a number of interesting and useful responses; for instance, its heart-rate decelerates and its breathing becomes shallow and rapid, helping it to become less perceptible to the eye and perhaps contributing to a decreased likelihood of the animal being over-looked by a visually scanning predator. Freezing is also associated with increased attention and decreased reaction times, allowing prey to become increasingly vigilant and ready to spring into action (i.e., flight or fight). Additionally, the lab rat becomes analgesic, activating the endogenous opioid system; this response reduces recuperative behavior (e.g., wound licking), because it would disrupt responses needed for immediate survival. Putting all of these normal, natural responses together increases sheer odds of survival, and are controlled by a system chiefly concerned with protecting the organism from predation. At times of threat, this system should "fire."

Although this one-way (i.e., in the presence of danger, react with anxiety) reasoning is normal, Arntz, Rauner, and Van den Hout (1995) eloquently described a second type of reasoning—bidirectional reasoning—that leads to undesirable, abnormal anxiety reactions. They reported that ex-consequentia (read as bidirectional or emotional) reasoning makes the person reason in a backward fashion. As with other people, those who suffer with anxiety disorders also respond with anxiety to truly dangerous situations, such as almost being run over by a car. That kind of response is still advantageous. On the other hand, anxiety-disordered people often also reason in this other, unique way. That is, when they *feel* anxious, they emotionally reason, or infer, there must be danger. After all, as most people recognize, anxiety should occur within the context or situation of threat and danger. So, when the anxiety-disordered person feels anxious, he or she understands or interprets that it *signals* the presence of such negative contexts, and, not surprisingly, the person responds as if in such situations. In essence, the person sometimes emotionally responds with anxiety when there is no car coming, and he or she may indeed respond like this to a variety of circumstances devoid of actual threat, or may represent benign or imagined (misperceived) dangers. These people are reacting in this bidirectional way because it *feels* like there should be danger around. Ironically, if the body and brain cannot tell the difference between actual, benign, and imagined, then it will respond to them equally.

Arntz et al. (1995) argued that ex-consequentia, or emotional reason-ing, plays a central role in the development and maintenance of patho-logical anxiety and fear. They reported that when patients are questioned about the specific danger in specific situations, the patient might very well present the argument that the experienced anxiety and fear is sufficient "proof" that there must be danger. They cite Beck and Emery (1985) as describing this type of emotional reasoning when suggesting patients use their feelings to validate their thoughts and that such behavior starts the vicious, self-sustaining circle of reasoning that there must be something to fear if one feels anxious. Collectively, this reasoning anomaly portrays itself in the following fashion: "If there is danger, I feel anxious" implies or infers "if I feel anxious, there must be danger." In their description of this bidirectional reasoning phenomenon, Arntz et al. hinted at a particularly compelling example of how to illustrate the fallacious nature of this way of reasoning, namely the "cow example." I have adapted this example and incorporated it as a standard story/metaphor for explaining emotional reasoning in a fashion to enhance information processing and integration. Otto (2000) suggested that the use of stories and metaphors in cognitive-behavioral therapy (CBT) provides a method for transforming therapeutic information, sometimes quite technical and dry therapeutic information, into a more palatable and easily understandable format. Such a modified format makes it much easier for patients to readily remember the information and apply it in real-life situations. Most patients I have treated tell me that there is no way to forget the cow illustration and find that it helps them notice "cow moments" when they are happening in their daily life. This is of central value, because emotional reasoning appears to be otherwise largely responsible for maintaining abnormal anxiety and fear. The metaphor/story, as I tell it in my own work with anxiety disordered patients, follows.

> People are interesting creatures, in that we are very adept at surviving. I have spent a fair amount of time investigating just how people "survive," and what I have found is that *how* we reason is quite influential in how people decide what is dangerous and not. After all, to survive we have to escape from or avoid danger altogether. As it turns out, as you well know, life has its dangers, so reasoning plays an important role in how well we do or fare in life. Unfortunately, in the reasoning department, there are some ways in which we tend to get ourselves into more trouble than is good for us. That is, sometimes when we reason that there is danger or threat, there really isn't, or we grossly overestimate just how dangerous some situation or circumstance really is, and as a result we feel anxious or at least quite uncomfortable when we really don't have to be. In the absence of such real situations, anxiety doesn't seem to help much, and if anything it tends to make life pretty miserable.
>
> Because you are sitting here with me today, I imagine you might also have some difficulties with feeling anxious a lot of the time, even when there isn't a directly discernible threat around; is that right? [Patient typically responds in the affirmative because he or she is seeking help for

some anxiety condition.] OK, well, anxiety is an interesting phenomenon, in that it is supposed to prepare us to act in the presence of some bad situation; that is, it typically prepares us to run like the wind or fight like a mad person when we are faced with some real danger. That way, we have a better chance of surviving. It isn't really *that* fancy, but it works like a charm when the chips are down. By surviving, we live to tell the tale another day, too, and, ultimately, to pass on our genes. Survival, then, is the actual goal of anxiety. People have in essence survived because we have the capacity to respond with anxiety. So, how does this reasoning business come into it all then? Well, it turns out that in the presence of threat and danger we all respond with anxiety, as it should be, so we can run away from—or avoid—the dangerous circumstance. So, imagine that danger triggers anxiety [I typically will draw on a whiteboard the relationship DANGER → ANXIETY]. Again, it should work like this, and it is good for survival in that anxiety will help you run or fight. The problem is this: many people who struggle with anxiety tend to reason the other way, too. That is, if they feel anxious, they reason there must be something to be feared around. [I typically draw the relationship DANGER ← ANXIETY.] Fortunately, danger isn't lurking around most corners these days, so a lot of the distress experienced, unfortunately, is really unnecessary. After all, who really *wants* to feel anxious when it isn't necessary? It feels bad! Make sense so far? Understand? [Here I am eliciting whether the patient has followed me to this point because I am about to launch into the metaphor (cow) part.]

OK, well, let's talk about something quite different for a little bit, but I think you'll find it really isn't so different after all. Let's talk about cows. [Here it is normal and expected that the patient initially looks puzzled, and if he or she looks too perturbed I usually ask him or her to bear with me.] Cows, unless something dramatic or strange has happened to them, have four legs, correct? [Patient usually agrees, even if puzzled by the line of discussion.] Well, let's look at a particular relationship then. If you have a cow, you have four legs, right? [Again, patient will commonly agree, and I draw the relationship COWS → FOUR LEGS.] Kind of like if you have danger, you have anxiety [pointing to the relationship DANGER → ANXIETY]. Well, let me then ask you the million dollar question. [Pause, to make the patient focus and expect that something important is coming.] If you have four legs, do you always have a cow? [Here I pause again for important effect, and allowing time for the patient to begin to form a beginning, naturally occurring insight ("ah-ha" moment) into the problematic relationship.] What else could you have if you had four legs? [Pause; patient might contribute something.] How about a horse? How about a dog? A cat? A table? A chair? How about anything which has four legs? [Pause.]

So, is it really true then, that when you have four legs you always have cow? [I typically draw COWS ← FOUR LEGS.] Why do four legs have to be a cow? [Pause.] I'll tell you why. It's because it *feels* like a cow. Four legs feel like a cow, much like anxiety feels like there's danger. If something feels bad, it unfortunately often becomes, or is reified into being bad, whether that's true or not, unless you question it. [Here I am making sure to illustrate the problematic connection between feelings and feelings that reify situations into being "true."] So, the next time you feel anxious, ask yourself "where's the cow?" to begin to question whether you might be engaging in emotional reasoning, or reasoning with how it feels. If that turns out to be true about what you are doing, then you might be feeling anxious when it's really not needed. After all, if you look around and can't see a cow, why should you behave like you're about to run for your life?

A vast majority of patients report, during follow-up assessments and interviews, that the multitude of stories and metaphors I use in my work with them stick. Some of them even go so far as to create metaphorical reminders for themselves to highlight the main themes discovered and lessons learned during treatment (e.g., some former patients have reported carrying around a picture of a cow [or cows] on a 3 × 5 note card as a consistent reminder that they may be prone to emotional reasoning and its effects if they stop paying attention to such processes).

It is quite understandable why anxiety-disordered people and people in general really feel so bad much of the time if they do not regularly question what they feel or believe. Emotion theorists have long portrayed certain basic emotions as adaptive response sets meant to protect against danger (e.g., Ekman, 1992, 1994; Izard, 1992; Panksepp, 1992). Without questioning them, these emotions and beliefs might as well be true, or absolute, because the person will most likely act on them *as if* they were true if he or she does not consider their veracity. When a person acts on something as if that situation is true, it by default becomes "reality."

Indeed, some emotion theorists (e.g., Russell, 1980; Russell & Mehrabian, 1977) have found combinations of emotions that, as a conglomerate, look in action and effect much like the two most common byproducts of anxiety and fear, namely withdrawal (i.e., escape) and avoidance. Specifically, they consider combinations of activation (arousal), pleasure (valence), and dominance (control) in portraying a system for how to formulate what happens in anxiety and fear experiences. Fear, according to their system, would be demonstrative of a combination of high arousal, low enjoyment, and low control; combined, because of the aversive nature of the combination, these often produce the behaviors of escape and avoidance. Again, people generally do not like feeling bad and generally act to reduce negative states.

Mowrer (1939, 1960) suggested, in his two-factor theory of fear acquisition and maintenance, that the autonomic response reactivity must be regulated to reduce escape and avoidance behaviors to a meaningful degree.

So long as situations feel bad, whether true or not, such problematic behaviors will continue. *Therefore, autonomic arousal and reactivity must be reduced to eliminate anxiety and fear to a meaningful degree and to improve overall individual functioning.* A more complete discussion of the role of negative reinforcement in the acquisition and maintenance of anxiety reactions and fear responses will follow. Nonetheless, escape and avoidance behaviors, including safety behaviors and reliance on safety signals, are central contributors to the maintenance of anxiety and fear (Craske et al., 2000).

Although most people who experience anxiety to any great extent can clearly say that something is (obviously) happening within their bodies, few can adequately explain the phenomenon or know exactly what does happen when they are exposed to a perceived or actual threat. A general lack of knowledge about processes of anxiety often contributes to irrational, fear-based reasoning about meaning of symptoms. Appreciating the predominantly fallacious nature of anxiety and the misconception that it occurs in the presence of danger (only) readily affords the practitioner insight into how easily people can give meaning to their symptoms that simply cannot be supported by facts.

In working to normalize the experience of anxiety with patients, it is often useful to provide detailed scientific explanations about the biophysiological processes involved. It is often the component bit within *biopsychosocial* formulations that patients know least about, and struggle most with understanding because it involves biology, neurology, and other highly complex chemistry issues typically outside many laypersons' educational backgrounds. Lacking such detailed knowledge and insight leaves many patients reporting that they fear the symptoms they are experiencing are demonstrative of being "crazy" or are precursors to going insane. Many are quite relieved to hear this is a common fear, but then also often go on to have questions about what exactly their bodies are doing and why they are doing it, if the experience is not indicative of impending major mental health problems. Depending on the sophistication of the patient, information can be tailored both for amount and depth. As a basic orientation, patients benefit universally from knowing that the response sets are adaptive, in that anxiety allows people to learn more quickly and perform better motorically and intellectually in preparing to meet challenge and adversity (Barlow, 1991a, 1991b).

When a more complex explanation is required, it is often most useful to explain what survival value each symptom experienced holds, and how that symptom is created, much like what is commonly done in the psycho-educational component of panic control treatment (e.g., Barlow & Craske, 2000; Barlow, Craske, Cerny, & Klosko, 1989). It is commonly most helpful and easier (more tolerable) for patients to start such a discussion by focusing on several specific symptoms more commonly experienced during anxiety. For instance, because an increased heart rate commonly occurs during stress and adversity, it makes a good starting point. It is important to explain that a pounding heart is related to a quickening heart rate, which allows the heart to pump blood more quickly to the major muscle groups engaged when one is running or fighting. More blood is needed for those high-demand activities, so the heart has to work harder to support such behaviors. If the heart rate goes up, the respiration rate likely follows in increasing quickness, often producing rapid, shallow (panting) breathing. This allows for more oxygen in the blood. This is important because many "fuels" are transported on oxygen molecules. Indeed, more fuels are typically required for running "like the wind" or fighting "like a mad person," so the liver dumps increasing amounts of glucose into the bloodstream for transport to major muscle groups. Because the major muscles need more fuel, the blood vessels in such groups expand, whereas blood vessels in extremities contract. Shunting blood away from extremities also serves the purpose of preventing excessive bleeding from points of contact initially most likely to face danger (i.e., hands, arms, feet, legs, and skin surfaces). Not only is blood drawn away from extremities and the skin, but also away from digestion (i.e., it does not serve an immediate survival value). Essentially, lots of responses occur that prepare a person to be best able to fight off an attack (become aggressive) or run away from such a threat.

For some patients who become more interested in the fine workings of these kinds of responses, a few additional, biochemical responses might also be described and discussed as to their specific survival values. For example, cortisone is described as being released from the adrenal glands to help inhibit allergic reactions during danger. Thyroid hormones are released to speed up metabolism, which is necessary for using blood sugar and other fuels most efficiently. Endorphins are released to help mask pain perception. Endorphins also produce a mild euphoric state, thought to instill extra hope and expectancy of enduring the situation. Cholesterol released from the liver helps keep up energy levels, and the blood's clotting capacity increases. Collectively, all of these autonomically driven responses collaborate to increase survival chances, through broadly and primarily supporting running away or fighting. At the conclusion of this kind of discussion, it is important to point out that most modern problems are not best solved through these kinds of responses anymore, even though these reactions are normal. These kinds of sympathetic nervous system behaviors are simply less relevant today, but continue because of eons of genetic transmission (Barlow, 2002; Borkovec, 1994; Paterson, 1997b).

In modern times, then, these bodily (biophysiological/emotional) reactions may no longer be the most adaptive response. When being threatened with foreseeable and immediate danger to life and limb by, for example, lions, tigers, and bears, then it is certainly still most advantageous to respond the way our ancestors did. On the other hand, in the current-day experience of everyday modern life, there are few wild predators roaming freely where people live, thereby making this kind of primitive "fight or flight" response unnecessary most of the time. Of course, in modern times more realistic, modern threats such as muggings and other physical violence may indeed still make this basic anxiety useful. Nonetheless, this is not true for most people most of the time. For modern threats (e.g., project deadlines, interpersonal disagreements, commuting) critical, creative, and meaningful thinking represents a significantly more useful response set. Such a response set is virtually required for the type of human functioning central to effective problem-solving, strategic planning, and, ultimately, modern-day survival.

Tryon (e.g., 1999, 2000, 2002, 2005) presented compelling arguments for integrating a novel and innovative learning and memory model for understanding exposure therapy, and using such a neural network model to provide both descriptions and predictions to patients about how and why exposure therapy works. Anecdotally, at least, it appears easier for patients to engage treatment when they can understand the process of change, and how to best support an optimal outcome. See chapter 2 for an explanation of parallel distributed connectionist neural network (Tryon, 2005) models.

CLINICAL IMPLICATIONS AND PICTURE OF ANXIETY DISORDERS

Anxiety is not simply about being too anxious but is instead more critically about the exhaustive ways in which people are affected by their unfortunate conditions. There are few, if any, aspects of a person's life (e.g., intrapersonal, interpersonal, social, occupational, moral) that remain spared from genuine impairment when someone is touched by an anxiety disorder. There is an incredulous amount of suffering associated with anxiety disorders, which is profoundly ironic when one considers that in theory anxiety is supposed to be helpful (which it is when people really need it). Because people typically no longer benefit greatly from anxiety reactions in modern circumstances, such continued responses do many people a great disservice. Yet, anxiety disorders are highly prevalent, and often take chronic and devastating courses when left untreated or undertreated (e.g., Maj, Akiskal, Lopez-Ibor, & Okasha, 2004).

Greenberg et al. (1999) reported an annual cost in the United States (alone!) of anxiety disorders as being approximately $42.3 *billion*. This is just the financial burden, although this financial cost is composed of many variables (e.g., direct mental health treatment [psychotherapy or psychopharmacology], lost productivity at and absenteeism from work, excessive utilization of primary care services). Beyond the basic economic impact, many people suffering with common anxiety disorders also have a difficult time sustaining employment, becoming married and staying married, and they experience inflated risk for suicide. Even by the worst pessimistic estimates of impact, the clinical picture is all but dismal.

Barlow (2002) reported that in recent years, anxiety disorders have accounted for approximately 31% of total mental health care expenditures. This stunning proportion is followed in costs by mood disorders (e.g., depression), which account for 22%. Comorbidity suggests that it is highly likely that a patient who presents with anxiety will also meet sufficient criteria for depression, and commonly also a second anxiety disorder. Depressed patients are also likely to experience anxiety, so whichever way the statistics are twisted and turned, anxiety shows up as a culprit responsible for enormous human suffering and its various, deleterious effects. Depending on which anxiety condition is considered, the Epidemiologic Catchment Area (Swendsen et al., 1998) study estimated the prevalence of *recognized* anxiety disorders as ranging from approximately 2% to 13% (1-year prevalence estimate). When considering the staggering numbers such percentages produce, it becomes additionally important to note that this large study never considered subclinical, but still otherwise problematic, anxiety. Taken together, this suggests anxiety is a much larger problem than can perhaps be truly understood or appreciated.

In trying to impress on graduate students the importance of learning how to treat anxiety disorders well, because such conditions will represent a disproportionately large segment of patient care in any setting they might later find themselves in, some students are occasionally skeptical about the real impact anxiety can have. Indeed, without proper perspective, it can be hard to fathom just how disabling clinical anxiety can be. Nonetheless, it would indeed be an error to make light of the effects clinical anxiety can have on people's lives. In training graduate students to deliver empirically supported treatments for such anxiety disorders, they also often question what it must be like, from the patient's perspective, to undergo some of the more challenging aspects of a complete CBT package, such as exposure.

During years of teaching, training, and supervising students and professionals in these methods, I have found that case materials help immensely to illustrate the impact that anxiety disorders typically impose, and they lend sometimes unusual insight into what it might be like to undergo directive treatment approaches and techniques. Fortunately, most anxiety disorders are now readily treatable, and many patients who undergo CBT often experience meaningful changes in both symptoms and in life functioning (e.g., Hersen & Biaggio, 2000). Often, people are so excited about the change that they wonder if there is some way to "give back" for the gift of freedom they have received. Some patients have spoken to mass media sources (e.g., radio, newspapers), whereas others have visited clinical and counseling psychology classroom settings. What many of them are hoping to accomplish through such public "airing of former laundry" is that someone suffering with the same or similar conditions will come to know that there are very good, tolerable treatments available. Additionally, when speaking to future practitioners, they often hope to inspire them to learn how to deliver strong, proven effective methods. Many patients have suffered for years or decades and have often tried many ineffective means of treatment, when protracted suffering really has not been necessary.

What follows next is a firsthand account by a former patient, whom I will call "Catherine." Catherine was a 27-year-old, never married Caucasian female who lived alone at the time of referral. She was referred to me after unsuccessfully undergoing a cognitive therapy (CT) trial for significant obsessive-compulsive disorder (OCD), which in her case was hallmarked by intrusive, ego-dystonic homosexual (lesbian) and pedophilic thoughts and significant avoidance of women and children. Before the CT trial, she had not sought psychotherapy previously because she had only been accurately diagnosed with OCD a few years prior. To a large degree, her condition went grossly misdiagnosed because of Catherine's inability to speak openly with health care providers about her disturbing thoughts, let alone the nature of them. In having her share her story here, I hope readers will come to see two principal things. First, I think the readers will come to connect with the horrific impact anxiety had on her, to see just how disabling her fear was, and what it must have been like to live in the personal hell she shortly will describe. Her story may sound astonishing to the naive reader, but her case is actually not unusual for OCD (see similar themes described by Sandra Bates, PhD, in chapter 4). Second, and perhaps more important, without meaning to intentionally detract from her personal experience and challenges, I hope readers will recognize just how treatable her condition was. If it seems like a challenge to conceive of treating a case like this one because of the (sexual) nature of Catherine's obsessions, it is more a reflection of practitioners' personal comfort levels and not the treatability of the case per se. As practitioners, we all have to acknowledge and expand our own comfort zones to fully help others. In chapter 4, readers can also find case illustrations of other, more stereotypically recognizable forms of OCD. When reading her case, it might be useful for readers to try to put themselves into Catherine's experience, to try to get a flavor first for what life must have been like before treatment, whether going through exposure-based treatment for these specific symptoms might have brought up any discomforts and how they might have been coped with, and what her life sounds like for the present and future.

I've had an anxious and somewhat obsessive disposition as far back as I remember, though I managed it fairly well until the age of 17. The clearly defined routine of childhood and my early teenage years gave me stability, but I worried a lot about things closely related to my daily life, usually about people liking me, or my appearance. There was always something to mull over in my mind, and it would keep me awake at night.

When I left school and moved to college at 16, things changed dramatically. My sister moved to university, a close friendship ended badly, and due to age and injuries, I stopped doing gymnastics. My life as I had known it for many years came to an end and so did my coping strategies. My confidence dropped and I was sad and lonely. Then, 4 months after I started college, my OCD started. It was dramatic and intense from the beginning. I remember the exact day it started (January 31, 1992) as the end of a life that included love and happiness, and as the entry into a world of fear, guilt, depression, and anxiety, all to an extent I had never known before or thought possible.

It began with nonstop thoughts of sex, lesbians mainly, and sometimes violence and an overwhelming fear that I might do some of the things that were in my head. Questions ran through my mind such as, "How do I know I'm not a lesbian?" My world and my beliefs about myself were tipped upside down. I had been attracted to boys from an early age and had never questioned my sexuality before. Everywhere I looked there would be fuel for my obsession. Sitting next to a woman, hugging a friend, or looking at pictures of women in magazines all caused my anxiety to worsen, which my mind interpreted as "proof" that I was a lesbian. Going swimming or getting changed with other females became a nightmare. Thoughts and images occupied my mind constantly. I had trouble concentrating, I didn't want to be alone, I had stomach problems, and my periods stopped. I began drinking heavily and started relationships with boys I didn't want. I felt numb most of the time and cried a lot. I felt selfish for being so miserable when nothing bad had actually happened. I just had these thoughts.

I thought things couldn't get any worse. Then I began to have the same vivid images and detailed thoughts about sex with children. The questions found a new topic, "How do I know I'm not a pedophile?" I was devastated. I had always loved being with children and had a job supervising children at a local leisure center. How could I even have these horrendous, repulsive thoughts? "I must be an awful person. Good people don't have these thoughts." I could find no way to stop the thoughts snowballing through my mind. I thought about death a lot and how I could kill myself. I thought I was going mad and if I saw a policeman, I'd imagine he was going to arrest me. I avoided situations that provoked the most anxiety, tried to distract myself and push the thoughts away, and I would repeat a word in my head over and over (breathe, breathe, breathe) when I felt particularly anxious.

For years, before accurate diagnosis and treatment, OCD ruled my life. I fluctuated between severe anxiety, caused in part by forcing myself to ignore my symptoms and carry on as normally as possible, and the inevitable depression that came with acknowledging my disturbing thoughts and feelings and knowing I could do nothing to curb them. Putting on a mask of happiness in front of people was exhausting. It took its toll on my body and I developed irritable bowel syndrome. I lost all sense of myself and what I wanted in life and couldn't face making decisions about a future I thought would be filled with the same horrible thoughts and feelings. I felt I wouldn't be able to get married or have children, something I'd always wanted. I stopped spending time with children where possible, but occasionally threw myself into a situation I feared to prove to myself that I wouldn't do any of the awful things that were in my mind. Of course, I never did, but my mind was unkind and would always raise a new question, "Just because I didn't that time, does that mean I never will?" In short, my life was devoid of any pleasant feelings, including love. And without love, there is no life.

There were brief periods of intense happiness and even calmness, which carried me through, but they were short-lived and my OCD would worsen again; the worst bouts were usually triggered by key events, like important exams, moving, or a relationship ending.

My OCD wasn't straightforward, which may partly explain why I went so long without a diagnosis. I had no easily recognizable compulsive behaviors, such as checking, counting, or cleaning. Instead, my compulsions involved more subtle mental rituals. I was also extremely afraid to tell doctors or counselors about the exact nature of my thoughts, as I felt they were so awful I might be considered a danger to others. This also made it difficult to diagnose. I did try to find out what was wrong with me, though. I read books, saw doctors, counselors, and psychiatrists, and tried alternative therapies such as hypnotherapy. I was offered medication but didn't want it as I felt that it was only masking the symptoms, which, of course, without a proper diagnosis, it was. However, in my early 20s, I learned about biological dispositions to depression and as things were so bad, I decided I needed medications. It helped to stabilize me and made it easier to sleep.

It was in February 2001, 9 years after my OCD began, that I was correctly diagnosed. I'd been seeing a psychiatrist for a year who had suggested abuse in my own childhood and possible lesbian tendencies as a cause, and who couldn't understand why I wasn't getting better. This only made me feel worse. He referred me to a psychiatrist at a local university for a consultation. Within 20 minutes, he diagnosed OCD and told me about CBT. I was skeptical, but willing to try anything.

I went to a bookshop and for the first time, found myself in a book, *Tormenting Thoughts and Secret Rituals* by Ian Osborne, which was specifically about OCD. It detailed cases of people with similar sexual obsessions. I cried as I read about a woman who was afraid to change her baby's diaper and a man who had intrusive thoughts of homosexual sex. To know I wasn't alone was a tremendous relief, though I also felt sad and frustrated that it had taken so many years, and I wasn't at all sure that the treatment would work.

Before I began therapy, I read about CBT. I'd recommend this, as CBT is based in scientific theories that make this systematic approach believable and easy to understand. Having a clear comprehension of the treatment made it easier for me to start, and, I think, more effective more quickly.

I started my treatment with a female psychologist. Aside from the nature of my obsessive thoughts, which I felt more able to divulge to a woman than a man, I also knew I'd be tearful and felt that this would be easier with a woman. My therapist was close to my age, which initially was a little difficult, but she was also friendly and open. She sympathized and empathized with what I'd been through while also encouraging me to focus on the treatment and the present situation. She was always on time to see me and remembered things I told her, about my illness, and about myself. She was also honest. I remember a homework assignment she'd assigned me that had caused me a lot of anxiety. It had to do with having a "on" day when I was to behave as I normally would, trying to push the thoughts away, and an "off" day when I was to try not to push the thoughts away. I found my first "off" day incredibly hard, as trying not to pay attention to the thoughts had the opposite effect. I was anxious and discouraged. I called her and left a message explaining what had happened. When she returned my call, she talked me through the difficulties I was having and told me to take the exercise a stage back. Then she apologized because she felt she had asked me to do too much too soon. This made me feel better, and I realized that therapists are also learning, as each client is different, and success is a matter of working together.

She focused largely on cognitive techniques that involved correcting faulty beliefs. She tried to make me realize that thoughts and actions are not the same and to recognize the importance of understanding this not only intellectually, but also emotionally. She also prepared me for further treatment I would have to go on to have, which was to involve the behavioral techniques of exposure and response prevention (ERP). ERP is an extremely powerful treatment, which I ultimately felt was more effective than the cognitive techniques. I believe I probably wouldn't have been able to embrace ERP without having learned some other techniques first.

I was forced to change therapists because my therapist left the university, which wasn't ideal, but looking back, it meant I received the benefit of two experts and developed trusting relationships with two people. I believe now that this change enhanced my experience of therapy and the results I got from it. I also had to start working with a man, which was a bit difficult at first, but I was forced to get over my fear of sharing my thoughts with a man. However, I found that my new psychologist, Dr. Rosqvist, was as easy, if not easier, to talk to than my previous therapist. He had a relaxed manner, was always on time for sessions, and was available outside scheduled sessions if I had a problem. He endeavored to find suitable times to see me around my work schedule, lent me books, and worked hard to thoroughly assess my specific type of OCD. I felt he tuned into who I was and that he really cared about my progress, which was wonderful. Here was a person who knew the very worst things to know about me, but he still believed in me. This helped me to believe in myself, to believe that I was still the person I had been before OCD.

ERP is an extremely powerful treatment which requires some commitment, as it can be somewhat frightening at times. You do eventually confront your worst fears, but a good therapist, like mine, will ensure that your treatment program is done in realistic stages that you are comfortable with. You are not asked to face specific fears before it makes clinical sense and before you have agreed to do so. It involves collaboratively creating a hierarchy of situations that are increasingly anxiety provoking and exposing yourself systematically to them one at a time until the anxiety drops for each one. It is necessary to work on this at home, too, which can actually make ERP a relatively inexpensive treatment since not all of the requisite work happens during sessions with a therapist. It also means the client is independent and doesn't overly rely on his or her therapist, making it easier for him or her to continue treatment activities autonomously when the formal treatment phase comes to an end.

When Dr. Rosqvist first explained what I needed to do in ERP, I was quite shocked and somewhat afraid. I couldn't believe that a psychologist was telling me that in order to reduce the frequency of my obsessional thoughts about sex, I had to develop detailed scenarios of them and think about them for intense periods of time. Initially, it seemed so perverted. I left the session wondering if I would go back. I questioned whether it was a real treatment and whether Dr. Rosqvist knew what he was talking about, professionally. I read some more on the subject and discovered it was indeed the recommended treatment and even though I felt somewhat afraid, I decided to give it a try.

At first it was difficult to put my thoughts on paper. I was afraid someone would find them and think I was a pedophile. I talked these fears over with Dr. Rosqvist and he helped me to see the situation more objectively. I started by making two lists of my obsessional thoughts: one for sexual thoughts involving children and another for sexual thoughts involving women. I then put them in order from most to least anxiety provoking. I started my exposures by tackling my obsessive thoughts about women. As these were less distressing in general, it was a natural place to start. My first exposure was looking at a picture of an attractive woman. I found a picture of a woman I felt was attractive in a magazine and looked at it until my anxiety diminished 50%. I had to force my mind to stay on the subject and not look away from the picture. Initially, it took about 90 minutes, but each time I did the exposure, the time it took for my anxiety to reduce to an acceptable level became shorter. I continued this until my anxiety returned to acceptable levels quickly. I moved on to using a picture of a woman in underwear and then to using specific ideas about me having sex with her. I had to keep the images and the words very vivid and provocative in my mind. After I mastered this exposure, I used a loop tape to record a sexual scenario with a woman and listened to it until my anxiety level decreased like before. It was extremely powerful hearing myself saying out loud the thought that had been upsetting me for so long. The first time I listened to it, I became quite distressed and upset, but because of the success I'd encountered with the other exposures, I found the courage to continue. It took almost 2 hours for my anxiety level to decrease that first time, but as I continued doing the same exposure, my distress level was reduced along with the time it took. After mastering this exposure in my apartment, I did the same one outside in a nearby park, using real women that passed by instead of the picture. I eventually reached my most anxiety-provoking exposure, which involved going to a women's-only sauna where naked women were and forcing myself to think sexual thoughts. I also spent time on beaches where women were topless.

After successfully doing exposures focused on women and sex, I felt confident enough to tackle the thoughts about children and sex, which were much more distressing. Dr. Rosqvist was supportive and encouraging and never made me do anything I wasn't ready for. The first exposure I did involving children was looking at a picture of a child fully clothed. The second was doing the same but with the word "pedophile" in my mind. The first time I moved on to my third exposure, which was looking at a picture of a child semiclothed, I once again became quite distressed and upset. I cried, but I managed to carry on with the exposure. I felt this experience was a breakthrough point and gave me the confidence to continue with more difficult exposures.

Eventually, I got to the stage where contact with real children would be extremely beneficial and important to my continued progress. Dr. Rosqvist had two children that he frequently used in exposures with suitable patients and he was willing to use them with me. This in itself was good for my confidence. Dr. Rosqvist was the only person who knew the depth and extent of my thoughts and he trusted me explicitly with his children. I was concerned that I would become distressed and maybe cry as I had done during exposures I'd done in my apartment. When I explained this to Dr. Rosqvist, he asked what I thought would happen if I did cry. I had thought it would be a serious problem, but he made me realize it wouldn't be. Of course, his children had seen people cry before and although they might have asked why I was crying, it would be possible to handle such a situation.

I decided on certain thoughts that I wanted to use during the exposure and met Dr. Rosqvist's children. We carried out the exposure at the office I always visited him in at the university. A longer slot than our usual appointment was scheduled to provide me with enough time to reduce anxiety. He stayed with me initially as the children got used to the situation but then left, leaving me alone with his little girl who was 3 and his little boy who was 5. The girl was not happy that her father had gone and her initial distress made my anxiety worse, which was difficult, but it enabled me to learn to deal with situations that made my normally high level of anxiety even more intense. I had to make sure I kept the sexual thoughts in my mind at all times. Dr. Rosqvist came back into the room sporadically to ask how my anxiety level was and then left again, until it had diminished to appropriate levels.

After 3 months of ERP, I felt much stronger and more confident. There was still work to be done, but I knew that I could do it on my own, as Dr. Rosqvist had all along been preparing me to act as my own autonomous therapist should I need to continue past the formal, active treatment phase. I started to make decisions about the future. I wanted to travel and go back to Europe. I made plans to go to South America, where I stayed for 5 months before returning to Europe. I continued my treatment independently in both places and found that I continued to improve further with the methods Dr. Rosqvist had shown me. Now, I use both cognitive and behavioral techniques if I feel bothered by the thoughts, which are now rare and only happen when I feel extremely stressed.

My life now is complete and full of love. Dealing with my OCD has meant that I can find out who I am. I can make decisions about my career, plan ahead, and have close friendships and relationships. I enjoy my time alone again and can concentrate enough to read novels and write short stories. Once again, I can believe that I will get married someday and have a family. Occasionally, I feel sad that so many years were lost to OCD and that I haven't done all I wanted to. I haven't traveled as much as I'd have liked or defined a career path for myself, which sometimes makes me feel behind others my age. Other secondary effects of my OCD sometimes rear their ugly heads too, such as finances. I didn't save or use my money well during the years I had OCD and I notice that now. It is important to grieve for this lost time, but also important not to dwell on it. There are also positives that have come out of my OCD experience. I appreciate simple pleasures in a way I didn't before and can put problems into perspective more easily. I understand others' suffering and am more compassionate. I know that no difficulties will ever be too large—if I can overcome my OCD, I can overcome anything.

The approach to treating Catherine's intrusive thoughts used ERP, as she indeed correctly labeled. This method of ERP is still the most clearly established efficacious psychosocial treatment for OCD available (e.g., Abramowitz, 2001, 2002; Lindsay, Crino, & Andrews, 1997; Rosqvist, 2002; Rosqvist, Thomas, Egan, & Haney, 2002). In her particular case, it was also the treatment of choice because she exhibited significant continued autonomic reactivity, which was *not* reduced through the CT trial. In fact, by her own description, Catherine reported the CT psychologist as backing down when Catherine became more distraught; unfortunately, backing down in this circumstance is akin to escape, which would only further cement Catherine's fears (obsessions) and increase her future escape and avoidance (compulsions).

Indeed, when she was referred to ERP treatment, Catherine scored in the severe range on the Yale-Brown Obsessive-Compulsive Scale (Goodman et al., 1989a, 1989b), suggesting an inordinate amount of impairment in functioning and significant personal suffering. In CT treatment, she had learned what obsessions were and how to try to interact with them in a more useful fashion, but the trial had failed to adequately reduce her autonomic arousal. She felt no increase in her ability to disregard, dismiss, or control her thoughts or reactions, and because the thoughts were also personally aversive, she remained disabled by the OCD. The central issue, and what accounted mostly for failure of the CT trial to effectively help Catherine, was the remaining lack of reduction in reactivity to feared stimuli (i.e., her sexual thoughts). Without directly reducing her biophysiological reactivity to certain thought content, Catherine simply could not dramatically improve.

Interestingly, another former patient once made a rather profound statement when she offhandedly commented on her personal perception on the role that anxious reactivity plays in preventing critical, creative, and meaningful thinking by saying, "when I feel that way [anxious], I can't think my way out of a wet paper bag." In fact, in the presence of significant arousal and activation, the brain and body are primarily automatically orienting toward preparing to fight or flee, making critical thought processes difficult to engage. To modern threats, again, it makes much more sense to stay cool, calm, and collected because in such a state (opposite of fight/flight mode), critical and creative thought capacity is preserved. *Therefore, autonomic arousal and reactivity must be reduced to eliminate anxiety and fear to a meaningful degree and to improve overall individual functioning.* At the end of the formal ERP trial, Catherine scored in the minimal range on the Yale-Brown Obsessive-Compulsive Scale, even meeting all of the necessary statistical requirements for the coveted status of "recovered" in her end-state functioning (Jacobson & Truax, 1991). A discussion will follow that explores the use of clinical significance measurement of meaningful change, because such statistical monitoring of progress can provide practitioners additional, concrete markers, and targets for outcome.

The nature of anxiety is such that it can be most helpful, even desirable, when one is faced with adversity of the caliber that basic survival is in question. Outside of such now-rare circumstances, anxiety is still useful when arousal is moderate as some activation is thought to be needed for optimal human performance (e.g., Yerkes & Dodson, 1908). When anxiety becomes too high, however, or it is chronic, human functioning is actually impaired. In this respect, as might be gleaned from the previous illustration of Catherine's personal description, anxiety can actually be quite disabling. Anxiety, it seems, in the form of many typical anxiety disorders, can tear a person apart and destroy the very essence of what makes life beautiful and exciting. It can bring an edge to being alive most people would not appreciate. The good news is that anxiety disorders are amenable to psychosocial treatments, especially exposure treatments. These methods are efficacious, effective, and efficient; in short, they ameliorate human suffering from anxiety disorders. Unfortunately, sometimes (as in Catherine's case) accurate diagnosis of anxiety does not happen, and correct treatments are not used, prolonging suffering and disability unnecessarily. As normal and as common as anxiety is, there are some inherent problems about anxiety that may make a diagnosis of anxiety difficult or not timely.

ISSUES IN THE DIAGNOSIS OF ANXIETY

Because anxiety is such a universal experience, it can be difficult to say, or at least agree on, just when it becomes problematic. *When* something is too much is such a subjective judgment. Although there is broad consensus that clinical anxiety is best identified by functional impairment (the why and how of problems), just what constitutes functional and impairment remains debatable. Nonetheless, there appears to be two domains of interest in understanding and conceptualizing the nature of anxiety, namely categories and dimensions of anxiety.

Although categorizing anxiety into distinct syndromes, or categories, holds inherent value (e.g., universal and common language for describing specific phenomena, billing requirements for codes, treatment selection), there are philosophical disagreements whether something so common as anxiety is not just a matter of degree; pathologizing anxiety within such a perspective is fundamentally problematic. The same argument can then be made that the differences between anxiety disorders are mere subtleties, and such distinctions should not be made. Perhaps anxiety, when problematic, should instead just remain a "neurosis."

All things being equal, there is now indisputable evidence to suggest there are clear and different syndromes of anxiety, which often require different solutions. For example, posttraumatic stress disorder (PTSD) is exemplified by some trauma (that could vary broadly from directly experienced to very obscure "traumatization") and three clusters of interference. There is the "reliving" cluster, which is typified by intrusive memories, nightmares, flashbacks, and so on. There is the avoidance cluster, in which the affected person tries desperately to avoid reminders of the event by trying to not think of the event, to not see things that remind him or her of the event, or to broadly avoid people or situations that might trigger memories. Last, there is the arousal cluster, in which the person is on edge, vigilant, irritable, has difficulties concentrating, sleeping, and making decisions. Together, these problems make up what is labeled *posttraumatic stress*, something that is quite unlike any other anxiety disorder. There may be an aspect of other anxiety disorders (e.g., panic attacks) that occur within the phenomenon of posttraumatic stress, but as a syndrome, the conglomerate symptom presentation of posttraumatic stress does not occur within other anxiety disorders. In PTSD, the patient is afraid of the event recurring and might attempt to actively prevent its recurrence. In panic disorder, on the other hand, the fear is not that some terrible event or situation will occur per se, but that the patient's own body will behave unpredictably and new panic attacks will happen. The fear there is not for external events but instead for internal events. The treatments for posttraumatic stress and panic may have some similar components, but differ in many significant ways and require differing treatment strategies. The two conditions may both need variants of exposure, but the way it is delivered and formed will differ significantly. Not knowing whether one was treating PTSD or panic disorder would represent a significant therapeutic obstacle. Therefore, categorical views have their place and utility, without suggesting anything further. Categorical information, as useful and directive as it might be, does not determine all in psychotherapy. From diagnostic information flows case conceptualization, something even more valuable than specific diagnosis as formulation lends clues to the controlling variables of the conditions under consideration. For example, people can panic for many reasons. Sometimes reasons are known, and sometimes they are not. Such dimensionality can change how treatment is focused. Likewise, depression can have many causes, and can have a variety of possible solutions. As such, dimensionality is again of central importance. It becomes important to understand both what sparks and what fuels anxiety and fear, especially when one is considering efficaciously treating such conditions with established treatments.

EPIDEMIOLOGY AND ETIOLOGY OF
ANXIETY DISORDERS

Even though anxiety can lead to suicide in some severe cases, in which people's sense of hope and expectancy for a return of normalcy has been lost, it is not generally felt that anxiety directly kills people. Some patients, especially among panic-disordered ones, often believe they are having a heart attack or a stroke when they are experiencing high anxiety. Yet, anxiety itself does not kill anyone. It is actually supposed to do the opposite. Nonetheless, changes in lifestyles because of anxiety can affect health status grossly; for instance, fear often produces significant avoidance as a principal byproduct. Avoidance frequently displays itself as a sedentary lifestyle, and other poor indicators (e.g., excessive use of alcohol and other substances, eating poorly).

Few people who have experienced anxiety or understand its impact would willingly sign up for it. Many would frankly rather die or be dead than feel what they feel during anxiety. It is a torturous experience. Julius Caesar is quoted as having said, "It is easier to find men who will volunteer to die, than to find those who are willing to endure pain with patience." The argument can be made that it would be equally difficult to find people who would be willing to endure anxiety with patience. This assertion is frankly supported by the research literature, which finds that anxiety is actually associated with an inflated risk for suicide. For example, Weissman, Klerman, Markowitz, and Ouellette (1989) found that 20% of panic patients have made a suicide attempt at some point in their lives. They, along with Coryell, Noyes, and House (1986), reported that the risk for suicide among panic-disordered patients was as high for those suffering from major depressive disorder. This substantial risk for suicide was also found to be independent from any comorbidity, ruling out possible contributions of both major depression and substance abuse (Johnson, Weissman, & Klerman, 1990). Taken together, this over-all picture suggests that anxiety is epidemiologically relevant. Carefully studying the incidence and distribution of (both clinical and subclinical) anxiety among people, and the conditions influencing the acquisition, maintenance, and severity of anxiety quickly reveals a pandemic condition with exacting consequences. Anxiety, for all of what it is supposed to do for people, is not a joke, but it is instead often a serious problem that leads both sufferers and practitioners to sometimes desperate measures to try to ameliorate the suffering. Sometimes, patients even go so far as to agree to have their brains cut (i.e., neurosurgery or psychosurgery) to try to alleviate the resulting "pain" (Jenike et al., 1991). Unfortunately, such desperate measures have been largely unsuccessful in producing meaningful changes and are filled with controversy, but are moreover notable because many patients who have undergone such severe interventions have not gone through an adequate trial of CBT with an exposure emphasis.

In beginning to acknowledge pandemic proportions and presentations of anxiety, perhaps through an increasing sense that anxiety disorders represent the most commonly presenting complaint in most mental health care settings, several epidemiological studies have been conducted to try to comprehend the scope of this problem (e.g., the Epidemiological Catchment Area [ECA] Study, the Edmonton Area Study, the National Comorbidity Study). The studies all agree that anxiety disorders are a prevalent problem, but disagree somewhat in exact numbers. The ECA study typically found high lifetime prevalences, ranging from 10% to 25% of the population (Bourdon et al., 1988). The study examining the Edmonton area in Canada found a lower lifetime prevalence rate of 11% (Bland, Orn, & Newman, 1988), with discrepancies between it and the ECA being mostly attributable to variations in interviewer instructions and statistical methods for determining prevalence (McLean & Woody, 2001). The National Comorbidity Study (Kessler et al., 1994) found lifetime prevalence for any anxiety disorder to be approximately 20%. This study also found prevalence rates being higher among women (31%), and that co-occurring conditions, whether depression, other anxiety, or substance, were commonplace.

Studying the causes, origins, and contributions to the occurrence of anxiety disorders is complex for a host of reasons. For one, how is it possible to parcel out, or separate completely, genetic contributions from familial modeling or vice versa? Let it suffice to say that understanding the etiology of anxiety and its effects is complicated and fraught with methodological challenges. Nonetheless, some potentially contributional variables are posited to exist, and all point to a natural and normal relationship between biology and behavior. Generally, a *biopsychosocial-spiritual* case formulation (i.e., a clinical description that contains a multitude and mix of data that describe who the patient is and, perhaps more importantly, why he or she is that way) will point to nomothetic, ideographic, and genetic variables that are most salient in producing individual presentations.

In this vein, there appears to be a genetic basis for anxiety (i.e., it comes into current day through eons of familial transmission). Family and genetic studies (e.g., Barlow, 2002) seem to point toward a dispositional loading for being anxious. What might indeed be heritable is a particular arousal capacity or disposition, or just how readily one becomes aroused and activated in the presence of stimulation.

What type of family one comes from does not seem to be a verdict in certainty for outcome, however; in my own work with a spectrum of anxiety conditions, I have worked with twins. In some cases, both twins have been affected by anxiety conditions. In others, only one in the pair seems affected by anxiety at all, whereas the other appears well adjusted and "successful" at life's challenges (e.g., advanced education, marriage, employment). This phenomenon suggests that genetics is not sufficient for the development of a recognizable anxiety disorder. What instead must be more completely true is that genetics is a necessary component bit, but it may not be sufficient for causing an anxiety disorder by itself. In this sense, genetics might be the necessary fuel for a fire, but without a match it cannot start an anxiety disorder independently. The sufficient part, then, would have to be activated by some life events through which underlying, necessary dispositions (fuels) are activated or accessed. In other words, some events would have to ignite the necessary fuel. Without fuel, a fire cannot burn; much in the same sense, without some disposition to react and respond in certain ways, an anxiety disorder cannot begin.

Additionally, it is thought that stressful life events (i.e., pivotal learning moments) contribute significantly to anxiety. For instance, it is broadly accepted that physical assault, sexual assaults, and motor vehicle accidents are disproportionately associated with the development of PTSD (e.g., Norris, 1992; Patrek, 2002). These kinds of experiences are significant events in anyone's life and are part of a diathesis of biology, psychology (i.e., how a person thinks and reasons), and specific events that may lead to recognizable forms of clinical anxiety. If nothing else, stressful events will serve to aggravate underlying dispositions toward anxious reactivity (e.g., Hammen, 1991; Lteif & Mavissakalian, 1995; Newman & Bland, 1994). Life events may not need to be especially aversive, but may also occur over years or a lifetime to eventually accumulate enough force to activate reactive potential and the sorted problems that result.

Although this is not meant to be a complete picture of the prevalence and causes of anxiety disorders, this brief review paints a picture of anxiety as commonplace and as multidetermined. Regardless of prevalence or course, for the individual anxiety disordered patient the news is phenomenal in that these kinds of symptoms and problems are treatable with well-tested and proven effective methods. The outlook for recovery is very good when the patient seeks the correct types of psychosocial treatment. Many people who struggle with clearly diagnosable anxiety problems do not seek formal psychological treatments for their conditions, which may seem baffling given how disabling anxiety often is. There are numerous reasons why someone might not seek formal help, ranging from stigma associated with mental illness to cost and practicality. Consequently, many people suffer needlessly for years.

Additionally, consumers of psychotherapy services might not know whether what they are getting in treatment is a good or bad product, or if the product they are getting is appropriate for their issues. Further, they might not know how to ask their provider why they are being asked to do certain tasks in treatment or whether there are other means of change available. Too many will blindly follow their provider's advice without stopping to ask why the treatment selected is being used and how specifically it will address the mechanisms of pathology of the specific condition. Many practitioners are not even clear on the mechanisms of pathology and change for particular conditions they set out to "treat," so it seems unreasonable to expect consumers of such products to be better informed than the deliverer of services. Ultimately, it is the responsibility of the practitioner to provide information about the proposed treatments so that prospective patients can decide for themselves whether they wish to consent to the proposed strategies. This is especially important when the practitioner will propose to use exposure methods, because there will be some discomfort involved. A thorough consent will include a complete review of the risk involved in treatment; for exposure work, it would mean carefully explaining that there will be some (albeit tolerable) discomfort necessary to reduce anxiety and fear in the end. In my own practice, I find it helpful to also discuss what such problems do when they go untreated or undertreated, for the sake of presenting a complete picture of what the various options and likely/plausible outcomes might be.

COURSE AND PROGNOSIS OF ANXIETY DISORDERS

Anxiety has a natural tendency to ebb and flow, as Catherine described in her own experience. Over a lifetime, anxiety disorders tend to chronically wax and wane with a whole host of biopsychosocial variables; however, even as fluctuations continue, the general trend is that anxiety, in an insidious fashion, gets increasingly worse over the years when left to fester on its own. Predictably, variables that will make anxiety and fears consistently and increasingly worse with time are many, but avoiding and escaping what makes a person feel nervous will always make such problems worse. This inevitability is supported by the fact that anxiety disorders represent, single-handedly, the largest mental health problem facing the world; in other words, it does not tend to improve naturally, but instead overwhelmingly worsens without some professional assistance.

There are a host of studies that suggest anxiety tends to take a chronic and worsening course without effective treatment (e.g., Agras, Chapin, & Oliveau, 1972; Katsching & Amering, 1994; Keller & Baker, 1992; Marks & Lader, 1973; Noyes, Clancy, Hoenk, & Slymen, 1980; Pollack et al., 1990). There are indications that some people show some improvement in anxiety over time, but the concerning truth is that the vast majority of people chronically experience clinical anxiety on a recurring trajectory. This is alarming because of all of the associated problems and costs incurred by anxiety disorders as a whole, and it strongly supports the notion that anxiety problems *should* be treated. In terms of recovery, anxiety looks especially poor. Compared with major depressive disorder, for example, which approximately 80% of sufferers recover from, only 18% of patients with panic and agoraphobia accomplish the daunting task of recovering from their ailment (Barlow, 2002). That again suggests that the vast majority of anxiety patients do not go on to recover without help. There are some limited data suggesting that anxiety disorders may not be as prevalent in older age (Flint, 1994), but by the time a person reaches old age the psychosocial effects may already have taken their toll if anxiety has remained untreated for a lifetime.

If the picture seems bleak, it really is not meant to sound as if prognosis is poor, for it is not. Instead, prognosis looks quite bright, with empirically supported treatments leading the way in reducing human suffering because of anxiety. Lots of different treatment methods comprise empirically supported treatments, such as modifying worry behavior, teaching applied relaxation and mindfulness strategies to reduce daily stress and arousal, using behavioral rehearsal and self-instructional training to better help people effectively reach goals, increasing appropriate problem-solving to solve real-life problems, and using cognitive and schema work to illustrate how to more critically evaluate one's experience and understand how beliefs and assumptions underlie maladaptive behavior. Chapter 2 will focus on one of the more established empirical methods for treating anxiety: exposure. Exposure is not necessarily a method that should be held out from these other effective methods as a champion per se, but it might be heralded as the single approach that most effectively and efficiently affects autonomic arousal and reactivity problems that so often play a central role in the maintenance of anxiety and fears. It behooves the prudent practitioner about to embark on treating an anxiety-disordered patient to carefully consider how exposure can play a role in an effective, overall treatment package.

CHAPTER 2

Description of the Behavioral Treatment Strategy: Exposure

You gain strength, courage and confidence by every
experience in which you really stop to look fear in the face.
You are able to say to yourself, "I have lived through
this horror. I can take the next thing that comes along."
You must do the thing you think you cannot do.
                                        —Eleanor Roosevelt

EXPOSURE: A DEFINITION AND EXPLICATION

In the 1960s, psychologists were beginning to more formally use a strategy called "exposure" (although its first uses can be traced back to the 1920s [Barlow & Durand, 1999]), a method that involved asking patients to face real-life situations that they perceived as frightening. As such, patients were asked to deliberately and repeatedly come into contact with circumstances that were anxiety-provoking (e.g., using public transportation and restrooms, spending time in crowded locations, driving alone, touching certain objects or animals). This, of course, was asking people to look fear in the face, as Eleanor Roosevelt put it. In much the same way, with a variety of refinements and some modifications, this is what is still involved in exposure treatments today; that is, patients are (basically) asked to deliberately confront anxiety-provoking thoughts, situations, and circumstances, which are objectively safe of course, until their arousal levels are reduced by at least half. Patients are also asked to perform such tasks again and again, until the repetition begins to lessen, or decondition, the anxiety reaction and fear response in the presence of the provocative stimulus. In short, patients are asked to face the stimulus until it seizes to be provocative.

On the surface of the description of exposure, it might sound like a cruel way to overcome anxiety and fear. Subjectively, it might not sound "good;" indeed, it might actually sound frightening and uncomfortable. In fact, it has been abandoned from time to time throughout history since its inception, and typically then in favor of some other behavioral technique that was perceived as less overwhelming, such as systematic desensitization (Barlow, Moscovitch, & Micco, 2004). When exposure has not been used, it has often been so because *practitioners* (not patients) have feared that patients will not be able to tolerate the exposure, that it would be too overwhelming or intolerable. This is rather ironic because patients are typically already overwhelmed by anxiety and fears when they seek treatment, and the overwhelming (pun intended) evidence suggests that if their anxiety and fears are not adequately resolved then the patients will remain overwhelmed for long periods, sometimes lifetimes. What could be crueler than a lifetime of agony from anxiety and fear? Is some short-term, yet tolerable, discomfort really *that* cruel? If so, then in comparison to what?

As it turns out for many anxiety problems, there are several cognitive-behavioral methods that are helpful, but few strategies appear to be as potent in producing *direct* and highly effective relief in the specific symptoms of anxiety and fear. This bottom line seems to be driven by what happens to these kinds of autonomic phenomenon when people do *not* face that which makes them uncomfortable through continued behaviors aimed at not looking fear in the face.

ESCAPE AND AVOIDANCE: MAINTAINING ANXIETY

Mowrer's two-factor theory (1947) provides the strongest argument for why anxiety and fear do not naturally or easily extinguish when people learn to escape from, or successfully avoid, feared stimuli. This "avoidance learning" model proposed, rather convincingly, that the failure of fear to extinguish is directly related to not being able to challenge and test fears in the *absence* of the feared stimulus, and hence it remains preserved and protected from extinction. Discovering what will actually happen in the presence of a stimulus can truly only occur in its presence, because everything else would be speculation of varying degree.

One predominant reason people have a difficult time allowing real-life outcomes to inform them about whether their fears are warranted or whether they are overestimates of the true state of affairs (or are completely correct, for that matter) is that when people consider doing what they are afraid of they commonly do not anticipate the average, or most likely, outcome. Instead, anxiety and fear networks prepare the person for the worst possible scenario; this "disaster preparation" leaves people feeling and thinking that truly horrible things will happen if they go ahead and do what they are afraid of.

Indeed, if the imagined, catastrophic outcome was true, then it truly would be "bad," so why tempt fate? What many anxiety-disordered individuals do not recognize is that *all* experiences in the world operate on a normal distribution and are under the influence of normal probability statistics. Instead of viewing world events through such a scientific frame, however, they instead subjectively come to expect, through grossly inflated probability estimates derived from how likely events *feel*, that if they do what they are afraid of (e.g., drive a car alone), then their worst fear will be highly likely, if not guaranteed, to happen (e.g., car crash). This belief is complicated and erroneously supported by two basic pieces of information, namely that when they do not drive they do not crash (i.e., avoidance pays off *every* time, whereas driving represents something akin to Russian roulette, where death sometimes happen)—and various media sources are filled with car crashes every day, lending credence to the belief that car crashes happen with enormous frequency.

Consider for a moment the local, national, or international news. How much of the news reporting is about "Average Joe" (maybe not the best choice of name anymore) and his average day. His average day, of course, looks extremely boring; he wakes up in the morning, takes a shower, has breakfast and reads his newspaper, commutes to work, performs his job functions, has lunch while chitchatting with colleagues, finishes the day's work chores, commutes back home, has dinner, watches television, and eventually goes to bed, only to repeat the whole boring scenario again tomorrow. What would the news be like if that is what people saw? Boring! People's lives are just that: mundane, repetitive, uneventful, and truly too boring for news to be documenting the lives of Average Joe or Boring Bill. No, instead what news outlets report on is Unlucky Luke who (against the best odds, actually) crashed on the way to work. Not only did he crash, but he broke his back and is now paralyzed from the chest down and is in a coma, and at home his seven children are going hungry after his wife ran off with another man, and so on. What also is not reported is Slightly Statistically Unusual Chris, Martha, Beth, and assorted others who actually had "average accidents" today, or fender benders. These kinds of accidents are not interesting and not *newsworthy* as nothing different, out of the ordinary, or statistically unusual actually happened to them. No life flights. No emergency 18-hour surgeries where the mangled person dies several times, but is successfully brought back to life. No sensationalism! No, these average, run-of-the-mill accident "victims" will just go on about their otherwise completely average lives, bar the slight dent in their fenders. So, consider for a moment just what kind of information people, especially anxiety-disordered people, are being bombarded with every day. Consider what that amount of death, mayhem, and otherwise horrific information might do to an anxiety-disordered individual's probability estimation capacities. Never mind that what is reported represents an extremely skewed statistical distribution of real-life, everyday, and common outcomes. The problem is that anxiety-disordered individuals begin to see the level of death and mayhem as actually being average and not as being a skewed representation. They begin to expect that terrible outcomes are much more normal and commonplace than a normal distribution would support, if normative information was used to calculate risk ratios. If everyone thought they were going to be killed in a car crash on the way to work today, and actually *believed* it, how many cars would be seen on the roadways today? Almost none probably, and perhaps those who would seek out driving that day are those people who actively are trying to commit suicide.

Avoidance learning operates very much on the same principle that makes Unlucky Luke and Average Joe influence what a person does when they consider whether they should drive to work today. More explicitly, what Mowrer proposed was that fear is initially learned and acquired through classical (i.e., autonomic, startle, or reflexive) conditioning, and is maintained through operant conditioning (i.e., what happens to a person before, during, and after the presentation of a stimulus). The person who is afraid of driving his or her car might have initially learned to be afraid of driving because he or she was startled by actually being in a car accident, being nearly hit, or seeing an accident (an unconditioned stimulus). The startle, or surprise and fear experienced (an unconditioned response) during the acquisition event, classically conditioned the response (e.g., release of adrenalin and endorphins, increased heart rate). Because the reflexive response occurred in the presence of a car, the car becomes the operant (i.e., control variable) that directs future similar automatic responses (conditioned response) through operant conditioning. Danger and threat have become attached to cars and perhaps anything else directly or indirectly associated with cars. This will likely lead to a desire to reduce contact with cars and associated stimuli because of their threat-signaling capacity, because feeling threatened feels bad, and because people are driven to avoid what feels bad; this produces avoidance symptoms (e.g., not driving cars, or having someone else drive). These avoidance symptoms are engaged to avoid the conditioned response of anxiety and fear, which was associated with the original trauma event.

This represents a basic, primitive, and almost primordial way of learning emotional material, such as fear-based information. Such basic

Proximity of Danger and Associated Behavioral Action Tendencies

Near	Moderately Close				Far

0 ---------- 1 ---------- 2 ---------- 3 ---------- 4 ---------- 5 ---------- 6 ---------- 7 ---------- 8

Faint	Fight	Flee	Freeze

	Defensive Aggression	Explosive Escape	
Tonic Immobility			Stop Movements
Dissociation			Vigilance
Behavioral Inhibition	Behavioral Activation		Behavioral Inhibition

Low Action ---------- 2 ---------- 3 ----High Action---- 5 ---------- 6 ---------- Low Action

FIGURE 2.1   Location of threat and related behavioral responses.

learning is conducted at a primitive, nonconscious substrate. This means the information learned is more directly stored in emotional defense and safety networks, which are more closely related to survival behaviors than in consciously aware centers of reasoning. As such, the information is used and accessed when a person feels threatened in an automatic, reflexive manner, and this type of information and response is not necessarily available for conscious cognitive evaluation before deployment.

This reflexive response safeguards against people doing too much thinking in the presence of threat, and instead produces more action. Recall that anxiety is a basic emotional response that in foundation signals, or primes, the person to get ready to act in the face of either actual or perceived threat (e.g., fight or flee).

Depending on the proximity of threat, there are four common response sets of actions that are geared toward helping the person survive (Figure 2.1). For ease of teaching patients about these types of responses, it can be helpful to refer to these as the 4Fs (which will be described in the following section). Many patients have reported asking themselves which kind of "F" they are engaging in to give them a better picture of what is happening to them in an everyday experience of anxiety or fear.

The type of survival action employed depends very much on the circumstance an organism finds itself in. For instance, when a threat is far away, the best course of action appears to be avoiding detection. If the threat is closer, but can be outrun, and an escape route can be seen, running away (fleeing) is the preferred mode. If the threat cannot be outrun, then fighting is chosen. Last, if the organism has been spotted, tried to run but was caught, and could not outfight its attacker, then playing dead is the best available defense. This heralds back to early times in human history when people were not yet entirely at the top of the food chain, but when people were more often dinner for some predator higher in the chain. These kinds of responses can often be observed on nature-oriented television shows, where it can be observed, for example, that antelopes on the African savannah do not move as a lioness saunters by in the distance, or that antelopes will try to spear their pursuer if caught.

In an effort to ensure that patients truly grasp the normal, adaptive nature of various anxiety responses, on an evolutionary level again, and specifically (scientifically) appreciate why the responses are happening, it may be helpful to use stories and metaphors to illustrate the primordial value of such responses. Two common stories I tell are about lions and antelopes on the African savannah and about smoke jumpers (forest firefighters who parachute into forest wildfire areas). These stories allow patients to listen to the fundamental therapeutic information, but allow them to superimpose their own, private information onto the stories in a naturally occurring fashion. I have loosely come to refer to these naturally occurring moments as "ah-ha moments," when, during some pivotal part in the story or metaphor, the therapeutic content "clicks" with some personally relevantly fitting information, which is then instantaneously imported into the generic story or metaphor. In such moments, the patients then seemingly independently derive, or figure out, therapeutically important information. Again, Otto (2000) reported that this way of imparting therapeutic information allows patients to encode the information in easily accessible formats, increasing the likelihood of using the information in the moments of their lives where it might be apropos. The two stories follow.

AFRICAN SAVANNAH VIGNETTE/STORY/METAPHOR

You were probably wondering where I was going with the cow illustration before, correct? [Here I alert the patient to the idea that another metaphor or story is coming, cueing them to put on a somewhat different thinking cap.] But it was a good way to learn about emotional reasoning. Well, I have another one for you that is very similar. Have you ever been to the African savannah? [Most patients respond in the negative.] No? Well, let me tell you a few things about the African savannah and about lions and antelopes that live there. Let's just say it's a tough place to live in; first of all, it's usually about 1,000 degrees during the day, but if you're a lion you nonetheless have to eat, and if you're an antelope you have to try your hardest not to be eaten. Like I said, it's a tough place to live. Now, you might not know this, but the savannah is perfectly flat. It's like a pancake, really. You can see for miles. This is a good thing if you are an antelope, actually, because you can spot a lion coming from a mile away. Let me also tell you that antelopes can easily outrun lions, so if you're an antelope you're in pretty good shape, both literally and figuratively. This presents sort of a problem for lions. After all, if you're a lion you still have to eat, but if the antelope can see you from miles away and they can outrun you, how the heck do you actually get to eat? After all, you have to *catch* your supper there! [Here I pause, giving the patient time to consider how one would actually go about catching something that can see well and runs fast. Most patients usually come up with some variation about hiding in the grass, but I quickly point out that there is not enough grass to hide that thoroughly to be able to approach undetected. Most patients then typically shrug their shoulders, and become inquisitive about how such a feat is actually possible.]

Well, it turns out that lions are smart animals. They're very, very smart. They are communal animals, meaning they live together in families. These families are in part made up of the young, which are too small and inexperienced to actually successfully take down an antelope even if they were sitting right on top of it. They are also in part made up of the old, or lame, or injured animals that cannot hunt successfully either because of old age, injuries, or other maladies. Then, of course, there are the middle-age, agile hunters who single-handedly could take down an antelope, if they could only catch up with it. All of these various family members have to eat, whether they are young and immature, middle-age and agile, or old and disabled. They all know it, too. That's why they're smart! Hunger is also a great motivator, because it makes them think hard and fast about how to catch the antelope. At some point, they recognized some common variables that would prove to be very useful to the purpose of catching antelope. They recognized that antelope would always run away from lions, which certainly makes sense if you're an antelope, right? [Here I am making sure the patient is following the gist of the story and gets the developing picture.] They discovered that the antelopes would even run away from a lion cub or an old, injured lion so long as those lions sounded big, scary, and dangerous. The antelope were not particularly discriminating what they ran away from, which sort of makes sense if you are the antelope; after all, you escaped from something you *thought* might kill and eat you. If you're an antelope, your job, basically, is to avoid and run away from lions. Doing so is good for your health. So, again imagine this flat pancake of a savannah, and then watch as the lions split themselves into two separate teams. [Here I will slow the rate of speech, and lower the tone of my voice to accentuate the "trick" that the patient is now expecting to come.] The two teams are split into the one that contains only the agile hunters, and one that contains only the young, old, and injured. The hunters go to that far end of a field, which has antelopes in it, and lay down completely flat. They are also very quiet and don't move. The other team goes to the other far end of the same field. In this fashion, the antelopes are now in the middle, still perhaps munching away blissfully at the savannah grasses. Soon, however, they begin to notice the second team made up of the young, old, and injured because they make no attempt at hiding themselves. In fact, they begin to make movements toward the antelopes, and make very hungry, frightening roars as they approach. [Pause for effect.] Let me ask you this: which way will the antelope run? [Pause for effect. Sometimes patients will spontaneously blurt out, "toward the waiting hunters!"] They will run away from what is frightening them, but when they do that they run right into the claws and mouths of the waiting, agile hunters. They really don't stand a chance, and the waiting hunters will take down enough antelopes for the whole family of lions to eat. In fact, the antelope would be far better off if they ran toward what frightened them, not away from it because then they run straight into worse trouble than if they would run toward being scared. In this respect, life of an antelope on the savannah is very similar to the anxiety you experience. That is, you tend to run away from—or avoid—what scares you, and you, too, would be much better off if you instead went toward what frightens you. [Here I will usually disengage the story for a bit to discuss examples of escape and avoidance behaviors the patient uses.]

Now, let's talk about animals on the savannah a little further still, OK? [Patients usually prefer these exercises to more technical presentations, although they are sometimes also needed.] It turns out there is a preferred sequence of four common survival behaviors. I'm going to refer to these four sets of responses as the 4Fs [begin to write on board], and you'll quickly see why. Imagine you are that antelope on the savannah. Your job is to not be eaten, right? That's right, you're going to *do* everything possible to increase your odds of sheer survival. It turns out that fuel and energy is critical to surviving on the savannah, too, so you don't want to expend anything unless you really have to. This way, when you really needed the energy, like when you might have to outrun a lion, you would have it stored up for that special occasion when you get to the "hundred-meter-dash-or-die." That's why *what* you do to survive follows a very predictable, sequential way of responding, which typically is related to how close a threat is to you in proximity. So, let's imagine you are that antelope on the savannah again, and you're laying down resting, perhaps munching some grass, and you happen to spot a lion walking by quite some distance away. After all, you can see really well, so you easily spot it as it goes by. What do you think would be your best strategy for survival in this encounter? [Here I pause for the patient to think and respond, and then write on the board: "Freeze."] Well, your best response would be to not move. Why would that be your best response? First, it conserves fuel for a later time if you had to run like the wind. So, if the lion did not see you, why should you run? Seems like a waste of energy, doesn't it? [Patients typically agree.] Second, do you know how and what lions, and most predators for that matter, see? [Pause for patient to think.] Well, they see in black and white, in monochrome vision. Not in color vision. Why is this important, you might be wondering? It's important because monochromatic vision is best for detecting subtle movements and outlines. Color vision is great for seeing crisp detail and the pretty colors, but if your objective is to see movements, then black-and-white vision is much more of an advantage. How do lions spot you, then? Is it because of your pretty colors, and so on? No, they see you when you move. Predators of all sorts are oriented toward movement. Therefore, your best bet, if the predator, or lion in this case, is further away, is not to move. They might not see you. If they don't see you, they will not try to catch you and eat you. This is also, by the way, the reason the stripes on zebras help them. When they run away from lions they do it en masse, or in a group; when they do that, it becomes very difficult for the monochromatically seeing lion to tell where one zebra begins and another ends, making it harder to bring one down.

So, now let's pretend the same scenario, with the lion walking by some distance away, is true, but that the lion spotted you. Then what is your best, preferred response? [Pause, and wait for patient to think and possibly provide an answer, then write: "Flee."] Your next best bet would be to run, and run like the wind. Run like you never have before. If you successfully run away, you will not be eaten. You might be tired, but you're alive. That's primarily because you didn't allow the lion to touch you, so anything you can do that will prevent it from touching you or stop it from touching you if it has started to will be important for survival. You can rest later, but for now you survived, and that's the important part. Well, next let's pretend that the lion saw you and actually caught up with you. You couldn't, for some reason, outrun it. What do you do now? [Pause, and write: "Fight."] That's right, you would fight like hell. Why would you, as a little fragile antelope, fight a big, nasty lion? Certainly not because you have some sort of Napoleon complex, but because lions have to be relatively healthy to survive on the savannah. Yes, there is an increased risk of being hurt because you might actually be touched by the lion. Still fighting, at this point, is preferable. Remember that life on the savannah is rough, it's hard! If you're a lion and you're missing an eye, or you have cracked ribs, or you have a punctured lung, you might just be out of luck. Last I checked, there isn't a lion emergency room on the savannah. Lions don't like to be injured because it might mean death for them. So, when a prey fights too furiously, even if it's smaller, the lion might just leave it alone, in favor of catching some easier, less combative prey later. Remember that lions are smart. Besides knowing they have to eat, they also know it's going to be much, much more difficult to do so with significant injuries.

OK, we are progressing along the normal sequence of preferred choices of actions, if our objective is to survive. The last response might be a bit more difficult to understand, but let me explain to you why, in a primitive way, the response of dissociating, "checking out," or fainting will help to protect you when all of the chips are down. [Write: "Faint."] Have you ever had the experience of being "scared stiff," where you just got so frightened that you literally couldn't move, felt frozen, or you actually fainted? [Some patients can relate to this experience, especially among rape trauma victims, combat veterans, and specific phobia patients who exhibit the vasovagal syncope fainting response.] Remember, I told you predators are drawn, or aroused, by movement? Well, have you ever seen a typical barn cat play with a mouse or a bird it has caught, and perhaps brought it to your house as a token of appreciation? Well, have you noticed why or when the cat finally stops "playing" with the mouse or stops swatting it around? When the prey stops moving, right? When it plays dead, or is dead, the cat stops. This is true for the big cats on the savannah, too. They stop clawing, scratching, and biting when the prey stops moving. So, if you're that antelope, for goodness sake, if you have been unable to fight off the lion, after being spotted and caught, then play dead. If you play dead you might still stand a chance. The only problem remaining, of course, is how one manages to be calm enough to look dead when there's a lion sitting on you, when you actually aren't dead! This is where your own body takes over to try to make sure you actually look dead, by preventing your body from fidgeting around and doing anything else that signals remaining life and struggle. This response only happens as a last-chance resort, again to protect you, but only after the other, escape-oriented actions have failed to work. When this paralysis response set in, you become less able to move, you become unable to make sounds or speak, you become numb to pain, and you will become disoriented or somewhat unaware of your surroundings. After all, if this terrible thing is happening to you, why be "present" for that? Interestingly, to further illustrate how sequential these behavioral responses are, when an animal or person comes out of one of these paralyzed, frozen states, they return right back to the immediately pre-ceding behavioral response, which is fighting. So, as you see, there are very adaptive reasons for why your body should be reacting the way it does, only for you personally, there are no lions after you. Your body, nonetheless, is acting as if there were. We need to change that.

Smoke Jumper Vignette/Story/Metaphor

Do you know what a "smoke jumper" is? No, well, as completely insane as this might sound, a smoke jumper is a firefighter who parachutes into the midst of raging forest wildfires. So, not only do they jump out of a perfectly sound plane, but they jump into fire! Sounds like a brilliant career, right? [I find that humor commonly puts a tolerable twist to otherwise challenging topics, and it allows me to lighten up the conversation; however, the appropriateness of humor should be based on individual patient suitability.] Well, smoke jumpers are an interesting breed, in that not only are they willing to work very hard at fighting fires in very remote areas, but, despite the way it might sound, they are very vested in surviving. They know that what they are doing is potentially quite dangerous. Fire can kill people quite readily, so it's not something to take too lightly. Knowing this, smoke jumpers carry some tools that are designed to help them survive. They carry shovels and picks to dig fire lines with and a whole bunch of other stuff to help them stop the fire. The main danger, assuming parachuting is safe enough to be survived, is that to stop the fire, the smoke jumper has to be on the side of the fire where there is fuel remaining. It does no good to have the smoke jumper on the side of the fire where it has already burned off the fuel. However, standing on the side with fuel, conceptually if not in reality, makes the smoke jumper fuel, too. The danger is that if the smoke jumper gets caught by the fire, he or she will burn up. That would be bad. So, in short, there is a safe side of the fire, which is the one where there is no more fuel, where the air is not superheated, and where there are not poisonous gases, and a dangerous side, which is usually in firefighting referred to as the "kill zone" for good reason. Follow me so far? [Pausing to be sure the patient gets the idea that being on the dangerous side is inherently bad, but a necessary evil for forest fire fighting.] Sometimes something very scary happens to smoke jumpers. Something terrible. [Here I slow my rate and lower my tone to draw attention and charge the atmosphere.] Sometimes, they become encircled by fire, meaning there is no way out. So, in such a circumstance, and because of the nature of fire that will want to burn any remaining fuel, they are in grave danger of becoming more fuel for the fire. They cannot actually outrun the fire, eventually, but instead they have to find some way to get to the other side of the fire, to the side where there is no more fuel and superheated air and toxic gases. However, this would necessitate going through a wall of fire. How does someone go through a wall of fire? How is that possible? [Pause, to wait for patient to think about it and see the clearly dangerous nature of the dilemma.] Well, they carry with them a piece of equipment that smoke jumpers only half jokingly refer to as a "slow bake." Do you know what that is? No, well, what it is, essentially, is a fancy space blanket. Not just the kind you can buy in the local camping goods store, but the $2,000–$3,000 kind you special order from a firefighter supply store. It is basically a one-person shelter that you can draw over yourself, so that you are underneath it against the ground. So what the smoke jumpers who wish to have a chance to get through a wall of fire have to do is to clear away fuels, such as wood and grass from a 10 foot × 4 foot rectangle, then lay down with the shelter over them and allow the fire to pass over them. This fire shelter has saved many lives because it is made to withstand extremely high temperatures, so that the fire can pass over the smoke jumper and allow him or her to emerge on the side of safety, where there is no more fuel. Nonetheless, smoke jumpers tell me it gets hot in there, almost hot enough to slowly bake something, or someone; hence, the name "slow bake." In this case, the smoke jumper has to go against eons of learning that says to run away from fire, and instead go toward it and even through it. The smoke jumper has to do what might seem unnatural to stand a chance of living. Anxiety operates very much like this, where everything is telling you to run away from the fire, to escape its searing temperatures and poisonous, superheated gases. Only problem is, with anxiety disorders, it's like you are encircled, like a smoke jumper in trouble, and you can run and avoid for a while, but sooner or later the only way you will be OK is to get through the fire, or in your case, face what makes you afraid. Just as smoke jumpers are trained on how to use fire shelters, we need to teach you how to use a fire shelter of sorts to get over, or through, your fears. Our fire shelter is exposure.

Although this system of classically and operantly conditioning encoding emotionally charged information is advantageous in some important, primitive survival ways, it also creates some unique problems. Primarily, the greatest problem still facing practitioners working with anxiety-disordered patients is how to properly access this type of information, as important autonomic response sets and behavioral activation codes are stored outside more conscious domains. Although conscious domains of operations may be available to both practitioner and patient to collaboratively work on and modify in ways that will better suit the patient in a modern world, autonomic reactivity and fear responses may not be as readily available for modification *unless they are directly accessed*. Exposure methods allow access to domains that otherwise cannot be readily entered and because such methods have a more direct capacity to extinguish reactivity and autonomic arousal, they are central to the adequate treatment of anxiety disorders.

Mowrer's model essentially describes the concept of negative reinforcement. Negative reinforcement refers to the strengthening of behavioral response sets through the removal of an aversive stimulus (e.g., something anxiety or fear producing). This kind of reinforcement is a more powerful agent of reinforcement than either positive reinforcement or punishment. Positive reinforcement often runs the risk of satiation effects, meaning that the reinforcer (e.g., food, money) is only reinforcing when the subject being reinforced views or experiences the reinforcer as desirable; that is, for food to be a reinforcer, a person would have to be hungry, or for money to be a reinforcer, the person would have to want something the money could buy. If the person was not hungry or had enough money already, those reinforcers would be irrelevant, and would consequently *not* be reinforcing. Therefore, a common dilemma is how a practitioner actually knows whether the patient truly is reinforced by a positive reinforcer.

Punishment, as a reinforcement strategy, is also fraught with challenges; for example, in the face of punishment, the punishment must be inescapable or the subject being punished will try to escape it. How often do people actually have that much control over another person? It is more likely that the subject being punished will not learn to stop the behavior being punished, but rather to only exhibit the behavior when the punishing agent is not around, or to simply avoid the punishing agent all together. Reinforcement is meant to increase or decrease behavior, but as such both positive reinforcement and punishment do only a minimally adequate job of the task. Punishment also has some inherent, potential moral issues. Is inflicting pain (a "positive" punishment paradigm, such as spanking) or removing some privilege (a negative punishment paradigm, such as a meal) all right? Many people do not think so. In fact, some countries (e.g., Sweden) have outlawed corporal punishment, so it is in some places illegal to spank someone (presumably an unruly child). Many countries do not allow the death penalty. Punishment is highly controversial in many ways, both on moral and pragmatic grounds. Beyond moral objections, for example, it is clear that physical violence teaches primarily using physical violence. Fundamentally, this is a problem for many people on many levels.

So, then, what is negative reinforcement, and why does it work so much better than positive reinforcement and punishment? By definition, negative reinforcement means going from something bad to something better. In essence, negative reinforcement means to take away something bad or unpleasant that by default (naturally) leaves the subject *relieved*. For instance, imagine being delirious with a fever and body aches because of a strong flu. That feels bad, and the person is, if the flu is bad enough, pretty much incapacitated. He or she is in a "bad way." Then, whether through medicine or time, the person begins to feel better; that is, the feeling bad is removed and is replaced by feeling better. That change for the better is inherently, naturally incredibly reinforcing, and makes it highly likely that the person will do again whatever he or she did to feel better last time should he or she ever feel bad again (i.e., the response that created feeling better is reinforced, increasing the likelihood it will be used again in the same or a similar circumstance). It is not even necessary to be all better, so long as the person feels just slightly better than before, akin to feeling a bit better after taking the aspirin or cough medicine (although not being all better yet). Feeling good is always preferable to feeling bad, which in essence is the backbone of the hedonistic principle on which survival is based. In a fundamental way, there are some experiences people are programmed to naturally fear because encountering such stimuli could threaten survival. For example, people naturally know if they fall from something high they might be seriously hurt, or even killed, so people tend to approach (especially novel) heights with caution. This caution is a natural response to something that signals possible danger. The same is true for situations such as deep water (people could drown), sharp objects (people could be cut or impaled), and a whole host of other basic threats to well-being and health. Being sick and feeling sick (nauseous) are other common experiences that come programmed for people at a deep, subconscious level as natural aversions. This is because in a primitive way, it could signal impending death or poisoning. Such primitive threats are responded to in autonomic, reflexive ways (e.g., vomiting when nauseous is meant to protect against poison) that are not necessarily available to or under the control of conscious thought processes.

The concept of *establishing operation* (Michael, 1982) refers to the idea that the practitioner must be aware that there are emotional states that are naturally reinforcing, such as what occurs within a negative reinforcement paradigm. So, anxiety for example, as an emotional state, is an establishing operation because it increases the reinforcing value of removing certain (aversive) stimuli and because it increases the frequency of those behavioral response sets that remove fearful stimuli (Sturmey, 1996). Establishing operation is intimately tied to the nature of negative reinforcement, in that it *establishes* what the individual will do to feel better (e.g., will avoid and escape to feel less anxious).

ROLE OF EXPOSURE IN REDUCING ANXIETY RESPONSES

So, how does exposure really reduce the autonomic anxiety response? This is a common question from both practitioners and patients. It is an important question, because the answer addresses the central mechanism of change of exposure. It is about the power to dramatically change just how easily someone becomes highly aroused, especially in circumstances in which the individual inaccurately responds with the kind of arousal that should occur in the presence of true and immediate threat to life and limb.

Exposure actually follows naturally from etiological models of anxiety and fear, which are built on learning theory. Because certain stimuli, whether they be thought- or situation-based, have taken on the capacity to elicit an (inappropriate) anxiety response, exposure deconditions this unwarranted response. In other words, strong reactions of anxiety and fear are reduced through repeatedly experiencing the aversive stimulus in the absence of actual, true threat or harm. After repeatedly not being harmed by the feared stimulus (e.g., not crashing the car when driving), it eventually ceases to produce the activation of the motivational system geared at helping a person survive. It stops responding with anxiety because the feared outcome (i.e., predation) does not occur. Fortunately, the human body is a system of conservation because it is a system for survival; when threat and danger are not imminent, then the body will conserve fuels meant to facilitate survival. Therefore, when an individual remains in the presence of what is supposed to be threatening (e.g., driving), and the outcome (e.g., car crash) does not happen, before too long the body will turn off the anxiety reaction, saving it for later.

So, how does exposure work? It works because it asks patients to face what they fear to be true without leaving (i.e., escaping or avoiding), so that, repeatedly, the survival system, which had been inaccurately responding to an imagined or benign threat, can stop or reduce its response. Exposure works by teaching the survival motivational system that it was reacting when it did not need to, responding, in essence, at the wrong time. The reason this deconditioning does not occur easily by itself for many anxiety-disordered patients is the typical fact they are not remaining with noxious and aversive stimuli for sufficient amounts of time for the survival system to recognize it responded in error. In fact, through escape and avoidance, the system learns, or is conditioned to believe, that it was successful in thwarting predation; hence, the next time the system (person) encounters the stimulus, it will enact the same sets of responses because it was *successful* in the past in preventing negative outcomes. Exposure forces the system to recognize its error, through giving it the opportunity to encounter better evidence for what is truly dangerous and not. Exposure forces the system to act on the basis of evidence, much like the scientific method treats beliefs and assumptions as hypotheses deserving testing; thus, exposure is akin to the scientific method step of testing hypotheses to derive information or data about the state of affairs. Avoidance and escape treats assumptions and beliefs as absolutes, and does not allow such to be tested or examined for their credibility. Exposure allows corrective information about the nature of threat and danger, and this new discovered information, in short, allows the survival system to respond more accurately, or at times when it is needed.

Why exposure works is a bit more complicated, however. Looking fear in the face, as Eleanor Roosevelt put it, is not enough. Something else has to happen for the exercise to be useful. In discovering evidence and "truth" (a scientific oxymoron) the autonomic, sympathetic nervous system has to be turned off by the parasympathetic nervous system; in other words, the individual has to experience *habituation*, or a decrease of arousal in the presence of what is feared.

HABITUATION AND EXTINCTION: ENDING INACCURATE ANXIETY RESPONSES

Habituation and extinction make up the backbone on which all exposure treatment is built. Habituation and extinction are the pivotal parts that collectively represent the mechanism of change contained within exposure exercises. They are distinct aspects of change, but both are required for long-term and meaningful reduction in anxiety and fear. Habituation and extinction are why exposure "works" and can only be achieved through exposure and repeated exposure.

The human body is a beautiful instrument of conservation, in that it tends to stockpile materials (e.g., adrenalin, endorphins, fat) needed for high-demand activities when they are not being actively used. This conservation tendency ensures that such materials are available when it really counts, and at other times of high use (e.g., athletics, hard physical labor). This response translates into a relatively quick return to not using such fuels as soon as the expenditure is no longer needed; in other words, if there is no adversity to face, or the challenge is removed, then the immediate and preferred response is either to not spend these precious commodities to begin with, or else turn off the expenditure as soon as the threat is removed. The human body wants to conserve, not waste. In a modern world, devoid of most meaningfully dangerous threats, this central tendency for storing and saving has turned into the bane and torment of people concerned with fitness and health.

Nonetheless, this phenomenon translates further into something even more beautiful, namely that anxiety is naturally self-limiting. It has to be. Because of the primitive tendency to conserve, anxiety, in the absence of something to fear, will stop. Recall that anxiety is an autonomic reaction that is largely biophysical, and that such response depends on the exact fuels the body wants to conserve in the absence of true threat. Anxiety, therefore, will not continue indefinitely, even though many patients often report it feels that way. It will stop when the conclusion is reached that there is no threat and the expenditure of the precious fuels is a waste, or the body is no longer able to pump out those products. Either way, anxiety is a self-limiting experience. It does not and can not last for forever.

This self-limiting nature should be very welcome news indeed to people who struggle with anxiety. However, people who suffer and struggle with anxiety, especially those with clinically elevated levels of anxiety, tend to not benefit from this self-limitation. This unfortunate reality is due to people's general intolerance for feeling uncomfortable. Hedonism suggests that people will do something to try to feel better when they feel bad. People are broadly intolerant of negative states, almost regardless of the domain involved (e.g., thoughts, feelings, physiological). In short, many people, especially those with significant anxiety, will be too impatient to wait around for natural relief and decline in arousal. They are too uncomfortable, and want to feel better as soon as possible. It goes against hedonistic tendencies to simply sit back and wait for such a desired change to occur. Running away (i.e., escape) feels better faster than waiting it out or looking fear in the face and waiting to see what will happen. Keep in mind, too, that all of the fuels dumped into the bloodstream and muscles are meant to help someone run or fight (not sit still!), so the person is already primed toward action. In this prepared state, running is easy and staying is hard.

People who are highly anxious tend to escape (Figure 2.2) from the circumstance that makes them feel bad. When they do so, their anxiety is often quickly reduced because they "escaped" the danger (which the physiological reaction signals *must* be there) and lived. Unfortunately, because of conditioning, the person has learned that the stimulus *is* dangerous (i.e., it has to be true that it is dangerous). Emotional reasoning often reifies this mistaken belief into an absolute truth that simply is not challenged, but is instead acted on as if the stimulus really is dangerous. Why else would they have escaped? Would it be necessary to escape if the stimulus was benign or nonthreatening? No. The action of escape *confirms*, or reifies, that the feared stimulus deserves being feared. This circular reasoning gives the fear credence. Otherwise, from a conservation mode or frame, it was all a waste. It also teaches the person two other, very important lessons that ironically set him or her up to continue being fearful in the future. First, if ever faced with the same stimulus again, or something similar, the person comes to think he or she should repeat the behavioral response set (i.e., escape) because it "worked" (i.e., distress reduced). Second, the person begins to believe that he or she should just avoid that stimulus altogether, because the expenditure of precious materials would not have to be performed if the stimulus were not encountered. Unfortunately, it is the rare fear that is so circumscribed, however, that it can be easily avoided in the world. Fears often generalize and make more parts of the world appear threatening because of the original fear. This operates through operant conditioning, which carries an enormous amount of capacity to form associations and connections from an original stimulus to both concretely and vaguely related stimuli. Nonetheless, conservation is always preferable, and easier to expend, and it is "safer" because a person is left with more rather than fewer reserves for another, future need. Conservation is easiest to achieve through avoidance of what would require action.

A significant problem with this mode of operation is that in an avoidant and escape model of survival, people can never find out what will happen if they actually looked fear in the face (i.e., faced what it is that makes them react and respond with anxiety and fear). They never obtain the evidence to either refute or support their beliefs, which then support their actions of escape or avoidance by default of being relatively all right when they do use such responses; after all, when they avoid or escape, the feared immediate outcome fails to occur. How can they, then, know if they are economical with how they are spending their fuels?

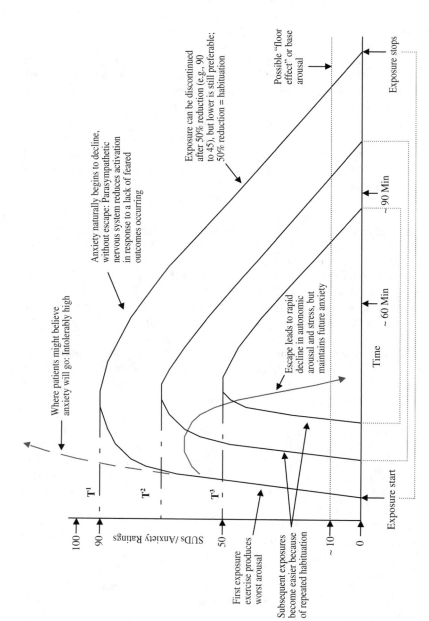

FIGURE 2.2   The normal, natural habituation curve and maladaptive escape curve.

Two-Process Theory (Negative Reinforcement) and Process

	Hedonistic Principle (Negative Reinforcement) Response Model	Exposure Paradigm (Endure Discomfort) Response Model
Stimulus: Trigger[2] situation	↑anxiety (or equivalent)	↑anxiety also
State 1: Aversive	Feel "bad"	Feel "bad"
Reaction: Desire to feel better (Hedonistic drive to ↓ "bad")	Escape[1] behavior response	NO escape response
State 2: Less Aversive/Good	Feels relief, quickly ↓ anxiety	Feels relief, but more slowly; nonetheless, ↓ anxiety still

Note: Escape[1] and Trigger[2] are net lessons: Escape behavior produces the relief and avoids the trigger in future.

FIGURE 2.3   Two-Process Theory: Hedonism versus exposure outcomes.

They cannot know, and therefore they keep spending, because continued expenditure continually allows people to feel all right in the moment. Thus they keep reacting with arousal because they have no evidence to the contrary that they should not. They keep reacting with stress to stimuli that do not warrant such reactions. They have become inaccurate in their response, reacting to more and new kinds of stimuli because their system is constantly pumping out chemicals that should be present only during danger. If they feel like something is dangerous, because physiologically it seems to be supported, then it becomes dangerous. Therefore, they become increasingly inaccurate, and respond more and more easily as they become more and more vigilant to all of the threats and danger they now perceive in the world.

Exposure, on the other hand, allows them to see this inaccuracy and helps them see that they are spending fuels at unnecessary times because it asks the person to not run away (Figure 2.3). When a person follows the hedonistic core programming, they principally learn that they need to use escape behavioral response sets to feel better, and that they should avoid the offending trigger in the future. In this sense, they become dependent on

escape-based behaviors and become largely avoidant so they will not have
to employ the escape-based responses. Because escape could conceivably
fail, it will always seem (from the hedonistic point of view) that avoidance
is a better response base, a "safer" choice. This exact preference is what
sustains fears long-term, because nothing contradictory can be discovered
through avoidance. Instead, what a person learns in the exposure is that
feeling better does not require any action per se, but that feeling better
can actually happen naturally with time, presuming the threat actually
does not represent any real danger. Additionally, they learn the feared
outcome did not occur, so an escape response would have been superfluous. Indeed, they most importantly learn that it was not necessary to
respond with anxiety and fear, and that anxiety is actually self-limiting.
With repetition of exposure, the body gradually stops responding in the
presence of the previously feared stimulus because it has learned through
experience it was not a threat. Repeated habituation, therefore, is what
produces extinction.

Extinction means the person no longer responds with anxiety and
fear to the stimulus, and the old response set has been made obsolete.
Earlier exposure will always seem more challenging to patients, because
they have little evidence yet to contradict what they believe and their
bodies are consequently quite reactive and responsive when presented
with the feared stimulus. However, as exposure is repeated, the exercises
should seem increasingly easier (presuming the same exposure is repeated),
because accumulating evidence informs the person of a more accurate
estimate of the state of affairs in which the reactivity is gratuitous. This
between-exercise reduction in challenge/difficulty is often called between-
session habituation. Although within-session habituation is important to
achieve, between-session habituation is even more important because it
theoretically demonstrates some deeper integration of new information
about what is dangerous and what is not. A lack of between-session
habituation (i.e., the same exposure exercise remains as hard as the first
time, or first few times, during subsequent exposure) signals a lack of
new learning and should be carefully monitored for. A careful investigation should be conducted to see what might be contributing to a failure
to integrate longer term information about threat, especially when within
session habituation occurs (see chapter 5 for some possibilities).

Four factors broadly influence the basic effectiveness of exposure:
frequency, duration, severity, and latency. In terms of *frequency*, the more
often a person can have contact with that which he or she fears, the more
quickly unreasonable fears can be deconditioned. Intuitively, this makes
sense in that with little contact, very little experience will be gathered that
directly contradicts what the person believes to be true. More experience

simply gives more opportunities to experience the threat as not threatening. How often the patient engages in exposure to face his or her fear is the first factor known to influence how quickly suffering is reduced. Roughly speaking, this means patients should engage in exposure exercises *often*, which typically means they should do exposure-based exercises between formal therapy sessions. This is, in part, why homework plays an important role in any exposure-based treatment package. Homework will also be important because it is preferable and pivotal for the patient to also engage in exposure work without the therapist present. Reasons for this will be explained in a later section.

In virtually the same tone, *duration* of exposure is important, if not absolutely critical, because it pertains extremely closely to habituation. It directly relates to habituation, in that habituation cannot occur unless there is a 50% reduction in personal distress (often termed Subjective Units of Distress [SUDS], which is often placed on a scale). A half-reduction in SUDS cannot be accomplished instantaneously; therefore, it will be crucial to continue the exposure at least until such a half-reduction has been achieved. If a sufficient amount of time is not spent, and habituation does not occur, the exposure will be ineffective. For most patients, a time frame of 1–2 hours is sufficient for normal habituation to occur. After they become accustomed to the exposure exercises and build some experience with finding or discovering that their worst fears do not come true, habituation can typically be accomplished in less time (e.g., 30–90 minutes). Ultimately, the SUDS ratings will determine whether it is prudent to exit the exposure situation, because exiting before the half-reduction is akin to escape and is detrimental to overall treatment progress.

Severity does not necessarily refer to the idea of only how difficult the exercise is, but is instead meant to ensure that a patient does not stay with a range of "safe," easier exercises that may be found low on a difficulty hierarchy. If the patient never performs any challenging exposure exercise, he or she is staying away from the fear, and a meaningful reduction in that fear is prevented. Severity means that the patient will have to face more difficult items in a fear hierarchy to ultimately overcome the fear. This does not mean that a practitioner should start the patient with hard items or what resides at the top of a fear hierarchy, because doing so would be engaging in flooding. Although flooding is a recognized exposure technique, it is not as effective in the long term, nor is it as tolerable for the patient. Starting in the bottom half of a fear hierarchy is important for many reasons, but principally ensures a greater likelihood of success and completing the treatment. Starting close to the top of a hierarchy, or moving too fast up a hierarchy, is one way to almost guarantee attrition and premature termination of treatment.

Situation	Fear Rating
Driving over the Steel Bridge at rush hour	100
Driving on the highway at rush hour, at dusk, and in poor weather	90
Driving on the highway at rush hour, in good weather	80
Being a passenger on the highway during rush hour	75
Driving on the highway in the middle of the day, in good weather	65
Driving on a city street at midday, when it is raining	65
Driving on a city street at midday, when the sky is clear	50
Turning onto a city street during traffic hours	45
Driving in a busy parking lot during business hours	35
Driving in an empty parking lot during "off" hours	25

FIGURE 2.4   Sample fear hierarchy for overcoming a phobia of driving.

Latency refers to timing. Specifically, it means how quickly after the command to start the patient begins. Procrastination and an unwillingness to start after the instruction has been given to commence cements further the credibility of the fear. If it had no truth to it, why would the person hesitate? The more the person waits and *avoids*, the more the feared stimulus remains feared. Indeed, poor latency (longer avoidance and hesitation) tends to make the fear worse because a lot of hesitation in approach behaviors is registered emotionally in the survival networks as signs of true threat. Hesitation reifies the fear.

Exposure work always begins with collaboratively establishing, or building, a fear hierarchy. The hierarchy is made up of increasingly difficult situations related to what is feared. For example, for someone who is afraid of crashing if he or she drives a car, that person would start in the lower part of the hierarchy, where "safer" driving tasks would be encountered (e.g., drive around an empty parking lot). Because success is realized in lower items (i.e., habituation is accomplished to lower items), then the patient moves on to the next harder step. The sequence of exposures moves the patient from developing comfort with the confrontational task with lower items (which may still be perceived as challenging in the beginning) to facing his or her most challenging obstacles and fears. For example, for the driving phobic, a last step might be driving across a challenging stretch of road or bridge under poor conditions (e.g., rush-hour traffic, rain, dark). Each step might also be broken into two-part stages, in which the first times the stage is performed, it is done when accompanied by the practitioner or significant other who has been recruited to support and facilitate the exposure exercises. Either way, the hierarchy progresses in challenge (Figure 2.4).

It is important that patients actively collaborate with the practitioner in developing the hierarchy, because no one knows the exact nature of the fears better than the patients themselves. Because of avoidance, patients may not be entirely in tune with the complete and full nature of the fears, so they may actually really need the assistance of the practitioner in more fully exploring the fears to be able to construct a meaningful hierarchy. A more common problem is that patients can readily identify what is at the very top of the hierarchy, or what is the most challenging, and what is really at the bottom, or what they can probably already realistically do with just some extra discomfort. The net effect is that there is no gray zone between the two, and without this, there is no material to "work up" with. With the material being bimodally distributed between "easy" and "hard" items, there is nothing that incrementally moves the patient closer to the end goal. If there is no such middle ground, then the patient would have to make a leap from easy to hard. This is often the byproduct of avoidance, in that as soon as the difficult stimulus is encountered, the patient escapes, learning no in-between approximations. Thus, without something "doable" in the middle, the patient might believe the distance between the bottom and top is too large, and he or she is probably right. Most patients experience large amounts of distress when they undergo flooding because there has been no preparatory middle-ground success. The leap straight to the top items may indeed be too hard, as the best literature suggests is true. In this sense, flooding, or going from easy (i.e., what people can probably actually do with some minimal prompting already) right to what is extremely hard (i.e., what they believe they cannot do, and consequently have not done), might just be bordering on cruel, unless patients request that type of approach specifically. Some people who have only a limited amount of time to spend at getting over their fears, such as an executive who literally has all of 2 weeks away from nonstop working in any given year, may even choose to go with flooding over gradual, hierarchical exposure because of pragmatic constraints.

PROCESSING CONNECTIONIST NEURAL NETWORK (PDP-CNN) MODELS

Tryon (2005) has offered perhaps the most scientific explanation for just why exposure therapy works. As with other authors (e.g., Rosen & Davison, 2003), he has put forth a strong argument that psychology should only list empirically supported principles of change, instead of trademarked, proprietary therapies (e.g., Barlowian panic control treatment). Listing such therapies, instead of the principles underlying such treatments, can promote and even facilitate the unfortunate establishment and proliferation of unscrupulous practitioners developing "new" therapies by adding one or more functionally inert components to already existing, established efficacious treatments. Although there may be agreement and professional/ethical requirements that only reliable and valid psychological tests should be used in psychological assessment, less consensus regrettably exists for psychotherapy. Tryon (2005) accurately suggested that the extent to which interventions are to be based and informed by scientific research is one of central professional debates of psychology today. Indeed, much has been accomplished in identifying interventions that meet minimal scientific standards (Sanderson, 2003), but this professional developmental push has not been without its opponents and strong critics (e.g., Hebert, 2003). It has been suggested that perhaps this opposition stems from the accusation that empirically supported treatments (ESTs) do not provide sufficient explanatory context for understanding patients' presenting problems. Although it would theoretically be possible to administer invalid or unreliable assessment measures or tests, most prudent practitioners (if they knew about lacking validity/reliability) would likely decide against such questionable action; similarly, many may feel that action without sufficient explanatory context is bordering on questionable or even unethical practice. Therefore, most practitioners will opt for a set of actions that most fully explain patients' issues, even if those actions mean they turn to "comfortable" theoretical tradition and interventions with which they are familiar (regardless of degree of empirical support such positions hold).

The surprisingly broad gap between science and practice flagrantly points to this practitioner need or desire to explain, even at the high price of empirical support (Tryon, 2005). Indeed, empirically derived outcome findings alone appear not enough to prevail on practitioners to use ESTs! Since the inception of ESTs, this lag of practice has been the norm, and it does not appear to be changing quickly toward any greater reliance on and use of ESTs. Capitalizing on this desire (possibly necessity) for explanation may in reality be how more practitioners could be increasingly persuaded to turn to empirical methods through scientific explanations of just how and why such interventions work. Understanding the hows and whys of ESTs turn them into empirically supported principles, and may provide the descriptive power practitioners appear to seek. Therefore, researchers and practitioners alike (e.g., Shapiro, 1995) are increasingly promoting that psychotherapy research should focus on just how effective therapies work, so that attention can be turned to matters of explanation as well as prediction and control. For instance, although philosophy and religion may explain much of what people want to understand, they can predict little that could be empirically verified or perhaps even falsified. Empirically supported principles, because they represent a shift back to or a return to scientific principles, just as hypothesis testing does, are capable of providing *both* explanatory theories and testable predictions. Mature sciences should provide capacity for explanations and prediction (Proctor & Capaldi, 2001; Tryon, 2005). Because principles behind how and why exposure therapy works have not been well explained, there may be a reluctance to adopt it as a treatment approach; thus, increasing insight into just how it does work (i.e., make its principles of change transparent) should promote its more widespread adoption and utilization. The burden of "proof" (a counterintuitive scientific term) rests with proponents of exposure therapy, not with its opponents. To date, proponents of exposure therapy may have correctly explained and fully described intervention effects of exposure, but as to a cogent and complete etiological explanation of anxiety disorders, its proponents may have fallen short. Indeed, a lack of widespread dissemination of ESTs may be disquietingly pointing to a remaining necessity to actually better *explain* therapeutic effects of exposure, rather than through predictions of outcome. Explanation and prediction, when truly given together, will describe more than necessary and sufficient procedural ingredients within exposure therapy, and thereby increase dissemination. This remaining need for explaining therapeutic effects has led researchers and practitioners alike to innovative mathematical and scientific models of memory mechanisms that learn, called PDP-CNN.

Psychotherapy is based on the fundamental principle that people learn. Tryon (2000) extended this basic premise to argue that learning plays an etiological role on psychological and behavioral disorders of all sorts, and that all people who benefit from psychotherapy learn something. In other words, learning is the active and necessary ingredient in change. Learning is perhaps the single most uniform empirically supported principle within psychotherapy; therefore, dissemination of exposure therapy hinges on better (scientific) explanations of learning within exposure. Learning is further based on memory and retention, and, as it turns out, there are many common biological structures to learning and memory, leading most scientists to see the two as interdependent structures and functions. From this stance, neuroscience has explored mechanisms of learning and memory, and this work has led to the development of formal network learning theory (e.g., McClelland & Rumelhart, 1987; Rumelhart & McClelland, 1986).

This careful examination of learning and memory has led to the acceptance that learning entails synaptic change, or brain plasticity. PDP-CNN models rely on mathematical models and equations to simulate synaptic change across learning trials (Tryon, 2005). Synaptic change has been proposed to imply a neural network architecture made up of a hypothetical three-layered feed-forward network of nodes. In such an architecture, all nodes in each layer are connected to all other nodes in adjacent layers so that nodes in the top layer are not directly connected with nodes in the bottom layer, except through the connective nodes in the middle layer. Connections between nodes and layers can be excitatory or inhibitory, as demonstrated by either positive (activating) weights or negative (not activating) weights. In this sense, layers of networks are made up of nodes (neurons) and connections between such layers (synapses). During learning and memory, activation "cascades" across the network, activating and inhibiting certain combinations of nodes, depending on synaptic weighting of connections for certain stimuli. Based on connections and weighting combinations, not all nodes are activated or necessarily activated or inhibited in the same combinations. Instead, stimuli have to go through a filtering (conceptual/abstraction) level before a response is produced or selected. The top layer receives stimulus input, as provided by perception processes. The middle layer is formulating concepts, which feeds to the bottom layer, where fitting behavioral responses are formed and elicited. Together, this cascade of connections and weights transforms sensory and perceptive data to behavioral responses. Depending on sign and magnitude (weighting) of connections, this transformation influences what the network "thinks" and "feels" about particular stimulus or setting events (Tryon, 2005). Through translating this network processing explanation to physical and chemical processes, psychology can move into the same arena as more mature, "hard" sciences, such as biology, chemistry, and physics (Wilson, 1998). Learning, or the mechanisms and effects of psychotherapy, entails changing size and sometimes the sign of connection weights that are related to constraints in a network processing cycle. Constraints can be thought of as limitations or restrictions that influence a person's capacity to reach the best possible solutions; the more important constraints that are satisfied, the better the solutions derived. Resolving constraints, through learning and memory activation by input, is largely what network theory describes. In this sense, PDP-CNN resolves dissonance to satisfy as many competing interests and constraints as possible, and settles the networks of nodes and connections into the best possible compromise (consonance) solutions possible to whatever problem is at hand (Tryon, 2005).

For some, this innovative and complex biological, chemical, and physics model for understanding humans may be intimidating. However, although the language may be more involved, practitioners are well familiar with the components that really make up this model for how to understand why and how people function. Practitioners know full well that their patients come to them, seeking services, with an already well-established and long developmental history. The top layer of nodes can be thought of as the results of sensation and perception within this history. Middle layers of nodes comprise various facets of cognitions and emotions, and the bottom layers are behavioral response repertoires that have been configured over such histories. The cascading process through these layers of nodes and connections arbitrates how individual patient's perceptions have given rise to fear-related cognitions, emotions, and behaviors. Practitioners' tasks involve creating dissonance and network instability, so that, through new learning cycles, new consonant states can be configured, which presumably will contain more reasonable response sets. Through presenting fear-related information, as is done in exposure therapy, patients behave "therapeutically" in that they engage in some desired output mode while faced with fear-related information. This is often referred to as "clamping" an output node, which creates network instability. Subsequent change occurs because patients' networks will seek consonance (i.e., decrease dissonance within the network) through an iterative gradient descent constraint satisfaction process wherein the learning process modifies connection (synaptic) weights, thereby producing network weighting that is consistent with desirable behavior as represented by output or response levels. Changing the weighting across the networks therefore makes stimuli cascade across the network into desired therapeutic responses, and through this process, new cascading patterns change causally mediating cognitions and emotions (Tryon, 2005). This PDP-CNN model of change allows sufficient explanation and prediction and has support from a variety of important, more developed sciences (e.g., neuroscience, neuroimaging, computer simulation). This model, as well as earlier, less neuroscientifically oriented models, points to the well-established fact that exposure works. The PDP-CNN model offers insights into just how exposure works.

TYPES OF EXPOSURE

There are a multitude of different versions of exposure formats, each being uniquely suited for particular types of fears, or serving a particular purpose. Each type of exposure will be discussed in turn.

In Vivo

Live, or in vivo, exposure is the all-time classic for exposure. It has served as a cornerstone for behavior therapy for decades (Hazlett-Stevens & Craske, 2003). Interestingly, more dynamic theoretical orientations (e.g., psychoanalytic, Gestalt), which are often critical of behavior therapy's "simplistic" focus on symptom relief, have relied on exposure techniques to treat neuroses (Foa & Kozak, 1986). Live exposure means that the patient is asked to confront, in real-life and real-time, the actual feared stimuli, whether gradually or more quickly. That is, if a person is afraid of spiders, for example, he or she would be asked to eventually handle spiders, although typically after working up through less directly confrontational exposures first because graduated exposure is more tolerable than flooding and has superior long-term effects.

One of the most recognizable forms of exposure has been *systematic sensitization*, first developed and used by Salter (1949) and Wolpe (1958). In this type of exposure, the patient is first taught how to deeply relax, and, once relaxed, the feared stimuli are gradually presented. If the patient finds he or she is becoming more tense, or more nervous and anxious, the stimulus is withdrawn until the patient can become deeply relaxed again, and then the stimulus is re-presented, again in a gradual fashion. The objective of this strategy is for the patient to be thoroughly relaxed in the presence of a feared stimulus, because this would intuitively and biophysiologically signal that the stimulus cannot be dangerous or threatening. After all, the human body is supposed to react with autonomic arousal in the presence of something threatening, so if the body is thoroughly relaxed (typically accomplished through progressive muscular relaxation), then the surroundings must not be threatening. Systematic desensitization capitalizes on the normal and natural anxiety reactions that should occur in the presence of danger, in that it sets out to fool or force the body into behaving in a relaxed fashion around something that is perceived as being bad by the patient. In doing so, the strategy makes the stimuli nonthreatening because the body ceases to be responsive to the threat.

There are two fundamental critiques of systematic relaxation and relaxation, in general, and their use in exposure. First, to be "successful," one has to be relaxed in the presence of aversive or noxious stimuli. This may work reasonably well for stimuli that have been deconditioned this way, but less well for new ones. The problem inherently is the idea that people are naturally aroused to a degree (i.e., base arousal; see Figure 2.1), and novel stimulation typically will increase such arousal. It is unreasonable to expect that people will be able to walk around life completely relaxed all of the time. People will become aroused in the presence of either stress or novelty, and they may not always be adept at relaxing or circumstances may not always be such that relaxation is appropriate. This represents a significant problem. The second significant issue with relaxation is that being relaxed precludes the possibility of habituation. Habituation simply cannot occur when a person is very relaxed, because a half-reduction of arousal simply is not feasible in the presence of a floor effect, or base arousal. Simply put, if the person is not more highly aroused, then he or she might not be able to experience enough relief that the body concludes the stimulus was not threatening after all. Without habituation, true extinction is not possible; therefore, relaxation has been very controversial in connection with exposure-based work (e.g., Borkovec & O'Brien, 1976; Craske & Barlow, 2001; Foa & Franklin, 2001; Foa & Kozak, 1985; Heimburg et al., 1990; Levin & Gross, 1985; Öst, 1996). Although the topic is controversial, it can be suggested that relaxation during exposure is contraindicated, generally; however, during much exposure work, diaphragmatic breathing is often used to keep patients from completely panicking while facing very difficult challenges (i.e., on a SUDS rating, keeping the arousal level to a 9 or 9.5 versus letting it become a 10). There are two important reasons to do so. First, if a person becomes completely overwhelmed and too highly stressed, he or she may leave (escape) the exposure before habituation occurs, which would cement further the irrational beliefs of danger and would serve to unnecessarily prolong treatment, presuming the patient returns. Second, when a person is completely overwhelmed, the last "F," or faint (dissociate, shut down, not be present), may occur. That is, the person may go into a self-preserving mode in which he or she is not present during the exposure, which is akin to avoidance; obviously, this also prevents habituation.

Critically, during exposure, patients must not do anything to diminish what they are supposed to be experiencing. That is, they cannot distract themselves, pretend they are somewhere else, think that what they are experiencing is not real, and the like. In other words, they must not do anything that detracts from what they are to experience. If they do, then that is similar to escaping. Therefore, it behooves the practitioner to watch carefully for very quickly falling SUDS ratings, because such a phenomenon might be indicative of some sort of escape behavior, even if patients remain in the presence of the offending stimulus. SUDS should be reduced slowly at first and then gradually begin to fall more quickly as about a half-reduction is realized; patterns other than such a gradual decline of arousal should be highly suspect and questioned as to whether patients might be engaged in some (unintentional) avoidance or escape behavior, whether overt or covert (e.g., not looking at the stimulus or thinking about something else). During exposure, the task is to focus on the stimulus and all of the danger that it represents, and nothing else that might shift attention away from it.

Some patients might not be willing to face their fears in this live format, although if done in a gradual, tolerable fashion, this typically does not present a significant problem. To combat this problem, exposure exercises will typically be conducted in the presence and under the guidance and support of the practitioner. The practitioner will model and demonstrate first, then ask the patient to also perform the exposure task. In this fashion, the patient gets to see, firsthand, exactly what he or she is supposed to do and then is supported and encouraged by the practitioner. After the work moves up the hierarchy, and more challenging exposures are performed in this manner, then lower items (already successfully performed) are assigned for the patient to perform independently (without the practitioner's presence and support) for homework. The practitioner should never push the patient into performing exposure exercises that he or she is not ready for or willing to do for ethical reasons, but also because if a patient performs a task only because the practitioner *made* him or her do it, then it will not be integrated as something that the patient really conquered. That is, such patients know full well that the only reason they did what they did was because of the practitioner, and they would never have been able or willing to do it if it was only up to them; therefore, if left to their own whims, they typically will behave as if the item has *not* been overcome and conquered. In fact, because of the likely stress and trauma potentially being involved with being pushed hard to do something they were not ready for or willing to do, the item may seem even harder to approach. Thus the strong and emphatic recommendation is to—under no circumstances—push patients into performing exposure exercises that they are not ready for or willing to do. In this respect, the only contraindication for exposure, and in vivo exposure particularly because it is exposure's most potent form, is an unwillingness to engage in exposure treatment and possibly three other conditions.

Exposure might be contraindicated for someone with cardiovascular disease, such as heart disease, because the arousal that can be brought on by exposure exercises might be too taxing for such conditions. Careful and complete consultation and collaboration should be standard practice for patients with medical problems, because a genuine risk for physical harm should be clearly ruled out. Only a qualified medical doctor can make such critical determinations, and for patients with medical conditions, close consultation should be ongoing throughout the active treatment phase. For some patients who exhibit the vasovagal syncope response, it may be necessary to alter treatment slightly to first teach them how to prevent fainting through applied tension (e.g., Öst, 1987, 1988a, 1988b; Öst, Fellenius, & Sterner, 1991; Öst, Lindahl, Sterner, & Jerremalm, 1984; Öst & Sterner, 1987; Öst, Westling, & Hellström, 1995). Exposure might also be against common sense for someone who is living in a genuinely dangerous situation of domestic violence. In the treatment of posttraumatic stress disorder (PTSD), there is often work conducted on feeling all right about being out and about in the world again, to reduce and eradicate beliefs that the patient's perpetrator or abuser will hurt him or her again, and to gain a better sense that the world is really a more moderately safe place. However, if there is any significant risk that the patient might actually run into the past abuser, then exposure that asks him or her to put him- or herself into vulnerable positions would be contraindicated. In such situations, live exposure might be eliminated or reduced in favor of in-imagination exposure. Last, exposure might not be a realistically helpful approach for psychotic or delusional patients, because exposure exercises might trigger problematic episodes. Again, careful collaboration with other treatment providers and prescribers in such circumstances would be warranted and should be deemed necessary before work with such patients using these methods can begin.

Nonetheless, some patients feel incapable of directly addressing their fears, and in such cases it may be useful to start with facing the fears in-imagination, or other "pretend" ways, such as virtual reality.

In-Imagination and Virtual Reality

Although in vivo exposure appears to be more effective than in-imagination, or "imaginal" exposure, there are many circumstances for which imagination-based exposure work is more appropriate. First, patients, as mentioned, might not be willing to face the real stimulus, but could be willing to face it in imagination. For this reason, some of the initial, worst reactivity and distress about provocative stimulus are reduced through in-imagination exercises, so the patient can move on to face fears in vivo. Some situations, such as lightning, thunderstorms, and tornados may realistically be impractical to recreate in vivo. For instance, one patient presented with PTSD after being injured in a landslide (see chapter 4); in that case, finding such events were essentially moot, so proceeding with in-imagination was necessary. Last, there may be situations that would simply be too dangerous (not to mention unethical) to replicate in vivo. For instance, treating a motor vehicle accident PTSD patient by having him or her crash cars would not be practical, safe, or ethical; in short, sometimes in-imagination (or other non-in vivo) methods represent the only prudent course of action.

In-imagination exposure suffers from the real dilemma of not being real. It is fantasy; that said, some people are capable of having such a real fantasy life that it appears as realistic as real life. On the other hand, many people are not cognitively flexible enough to be able to create enough detail for imaginal exposure to be effective. It is clear that people just vary in their imagery ability (Kosslyn, Brunn, Cave, & Wallach, 1984). For in-imagination work to be powerful, it has to seem real. Stimuli appear real when they manifest the capacity to tap multiple human senses (i.e., sights, sounds, smell, taste, tactile); that is, the more senses involved in imagination work, the more real seeming and effective the exercise will be (Borkovec & Sides, 1979). Reality will be important, if not critical, for translation purposes to real-life stimuli. Other important factors in bringing imagination alive, such as the more conventional human senses, are also proprioception (sensing the position of one's body in space) and human emotion. The more emotion and sense of physical and emotional involvement with the imaginal scene, the more real the situations will seem.

A technology that has been used to enhance in-imagination exposure is virtual reality (VR). Although in its developing form VR seemed much like a first-generation computer game (i.e., not real seeming), the current VR technology is much further advanced, to the degree that it can predictably and more readily induce the kinds of autonomic reactions necessary for habituation and extinction. Notable, when VR is used it typically follows a graded format and is then suitably called VR-graded exposure therapy (Wiederhold, Gevirtz, & Spira, 2001). VR allows people who are low in imagery ability to derive more benefit from imagination exposure, because it helps them to imagine in much more graphic (pun intended) detail what they are to experience during exposure. Indeed, VR does not have to rely on a patient's own internal capacity for internal imagery, but instead introduces an external source to "trick" the brain into being more creative. On a low-technology end, this is often done with pictures and audiotapes, too, but VR encompasses obvious advantages and potential drawbacks (e.g., cost and availability). Besides producing more realism into imagery, VR is also safer (as is standard in-imagination exposure) than in vivo exposure. It allows the person to sit back in an artificial but otherwise safe environment and experience aversive stimuli. The artificiality of the treatment approach may have theoretical, negative impacts on relative effectiveness when compared with live exposure, but then any exposure that is not live will suffer from the same predicament of the patient ultimately knowing that what he or she is doing is *not* real. This can be akin to a safety behavior or mechanism that will diminish the impact of the exposure, ultimately reducing the comparative effectiveness to when a person encounters a real stimulus (Rosqvist, Sundsmo, MacLane, Cullen, Clothier Norling et al., in press). Nonetheless, VR exposure has good support as being an effective treatment strategy for common anxiety disorders, such as claustrophobia (Botella et al., 1998; Botella, Villa, Banos, Perpina, & Garcia-Palacious, 1999; Bullinger, Roessler, & Mueller-Spahn, 1998), arachnophobia (Carlin, Hoffman, & Weghorst, 1997), public speaking (Botella et al., 2000; North, North, & Coble, 1998), driving (Jang, Ku, Shin, Choi, & Kim, 2000; Wiederhold & Wiederhold, 1999), and social phobia (Wiederhold & Wiederhold, 1999).

Loop-Tape, Disaster Scripts, Pictures, and Other Methods

There are many ways to enhance imaginal exposure and they all aim at bringing into play a mix of human senses, emotion, and motoric behavior. Exposure by loop-tape is a common method for burning out reactivity to noxious stimuli, such as words, sounds, and sentences. It is also commonly used to enhance and supplement in vivo work by bringing into play aspects that otherwise could not readily be present in a situation. For instance, for the obsessive-compulsive disorder (OCD) patient "Catherine" in chapter 1, adding a loop-tape with the message "pedophile" increased the challenge (and effectiveness) of the live exposure of watching children in the park. This may be necessary to thoroughly extinguish aversive thoughts that might otherwise continue unchecked. Rachman (Emmelkamp, 1982) conceptualized intrusive thoughts, images, and impulses as *aversive stimuli* that are commonly and effectively treated systematically by exposure by loop-tape (and pictures for imagery material), so that the patient can habituate to the thought content. This procedure can also be effective in reducing extreme emotional reactivity to such intrusions, and thereby lowering overall daily distress levels. Reducing this kind of maladaptive overreactivity appears to also allow more patients to effectively engage in vivo exposure (van Oppen & Arntz, 1994; van Oppen & Emmelkamp, 2000; Wilson & Chambless, 1999). With too much charged content, it may simply be too much to face live exposures.

For practitioners unfamiliar with how to create a loop-tape, there are no steadfast rules, but several guiding principles exist. By definition, a loop-tape is a cassette tape without a true beginning or end, where it is instead an endless loop. The most common standard use for such tapes in more conventional ways than psychotherapy is for answering machines. Historically, answering machines contained different tapes. One tape was a loop-tape, typically only 20 or 30 seconds long, but sometimes up to a couple of minutes, which contained the greeting message (e.g., "Hello, the Johnsons aren't home, please leave a message after the beep"), and the other was commonly a regular or standard tape on which callers would leave their messages. Depending on the machine, the second tape was either somewhat shorter to limit how long a message a caller could leave, but it was usually 45, 60, or 90 minutes so multiple callers could leave somewhat detailed (longer) messages before cumulative messages were heard and erased. For the purposes of creating loop-tapes, the first greeting tape is obviously the one of primary interest. Although many answering machines are now going to a digital format, and thereby making tapes obsolete, loop-tapes of varying lengths can still be purchased at retail stores (e.g., Radio Shack) at reasonable prices (e.g., 20- or 30-second and 2-minute loop-tapes selling for approximately $5.00/tape). There are also specialty manufacturers of loop-tapes who make high-quality loop-tapes of various lengths, but they tend to be quite expensive in comparison to retail versions (i.e., $15.00 to $20.00 for a single tape of various lengths). As retail stores increasingly convert toward digital technology, more expensive loop-tape versions may be the only remaining option. Reasonably priced 1-, 2-, and 6-minute endless loop-tapes can still be purchased at the Cassette House (www.tape.com, 1-800-321-5738) and similar online businesses (e.g., www.tapeplus.com). However, it should be noted that *any* tape could be functionally used like a loop-tape by simply recording the content onto a standard tape repeatedly (e.g., 10–20 times), and then simply rewinding it when the last time through the "message" has been heard by the listener. Standard tapes may also need to be used if the script does not lend itself to a maximum 2 minutes, which is the longest loop-tape still available at electronics stores.

To set up a loop-tape, practitioners need to assist patients in developing a script that contains the target message (see the following section for a more complete description of developing scripts). This script is then timed when read multiple times to be sure it will fill the specific tape (length) being used. After a few rehearsals, to ensure that both the content can be fit onto the tape and patients will not stumble too much over the words, the provocative "message" is recorded onto the tape using any standard cassette recording device that has a microphone. Several recordings may need to be made before the message fits well onto the specified length and the message is delivered effectively onto the tape. The tape is then listened to for what the final product will sound like, and if it meets the requirements, it is given to the patient to listen to on a determined schedule. Because many patients may feel awkward about saying their feared scenarios aloud, they may need to practice simply saying the words multiple times to even be able to make a recording of something they more normally might have tried to not think, let alone say aloud. The words should match the language and tone with which they occur in the patient's mind, so some exploration may be necessary to discover what the actual words and their quality and quantity are.

"Disaster scripts," or written worst-case scenarios, are other common ways in which patients can extinguish reactivity to themes of content in a story format. Often, in OCD, generalized anxiety disorder, and social anxiety disorder, because they are extensively cognitively fueled, patients experience persistent and pervasive catastrophic themes, or lines of maladaptive, frightening thinking. To reduce the intrusive and aversive nature of these story-like thinking patterns, such scripts are used to rein in excessive reactivity and personal distress.

Following are two examples of disaster scripts from a patient who met diagnoses for OCD, generalized anxiety disorder, and PTSD. She exhibited extensive intrusive, ego-dystonic thoughts about harming her children and becoming sick in various ways and dying. These kinds of thoughts caused her extensive distress, and she spent many hours each day trying to convince herself that she was a good mother and was not dying. Ironically, she was one of the most caring mothers anyone could meet, but it is a good illustration because OCD typically attacks what people care most about. In her case, it was her children and her health (which was related to being able to care for her children). Using Rachman's formulation of these kinds of thoughts as aversive stimuli, they were extinguished using disaster scripts, which were also put onto loop-tapes. The first script, below, is the most challenging script "Beth" developed during treatment. It was only developed after going through many other, increasingly difficult scripts. At first read, it is probably a difficult script to read for anyone. In light of the fact that she loved her children and would never do anything ever to hurt them, readers may wish to try to imagine having these sorts of thoughts throughout the day. When reading the script, readers should also understand that Beth wrote the script independently of detailed directions for what content to use; the only direction she had was feedback on previous scripts about how to make them "good," meaning able to provoke emotion, and a variety of human senses and emotions. She reported becoming distressed when writing the script, but was then increasingly able to read the script, and in the end (while hearing the story on a loop-tape) she was able to not become reactive to the content (i.e., her SUDS scores did not change from her base arousal levels when hearing the story script, even when there was nothing else to distract her). She had successfully extinguished the obviously horrific content, much like she had with a multitude of other scripts before. She reported feeling very relieved to not be thinking these kinds of thoughts when she was in the company of her sons, and if she occasionally had a thought like it in their presence she did not remain reactive to it. Losing her reactivity for the content meant that she lost a lot of personal anxiety and fear. The second script is based more around health and dying and is representative of what an earlier script looked like. When reading the scripts, notice all of the emotional language, and clear, descriptive detail, and the pervasive present tense; taken together, these factors make the script come to life, seem real, in a way that it results in emotions a person might feel if the situation was real. For obvious reasons, this exposure is in-imagination.

SCRIPT 1: KILLING THE CHILDREN

My two sons and I are in the kitchen, preparing after-school snacks. They're both chatting amiably about their day. I'm asking if there's homework and we agree on a good time to do it. My 10-year-old son, "Alex," asks if he can have a bagel and I say, "Sure." He asks if I can cut it in half for him. I select a large bread knife from the block on the counter, and as I'm walking past Alex I'm gripping the knife tightly in my hand and I'm feeling an overwhelming urge to stab him. I am looking at the back of his shirt and imagining the knife going in. I no sooner think it, and my hand jerks forward and the blade is disappearing into him. He cries out and turns around and looks at me searchingly. He looks to me for help, not realizing what I've done to him. His eyes are wide and glazed as he stares at me in disbelief, unable to speak. He falls over and is trying to reach around himself because the knife is still in his back. Something comes over me; this rage I've had pent-up. I feel like I've done it now, and I'd better finish the job. My heart is racing and I feel like a machine, I can't stop. "Bill" is yelling, "Mom! Alex is stabbed! You stabbed Alex!" I'm telling him to shut up. I'm bending down and with a sickening twist I take the knife out and push him by the shoulder to turn him around. I'm stabbing him again, this time in the chest. He is an overweight child and I have to push the knife in extra hard. He tries to struggle, and keeps yelling, "Mom! NO!! Don't!! What are you doing?" His eyes are wide with terror and his skin is drained of color. I pull the knife out quickly this time and I'm looking him in the eye. "You stupid little fuck!" I'm repeatedly stabbing at him while he bleeds helplessly. His eyes finally shut and he stops moving. His clothes are all bloody and there's a growing pool of blood beneath him; it looks black against the brown linoleum. I've killed him, my son is finally dead. All those times I've pictured it, now I've finally done it. Bill is pulling at me but is trying not to get in my way, too. He's screaming in absolute horror. Satisfied that Alex isn't going anywhere, I take the knife out of him one last time and turn to Bill. He is running away, screaming in a crying way, and I quickly overtake him. At 13, he is all arms and legs, wiry and tall. I'm stronger, but as I grab him by the arm, he swings his bent arm upwards and nails me in the jaw with his elbow. Enraged, I get stronger. With my right hand, I stab him in the arm, missing his chest as he turns. He screams, "Why are you doing this?? Jesus Christ, you're crazy! Mom, please stop it!!" He's sobbing as he tries to get away, but I stab him all over, wherever I can get him. In our struggle, we fall to the ground. I stab him until his shirt is bloodied and he writhes on the carpet. He starts to sputter and choke and blood is coming out of my son's mouth. He is vomiting, and it's his school lunch mixed with blood. "Die, you little shit! You sick little fucks have kept me from living my life!" He passes out into death and I stand up to go look at Alex in the kitchen. His hair is matted and wet, and his face is streaked with blood.

He's still just a large lump where I left him, laying on his back in his own blood. I go to him and lift one of his hands and let go. It drops with a thud onto the linoleum, splattering blood. I've killed my children. I'm looking for the phone and see it on the counter by their backpacks and school newsletters. I call "Arthur" [Beth's husband] and tell him what I've done. "Alex and Bill are dead. I've killed them." There's a pause and in a dead voice he says, "What?" I tell him, "You better come over here...now." He's about to react but I hang up and dial "Matthew," my sons' dad. When he picks up the phone, I think how his life as he knows it is about to change. I very suddenly get very, very scared as I realize what I've done. I can't speak. Matthew says, "Hello!" again. Out of my mouth comes an anguished wail as I stare down at Alex and the reality of what I've done sinks in. I take the phone into the hallway where Bill lays and I scream when I see his lifeless body. " 'Susan'??" Matthew asks. I say, "Oh my God. Matthew, you've gotta come home. Just come home. Now...Just come home!" I hang up the phone and wait, my sons lying dead.

SCRIPT 2: DYING OF AN ASTHMA ATTACK

Tonight it doesn't seem to matter that I've used my inhaler twice, I still feel wheezy. It is scaring the shit out of me because I can't take a full breath. And if my inhaler doesn't work, then I'm fucked. So I go lie down, but instead of relaxing, my breathing is becoming worse, and every breath is a chore. My lungs are feeling so small and tight, and air is just not getting in. I can't exhale and my throat is caving in with every inhalation. My mind is frantic with thoughts of having to go in to emergency. Nothing is helping. Pretty soon I'm panicking as well, which makes it much worse. I'm getting "Smith" to take me to the hospital. I don't want to go because I'm so scared and because I don't know how I will get treated with all of the cutbacks. It's raining tonight and Smith runs out of gas on the way. I am in panic overdrive now and I can hardly breathe. Smith leaves me alone in the truck while he goes the 2 miles for gas. I am so scared and panicky. I'm crying and I'm starting to freak out. My airways are getting smaller and tighter until I am gasping for every breath. I'll never make it. I get out of my seat and open the door of the van, I need to get help. But I am so out of breath that I fall down on the wet street and am too weak to get up. I'm struggling for air and for a very frightening and agonizing while I take my last breaths until my lungs can't take it and they shut down.

Imaginal exposure can also be performed with pictures and videos. For instance, Christine (see chapter 1) used a variety of pictures both of adult semiclothed and nude females and semiclothed and nude children. Much of that work was preparatory work toward doing more challenging in vivo exposure exercises. For example, Christine went to a women's-only athletic club and used the sauna and steam room for the express purpose of being around nude women while purposely thinking some of the sexual thoughts that used to be very disturbing to her. Without doing some of the preparatory work, with pictures, she might not have been able to make the leap to being around nude women. Likewise, with children, she might not have been able to give baths to a friend's young children had she not progressed from pictures of children in various stages of dress, which prepared her for being with live children in the office. Similarly to Beth, Christine believed her thoughts meant she was a horrible person and that her thoughts must have meant that secretly she wanted to do the terrible things she was thinking. For such purposes, it might be worthwhile to point out that keeping magazines around the office will make it easier for a patient to begin such exposures, because they may be reluctant or have far too difficult a time going to buy a copy of *Parenting, Cosmopolitan,* or *Playboy.* A prudent practitioner who does any amount of imaginal exposure work will quickly begin to assemble a collection of exposure materials, among which might be all sorts of pictures and videos. For instance, combat veterans and needle phobics are both commonly asked to watch the movie *Pearl Harbor* repeatedly, because it contains graphic scenes of combat and troops being inoculated (receiving injections). Following is an example picture (Figure 2.5) of a child partially dressed. To most people the picture is benign, if not cute; however, in the hands of someone who for some reason has anxiety reactions or fear responses around children, it might serve as exemplar material for exposure (Figure 2.6). The picture is just of a normal, everyday child, but he might serve as a trigger for inappropriate and inaccurate reactivity to an anxiety disordered patient such as Christine. When everyday magazines are not able to provide provocative enough pictures, it is often possible to use broadly available books for exposure purposes; specifically, around lesbian obsessions, *The Whole Lesbian Sex Book: A Passionate Guide for All of Us* (Newman, 1999) could be used. Had Christine been male and had comparable male ego-dystonic homosexual obsessions, then *The New Joy of Gay Sex* (Silverstein & Picano, 1992) might have been used instead. In either case, practitioners will have to seek out resources that can serve as props for exposure exercises.

Preparing and writing disaster scripts follow some basic rules and guidelines. The script needs to be in the first person (i.e., "I feel"), present tense, and contain as many senses and perceptions as possible (e.g., sight, sound, smell, taste, tactile) to make the script as real as something not real can be. Whatever the person can write to make it sound like the "story" is happening now, in present time, will make the script most effective (i.e., it will activate the fear-based network connections). Again, as with

FIGURE 2.5   Semi-nude child.

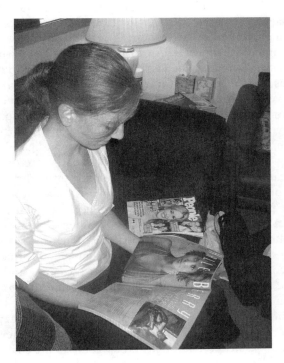

FIGURE 2.6   Imaginal exposure with pictures (mock patient).

creating a loop-tape, patients may have to give it several tries before they are able to produce a "good" script, and this tendency is primarily an artifact of naturally not wanting to think about or describe the content in this fashion.

Interoceptive Versus Naturalistic

Some patients need specific exposure to feared internal states and experiences, such as a pounding heart, labored breathing, or sweating. Fear of these sorts of experiences is commonplace in panic disorder (PD), whether with or without agoraphobia. Much of panic control treatment (Barlow et al., 1984; Barlow, Craske, Cerny, & Klosko, 1989) uses *interoceptive* exposure, or exposure to internal signals of danger (e.g., rapid heartbeat, tightness in the chest, upset stomach, dizziness). In essence, the patient is exposed to internal states that are feared. Ironically, the internal states feared are the very internal behaviors that are supposed to signal danger; in this respect, this type of fear of internal events has been referred to as "fear of fear" (Otto, Jones, Craske, & Barlow, 1996; Otto, Pollack, & Barlow, 1995) because PD is demonstrative of a condition in which the patient fears the cues signaling fear. They are afraid of feeling afraid. Much of the interoceptive work is done through inducing feelings of fear, or panic, to happen. This can readily be accomplished through various physical exercises. For instance, for patients who fear dizziness (often because of concerns that it means they are going crazy or having a stroke) several common exercises are used, such as spinning around in a chair, or simply standing and spinning. Sometimes spinning one's head with eyes closed also works well, especially if the participant then quickly opens his or her eyes and looks into a bright light. Patients who fear choking or feel as though they cannot breathe are often asked to do what is called "straw breathing." This entails trying (trying being the operative word) to breathe not through straws, but through coffee stir sticks. Most people are able to breathe through a regular straw (e.g., a straw from a restaurant), especially if they slow their breathing down and focus. Breathing through a stir stick is much more difficult, and more readily induces feelings of choking or being unable to get a breath. This, as uncomfortable as it might sound, is the point and purpose of interoceptive exposure; that is, feelings of panic are *not* dangerous, but may feel somewhat uncomfortable at worst and will not last. Neither do feelings of panic signal that a person is dying, going crazy, or having some sort of medical problem (e.g., many people believe they are having a heart attack or a stroke, and often end up going to the emergency room only to be told there is nothing wrong with them). As the *Diagnostic*

FIGURE 2.7   Interoceptive exposure (mock patient).

and *Statistical Manual of Mental Disorders*, 4th edition, text revision (American Psychiatric Association, 2000), points out, panic attacks are common occurrences. Although many people have panic attacks throughout their life, some go on to develop panic disorder. It is important to point out that panic attacks are not diagnosable events by themselves, but instead they are the building blocks for other disorders, including PD. Panic attacks also co-occur with a range of anxiety disorder, so it is the prudent practitioner who will include modules from panic control treatment for anxiety disorders in which panic attacks occur comorbidly (even when failing to meet criteria for PD).

While in PD, for example, the patient really only needs his or her own body to have the instrument of exposure. For many other kinds of common anxiety conditions, patients need *naturalistic* settings to access the instruments of exposure. This might entail searching out places that can produce anxiety and fear (e.g., heights for the height phobic, vast open places for the agoraphobic, and tiny little places for the claustrophobic) naturally. For some patients, the exposure becomes about going to a very specific place or setting. For the PTSD patient, for instance, it might entail returning to the scene of the car crash. It is noteworthy that even when people go to either a specific or a general naturalistic setting, they are bringing with them the instrument required for the exposure: their bodies (e.g., climbing stairs to produce a rapid heartbeat; Figure 2.7).

The human body is still what signals whether something or some setting is threatening or dangerous. If the body does not react, the circumstance is likely not a menace. Sometimes the panic-disordered patient experiences panic attacks in natural settings, which may lead him or her to becoming agoraphobic, or avoidant of going out. Agoraphobic avoidance can be both for open and closed (small) spaces. Such avoidance may make it difficult for such patients to actually come to practitioners' offices, so traveling to natural settings may be a requirement if treatment is to be provided. On the other hand, many agoraphobic patients may be very well able to come to a practitioner's office, and that practitioner may not have time to venture out to natural settings. In such circumstances, relying further on imaginal exposure can provide a bridge between in-office and naturalistic exposure. Practitioners may indeed use various pictures to supplement imaginal exposure (Figures 2.8, 2.9, and 2.10).

Therapist-Directed and Partner-Assisted Versus Self-Directed

Exposure can be carried out with a variety of people present. Obviously the prime player (patient) is required, but after that the selection of people playing both directing and supporting roles can vary broadly. Who is present is also often a factor of where the patient is in the treatment process. In the beginning stages, the practitioner providing the treatment will likely be present for multiple reasons. First and foremost, in the beginning, it will be important that the practitioner demonstrates (models) each of the exposures before the patient performs them. That way, patients can know precisely what they are supposed to do, because they can observe firsthand how to perform the actions of the exposure exercise. This ensures the patient has a clear picture of how to correctly perform the activity, but modeling the exercise also provides information about what not to do. That is, many people with anxiety tend to engage in safety behaviors when they are anxious; such behaviors impair and sometimes even prevent habituation, so knowing what not to do is at least as valuable as knowing what to do. Second, in the beginning, it is important that the practitioner praise patients for work well done and provide encouragement and support to keep going through the exercise when thoughts about stopping too early might creep in. This is common in exposure exercises, in that some patients may want to stop because of the discomfort and the fear. Nonetheless, doing so is contraindicated until habituation is accomplished. With the practitioner present, patients are more likely to continue to go through the exercise and to not stop it prematurely. Left alone, especially if the exercise is at all too challenging for patients' developing capacities, they might quit.

FIGURE 2.8   Agoraphobic imaginal exposure picture 1.

FIGURE 2.9   Agoraphobic imaginal exposure picture 2.

FIGURE 2.10   Agoraphobic imaginal exposure picture 3.

Because it is unlikely the practitioner will be able to spend large amounts of time with the patient in all of the exercises necessary to completely conquer a fear (or multiple fears), it is often very helpful to enlist the support and assistance of "significant others." Exposure work conducted with the help of a significant other is often referred to as *partner-assisted* exposure. In such an arrangement, someone else other than the practitioner is the support person for the patient doing the exposure work. Typically, that person might be a spouse, partner, friend, or colleague. Regardless of who the person is, it must be someone who the patient feels somewhat comfortable with and who the patient, more importantly, trusts. Exposure work is sometimes difficult, and the last experience a hardworking patient needs is someone ridiculing him or her for not being able to do what to others seem rather benign activities. What the patient needs is effective and supportive support and encouragement, so such requirements might limit who could be a "partner." It will be important, with the permission of the patient of course, to orient and minimally train the significant other, because he or she may do some common things that are countertherapeutic. For instance, when someone is anxious and nervous, it is common human practice to assure him or her that everything will be all right and that nothing is wrong. In fact, for the purposes of what needs to happen in exposure, this would be the wrong approach to take, because the patient needs to experience complete vulnerability in the face of fear. Reassurance that the patient will be fine and there is nothing dangerous around might eliminate vulnerability and consequently interfere with the patient's ability to habituate naturally. Without normal habituation, there cannot be any extinction; therefore, it becomes important to sufficiently prepare a partner to be effective. For patients who are disabled to the point that they are house-bound and living with family, it is often helpful to direct the other family members as to how to best interact with the patients and to not unduly upset them, but also to not facilitate the continuation and maintenance of symptoms. Participation in patient symptoms by other family members is often referred to as "family accommodation," and is something that frequently occurs across anxiety disorders. It occurs for predictable reasons; that is, when a person is anxious, worried, and distressed, often so is the rest of the family. So, often times, the family members will do certain things to put sufferers more at ease. Although this is typically well-meaning, or perhaps done out of desperation (because the anxious patients might become hostile and angry when others around them do not accommodate their concerns), what people tend to do to appease sufferers usually falls along the lines of two basic modes of behaviors: escape and avoidance. The other people, although often well-meaning, will allow patients to do something for them that falls into either category. So, for example, family members who live with someone socially anxious go out to get the mail from the mailbox (where public scrutiny would be possible), and they do not throw parties for friends and acquaintances because they know that the sufferer becomes uncomfortable, awkward, and perhaps even irritable in the presence of groups of people, sometimes even those the person knows already. This problem of family (symptom) accommodation has to be addressed to be assured that the assistance that such an arrangement would provide will not work out to be counterproductive and countertherapeutic. Additionally, it would be important to assess the relationship quality between the patient and the proposed partner; if the partner is less emotionally tied to the patient and his or her symptoms (i.e., is able to remain objective and not emotionally charged or drained by the experience), he or she will be more effective. There is some literature that suggests that certain types of relationships should be avoided when selecting an exposure partner, namely that the support person cannot have a hostile or otherwise negative relationship. In this sense, it is usually easier to pick a nonfamily member for an exposure partner. Ultimately, how effective of a partner the person will be will determine whether he or she would make a suitable, therapeutically advantageous addition. A specific advantage that such a person could add to the treatment package is that this person (provided the circumstances are right) can often go to places where either the practitioner cannot go or might be ethically questionable (e.g., a spouse can accompany the patient into bathrooms).

In the end, *self-directed* exposure will play a significant role in combating personal anxiety and fear. If the patient cannot perform the exposure tasks independently, the basic ethical principles of autonomy are at risk. Part of the overarching objective in exposure treatments is to provide the patient with increased personal choice, or autonomy, to again be able to independently perform chores of daily living (e.g., driving). If the patient never progresses from accompanied exposures to independent exposures, the risk is that the association for success is the treatment provider. This goes against the ethical guidelines of supporting and facilitating personal freedom. How self-directed treatment is best encouraged and supported is, fortunately, rather straightforward. Initial exposures, regardless of level of complexity and challenge, should be modeled and accompanied by the practitioner. After there is movement up a fear hierarchy, the next move toward fostering independence is to start the patient on performing exposures they have accomplished when accompanied. That is, they begin performing the exposure exercises that they have completed and succeeded at with other support. It will remain important to continue to direct and guide new exposures, because doing so ensures greater likelihood of successfully completing the novel tasks and safeguarding correctly performing those new tasks. Additionally, there are overarching strategies contained within cognitive-behavioral therapy (CBT) that safeguards autonomy and independence, such as focusing formal parts of the treatment on activities that teach the patient to become his or her own therapist. After all, they know themselves better than anyone else, including their therapist. In this respect, CBT often portrays itself as a "coach" or guide and makes it in other ways very clear that the patient is as much, if not more, a collaborative part in the treatment. In this way, treatment is seen as a team activity, within which the patient plays a central and guiding role. The patient's task is to learn how to become his or her own best therapist or best attorney; the practitioner serves mostly a supporting role, much like a computer technician might come to a client to load new software onto the patient's computer (only the person *is* the computer). After the sharing of software is complete, the patient no longer needs the service provider. In this same sense, CBT is oftentimes split roughly into thirds. In the first third of the treatment package, the treatment provider is acting very much in the role of therapist or expert who has the latest new software updates to provide. In this respect, the first third of treatment is spent downloading a lot of information (e.g., psychoeducation, basic problem solving) to get the patient ready to be able to collaborate more equally with the therapist, who in the middle third of the treatment shifts roles slightly from expert to equal collaborator. Also during the middle stage of treatment, much of the heavy therapy work is performed. Here the patient is still supported more directly by the therapist, but the patient begins to play an equal partner in the treatment; however, he or she has yet to fully become his or her own therapist or expert at how to solve problems. In the last third of treatment, the treatment provider is shifting out of the role of therapist, and really ceases to provide those kinds of directive services and shifts instead into the role of supervisor. Here, the patient shifts roles from being equal collaborator toward budding expert, in which he or she takes on the role of being therapist. In this stage, the patient takes on the responsibility of designing and implementing exposures and other treatment tasks, much like a "true" therapist might. In interactions with their "former therapist" (who has become the supervisor instead), patients then act as supervisee, where they bring information about how the treatment is going and what they are projecting forward as future treatment targets and tasks.

Hierarchical Versus Flooding

Whether exposure is to be conducted on a graduated, systematically hierarchical manner or faced in the more wholesale, perhaps bordering on brutal fashion of flooding, it is to be collaboratively decided on by patient and practitioner. It is the job of the practitioner to advise the patient about what is known about the two formats, what prospective benefits and cost might be, and provide any additional information that will be necessary for the patient to ultimately decide which version he or she will choose. The central, ethical importance of choice cannot be underscored enough because the patient will be deciding on treatment routes that, by design, will produce some discomfort. The practitioner will have to be careful to completely explain that more discomfort does *not* necessarily lead to increased gains, but that a willingness to endure more challenging exposures may very well lead to similar results more quickly. Larger gains do *not* come from larger pain. The debate should instead really be more focused on how quickly the patient would like to improve functioning and how much personal distress (within limits) he or she is willing to experience. Exposure treatment does *not* have to be intolerable; in fact, best therapeutic effect is contradicted by exorbitant arousal, because the body will, reflexively, begin a shut down (dissociation) program to protect itself. Such a mode during exposure will prevent habituation, thereby preventing extinction. If between-session habituation is not apparent, then it could be an indicator that the exposure exercises being conducted are too hard and are leading to a lack of integration of pivotal information. This, in turn, leads to the patient having similar difficulties in subsequent exposures; that is, because he or she has not habituated to the stimulus, he or she cannot experience it as any (significantly) less distressing.

Flooding is based on Stampfl and Levis's (1967) implosion therapy, in which patients were instructed to imagine, for long periods, horrific and utterly terrifying scenes related to their fears. The objective of flooding, then, is to have the patient become as anxious as possible. The implosion/flooding sessions were conducted in this manner until the patient's distress and arousal declined. To their credit, Stampfl and Levis operated from the principle of extinction (the key ingredient to genuine relief!) when proposing that classically conditioned fears would extinguish when the stimuli were continuously present (i.e., when escape and avoidance was prevented). The key to flooding, as with any type of exposure, remained the duration of the exposure; too short of an exposure would not extinguish fears, because habituation would not occur, and would instead more than likely increase fears because of what escape teaches people. Although therapists at the time first believed that exposure needed to be as intense as possible, it was quickly realized that the key ingredient was not necessarily the intensity but instead consistent habituation (Hafner & Marks, 1976). Leitenburg and Callahan (1973) found that gradual exposure was more effective than the flooding method.

All of the benefits and costs of flooding should be carefully weighed before starting such a program, and if the patient chooses to proceed, he or she needs to very clearly understand that the work might seem intolerably hard at times. If the patient still wishes to proceed, it would also be centrally important to make sure he or she knows and appreciates that starting such an approach and then finding it simply too hard still leaves alternative routes as an option. Because they start flooding, it does not preclude shifting and changing to graduated exposure later. Again, this would also support the notion of personal autonomy to make independent decisions. No matter which version the patient chooses, the critical within-session experience is that escape and avoidance need to be prevented or completely blocked, because doing so, theoretically at least (if not practically also), directly influences the key variables of frequency, duration, severity, and latency.

Single-Session Treatment

Lars-Göran Öst (1989b) developed an extremely rapid exposure treatment approach he termed single-session or one-session treatment for specific phobias. Although this at first might seem an ambitious task, to treat phobias in only a single session, it should be noted that the single sessions used for this treatment are longer than a usual exposure session. Öst's single session typically could run as long as 3 hours, with an emphasis on bringing anxiety and arousal in the presence of the feared stimulus as low as it could get in the allotted time. Additionally, it should be noted that the phobia treated with this approach typically would be a specific phobia, and as such would be a relatively circumscribed or limited phobia (e.g., fear of spiders). If the fear is more pervasive and not isolated to some single, specific fear, this approach might not be sufficient to completely extinguish reactivity and fear. The actual treatment session is also preceded by an interview session, in which a functional analysis is performed and pertinent information about the fear is gathered, a rationale is provided, and information for what will happen during the prolonged exposure is given (e.g., how the person will face the feared stimulus, how SUDS ratings will be assessed).

For maximum impact and effectiveness, the Öst one-session exposure treatment is an in vivo exposure and it does not end until at least a half-reduction is realized. High arousal, unlike flooding, is not necessarily needed, neither is it a goal, so long as no escape or avoidance occurs. The exposure used in this treatment is more like a series of behavioral experiments, in which patients state what they fear will happen if they do certain things. The feared activity is then performed to see if the feared outcome about the specific fear actually occurs. The exposure is always preceded by therapist modeling of correct, desired actions.

This type of exposure is considered a massed exposure, in that multiple exposures with the stimulus are performed. So, for example, a blood phobic might get finger-pricked several times, have several subcutaneous injections, and a few venipunctures all during the one session (Öst, 1997). Its use is primarily indicated for spiders, snakes, birds, wasps, blood/injection, and other animals (e.g., dogs, cats, horses, cows) and insects, but it has also been used, more interestingly, with claustrophobia and fear of flying (Öst, Brandberg, & Alm, 1997).

Artificial Settings, the Natural Environment, and Ecological Relevance

Even with the wealth of literature that is available supporting the positive impact of exposure therapy, this kind of treatment is not without its troubles. Indeed, some patients are not responding favorably to exposure, with up to 30% of patients, for example, appearing refractory to exposure and response prevention (ERP) treatment for OCD, and dropout rates (i.e., premature, early termination) average around 20%

(Baer & Minichiello, 1998; Foa, Abramowitz, Franklin, & Kozak, 1999; Koran, 1999; Kozak, Liebowitz, & Foa, 2000). Taken together, these phenomena combined could appear to suggest that up to 50% of patients who attempt this now standard approach for treating OCD are not adequately helped by traditionally delivered ERP (McLean et al., 2001; Salkovskis, Richards, & Forrester, 2000).

Despite these seemingly negative findings about OCD, there is significant and meaningful hope for refractory, severe, and chronic patients. In fact, preliminary data suggest that delivering a standardized CBT product, focused on in vivo ERP components, as a home-based intervention, may be modified enough for a positive treatment response to occur in many refractory and challenging patients (Rosqvist et al., 2001; Rosqvist, Sundsmo, MacLane, Cullen, & Cartinella, in press; Rosqvist, Thomas, & Egan, 2002; Rosqvist, Thomas, Egan, & Haney, 2002; Willis, Rosqvist, Egan, & Baney, 1998).

Although ERP was originally designed to be applied in a hospital setting, the treatment can be administered in the patient's natural environment in a more cost-effective manner and in a fashion that results in superior maintenance of treatment-produced change (Emmelkamp, 1982; Emmelkamp, Kloek, & Blaauw, 1992). In more recent years, health care, including psychotherapy, has seen an increasing trend toward clinical care that is both less restrictive and more cost-effective (Levendusky, Willis, & Ghinassi, 1994; Mesh & Loeb, 2002; Willis, 1994). Rosqvist et al. (2001) investigated delivering ERP exclusively in natural settings with a group of 11 refractory patients through a home-based delivery system. Their findings suggested that approximately half of the patients treated in the presence of genuine (not analog) cues improved significantly. For others, it additionally served to facilitate transition into an OCD day-treatment program, which had been previously impossible because of significant OCD symptoms. They concluded that home-based ERP is an alternate product that should perhaps be offered to patients who have, for various reasons, failed to benefit in more conventional settings. Understanding nontraditional or natural settings remains challenging.

Much research on the treatment of OCD has focused on traditional delivery settings (i.e., hospital settings, whether inpatient or outpatient; e.g., Baer, 1993; Calvocoressi et al., 1993; Drummond, 1993; van den Hout, Emmelkamp, Kraaykamp, & Griez, 1988; Hoogduin & Hoogduin, 1984; Pollard, 2000). Limited research has investigated treating OCD away from outpatient and inpatient treatment facilities (e.g., Boersma, den Hengst, Dekker, & Emmelkamp, 1976; Emmelkamp, van Linden-van den Heuvell, Rüphan, & Sanderman, 1988; Emmelkamp, van Linden-van den Heuvell, Rüphan, & Sanderman, 1989). Research available on exposure treatment in naturalistic settings (i.e., *not* analog settings) suggests that nontraditional delivery of exposure to challenging OCD patients may be, at least in part, responsible for meaningful change. Notably, such results were attained by relying on established methods of habituation and extinction, only altering where the delivery takes place. This seems to suggest that natural settings appear capable of reducing problems with generalizing gains that some patients appear to experience when leaving traditional treatment settings (e.g., Emmelkamp et al., 1989; Steketee, 1993).

The implications of using natural settings as delivery vehicles for exposure treatments become even more interesting and compelling if treatment-refractory patients demonstrate positive findings, because they may otherwise continue to represent a greater utilization risk or burden, leaving practitioners unsure of what to do for them (Rosqvist et al., 2002).

Ecological relevance may indeed play an important role in how the aforementioned, and other anxiety-disordered patients, obtain meaningful change. Specifically, ecological relevance refers to the setting or location in which the treatment is delivered. A common concern of practitioners is the disappearance of improved behavior and reduced fear when the patient returns to his or her natural environment, which, for obvious reasons, may be an exacerbated problem for the inpatient treatment of OCD and other severe anxiety disorders. In analog residential settings, the patient is completely removed from natural settings in which he or she will eventually have to function. This can potentially create substantial problems with at least transportability (i.e., capacity to bring any gains home), if not generalizability (i.e., applicability of any gains to a different setting than that which the gains were made in).

Practitioners have not harnessed the enormous influence of the natural environment toward therapeutically congruent ends; instead, early observations have been made that the natural environment has often actually been established as the enemy of therapeutic intervention (Tharp & Wetzel, 1969). This tragic stance remains largely in effect today, at least in North America. Although it is recognized, and sometimes even acknowledged, that significant potential for behavioral change lies in the natural environment, researchers and practitioners outside Europe and Scandinavia have largely failed to use such settings routinely as a *primary* delivery site, opting instead to rely on outpatient care and higher stepped, more restrictive (analog) care settings. In North America, this is influenced by a pervasively restrictive insurance industry, which dictates where and how services can be delivered and by whom. Consequently, this translates to most patients receiving exposure treatments in traditional settings, no matter how compelling indications for use of natural settings might be. When a patient does not respond on the least restrictive level commonly used, the outpatient clinic, the strategy employed sometimes follows an increase in stepped-care level, which can lead to an inpatient or residential treatment approach. This de facto standard practice is often used instead of considering delivery in natural settings, which (not unimportantly) represent a significantly more cost-effective treatment option when compared with more restrictive hospital settings. Indeed, even self-treatment of anxiety can in some instances be effective (Fritzler, Hecker, & Losee, 1997). However, in a few cases, when a patient has "failed" both conventional outpatient trials and inpatient programs, the treatment suggested could progress to the most restrictive, invasive level of psychosurgery, even though efficacy of psychosurgery for refractory anxiety has not been clearly established (Jenike, 2000). When such dramatic and potentially costly (i.e., both financially and health risk-wise) steps have been taken, careful attention to whether or not naturally occurring environments might have made a difference often have not been carefully considered. In fact, psychotherapy practice tradition has all but ignored natural settings, even when it is clear that discrepancies exist between analog settings and the waiting community needs.

Nonetheless, in spite of tradition, one field in psychology that frequently conducts therapeutic interventions in the natural environment is the field of applied behavioral analysis. In this field, practitioners conduct single-subject research and provide treatment for a variety of patients who exhibit an array of behavioral problems, including anxiety disorders. The research and treatments they conduct take place in many settings, but extensively rely on natural settings in which symptomatic behavior occurs. To ensure that a problem behavior can be successfully treated, an applied behavioral analysis practitioner conducts therapy in the same historical and environmental context in which the patient displays the problem behavior. This ensures that the environmental cues encountered are the natural cues that naturally trigger anxiety and not a re-creation of the cue in some faraway, analog clinic setting that is little like the setting to which the patient later has to return. In addition to providing direct, meaningful therapy in such settings, the practitioner also often conducts training of significant others to ensure that the interventions are supported and continued, even after the practitioner is no longer in the environment. This approach and system aspires to the highest ethical guidelines of promoting self-efficacy and independence. In this fashion, by relying on ecological relevance and the monumental power contained in natural settings, the practitioner is better able to ensure generalizability and perhaps even enhanced effectiveness of the interventions.

The U.S. Environmental Protection Agency, in its Ecological Risk Management Training, defines ecological relevance as "one of the three criteria for assessment endpoint selection," and further points out that "ecologically relevant endpoints reflect important characteristics of the system and are functionally related to other endpoints" (U.S. Environmental Protection Agency [n.d.] retrieved April 10, 2005, from http://www.erg.com/portfolio/elearn/ecorisk/html/resource/glossary.html). Although this definition comes from outside the field of psychology, the definition and subsequent observations still hold. In clinical psychology, this definition means ecological relevance is an element in the assessment of treatment intervention selection. Therefore, ecologically relevant interventions reflect characteristics of the environment in which the patient lives and the interventions are functionally related to other aspects (e.g., job, personal life) of the patient's life.

Examples of ecological relevance can sometimes come from research work outside of psychotherapy. In neurocognitive assessment, for example, Makatura, Lam, Leahy, Castillo, and Kalpakjian (1999) evaluated the accuracy of memory impairment classification (none, mild, moderate, and severe) when using an ecologically relevant test (i.e., those that measured memory used in everyday situations, such as memory for routes) and when using theoretically based tests (i.e., those that measure the theoretical construct of memory but are not necessarily tasks performed in daily life). Interestingly, but perhaps not surprisingly, they found that the ecologically relevant test outperformed the theoretically based tests and hypothesized that this measure may take into account those compensatory mechanisms that patients use in their environment. Consequently, this test "can aid in making hypotheses about the types of problems an individual may encounter at home, work, and the community" (Makatura et al., p. 65).

This memory example highlights the importance of ecological relevance in assessment, and as such is arguably of central importance in psychotherapy, too, because treatment interventions should logically flow from what assessment suggests would be helpful. Although the theoretically based tests may have been technically more sensitive, being able to pinpoint the exact point at which the memory fails, the ecologically valid test was able to evaluate what the impairment actually meant in the patient's day-to-day functioning. Knowledge for knowledge's sake may be interesting to the practitioner, but does it really help the patient? Bringing this example back to the therapeutic setting, teaching a patient the skills needed to become more effective in the environment within an office, or analog, setting may give the client some knowledge and insight into the condition, but will it really transfer into action in "real" settings? Some patients can make this leap, but not all. For those who find this difficult, an ecologically relevant treatment approach will ensure that the common problems of generalizability and transportability are directly addressed.

CHAPTER **3**

Research Basis of the Phenomenon and Its Treatment

Science is simply common sense at its best that is,
rigidly accurate in observation and merciless to fallacy in logic.
—Thomas Henry Huxley

EMPIRICAL BASIS FOR EXPOSURE WITH ANXIETY DISORDERS

No one, especially third-party reimbursers and managed care, is interested or willing to pay for treatments that do not work or are only marginally useful. Although many treatments can arguably be "useful," the general trend in the health care industry is a move toward demonstrating treatment efficacy (i.e., treatment works), effectiveness (i.e., treatment generalizes to everyday clinical treatment settings and private practice), and efficiency (i.e., therapeutic change is attained reasonably quickly and long-term work is undesirable). No insurer remains eager to pay for improved insight, self-understanding, and actualization without appropriately accompanying symptom relief. Health care today is primarily, but fortunately not exclusively, focused on personal functioning. Trends suggest, however, that insurers pay for treatments that directly influence and improve symptoms that keep someone from, for example, working, or in other ways prevent someone from being a contributing, meaningful life participant.

This reality has led to a greater adaptation of the medical model, or science-based models, for evaluating which treatments to use with patients to deliver an optimal impact. This shift in psychotherapy practice, some will argue, is a shift away from the traditional art of psychotherapy toward therapy by the numbers (e.g., Silverman, 1996; Smith, 1995). The assertion is that empiricism and this science-focused approach to ameliorating human suffering is too technician-like in basis, and that it consequently loses the trees for the forest (i.e., does not see the patients for the science). Although the position that empirical approaches make patients fit the treatment has been put forth, and defended both vigorously and emotionally, the good news for the everyday practitioner who also has concerns about reimbursement for services and about connecting with patients is that using an evidence-based approach does not have to be unfeeling and disconnected from patients, uncaring about patient needs, or lock-stepped to manuals. The news is good indeed; not only can empirically oriented practitioners foster strong, creative, and flexible connections with their patients, but practitioners are also highly likely to feel effective and able to facilitate meaningful positive change in patients. This happens through the systematic application of evaluated and supported methods that have been deemed to affect the central mechanisms of some pathology in question. Empirical treatments (again, whether for good or bad) are also highly reimbursable.

Accountability is a catchword apropos for the current health care system; it has become increasingly necessary to demonstrate the need for treatment and that, when warranted, such treatment will be selected from accepted (supported) effective methods. Whether this is, from the collective voice of psychotherapy practice, healthy and appropriate can be argued. For a more thorough debate of common concerns about "going empirical," see chapter 7. As a result of shifting toward established treatment methods, there has been increased work at researching exactly what does seem to work and for what types of problems. This line of thinking adheres to a medical model of thinking and has produced a significant set of clinical practice guidelines for which approaches have been demonstrated to help. Lots of treatments can be argued to be helpful, but from a practice guideline standpoint, help is better thought of in terms of whether or not something "works" or addresses central and specific mechanisms of pathology and change. In this way, then, there is an abundance of literature describing research findings about a whole host of different problems, giving direction to practitioners about what is more likely to work for particular patients and problems they face. Even when there is a lack of research in a particular phenomenon, the empirical model for practice suggests a systematic mode for practice that relies on the scientific model for problem-solving.

With an eye on the scientific method, it will be easy to "smell out" scientific wannabes. Greg Bear (1999) reported that "they smile funny when they talk" when he suggested that scientific wannabes stick to their facts when such facts can be clearly demonstrated as false. Perhaps most poignantly, he suggested that the scientific wannabes' ends define their means and discourse. Put differently, one might ask why some practitioners are so bent against adopting empirical methods, especially in light of their proven nature; what exactly is the end that they are trying to preserve through resisting? Is it an orientation loyalty issue (keep in mind that cognitive-behavioral therapy [CBT] is overrepresented among accepted effective approaches)? Is it a financial issue (concerns of not being reimbursed for psychotherapy services are real for many)? I would make the strong argument that, on a process level, not content level (because that will differ from one person to the next), it is a fear issue. However, no matter what the reason is, this fear translates to scientific wannabes saying and doing things that do not fit "scientific grammar," as Bear puts it; you can get something for nothing, different cultures see nature differently, so nature must follow different laws for different people, numbers are too precise to be reliable, and so on. Bad science can perhaps tell a very entertaining story (i.e., lots of psychotherapies can be very *interesting*), but it fails the scientific grammatical test just as much as suspect stories of modern charlatans and other scientific wannabes. Bad science is a real problem because it is only able to tell people what they want to hear (e.g., one can get something for nothing) and not what is more likely to be true. What is true about anxiety disorders is that without addressing the central mechanisms of the pathology, the patient will likely not realize improved functioning because the symptoms are often disabling. This is the truth about anxiety disorders, but some (charlatans) want to tell the entertaining story that other, more compelling (read as *interesting*) approaches also work. Lots of psychotherapies are interesting, but fewer have good scientific support as actually being helpful enough to be thought to *work* or solve problems in functioning.

This disagreement about what constitutes "working" prompted Division 12 (Clinical Psychology) of the American Psychological Association (APA) to put together a task force (the Task Force on Promotion and Dissemination of Psychological Procedures, which later became known as the Committee on Science and Practice) to identify which psychological interventions are empirically validated. The reports that this task force put forth met with both praise and opprobrium (Chambless & Ollendick, 2001). These reports supported the controversial notion that psychotherapy *should* be based on science. It is important to point out that this task force was not necessarily self-generated, but grew instead out of the growing gap between actual scientific advances in the development and evaluation of psychotherapies and the relatively minimal (dismal, really) impact such developments had on actual clinical practice (Herbert, 2003).

The findings published by this task force have all but disenfranchised psychotherapies that are not directly oriented toward symptom reduction of specific psychopathologies. With health care costs skyrocketing to the point of bankrupting entire systems, which is true in many locations nationally and internationally, what kinds of care should be reimbursed becomes an important question. Should psychotherapies that do not directly affect symptoms be reimbursable? If so, should health care systems pay for members' idealistic pursuits of personal enrichment and self-actualizing? These questions are difficult to answer without intense controversy ensuing, so these questions will chiefly remain rhetorical here.

These questions are predominantly questions only when third-party reimbursement, or insurance, is to pay for services rendered. If a patient pays out of pocket, these questions do not perhaps seem as pressing. They should be. Standards of care should not be flexible depending on the source of payment; the same high, professional standards of conduct should be followed for a utilization review board and individual (self-pay) patients. Managed care is in place today *because* of the fraudulent, fleecing behaviors of therapists who were taking advantage of patients and reimbursing policies. Practitioners should be extremely careful to not continue in such ways, for if managed care seems like a foe now, then it might seem like a demon before long if lax practice behaviors continue. Ultimately, it will affect the care provision for patients who really need help; with continued misbehavior and questionable practices, psychotherapy might not be available to those who truly need it. "Treatment" without discernible, meaningful effect only serves to further drain an already low reserve or pool of funds denoted for psychotherapy.

Accountability is good for patients, because it preserves the integrity and honesty of services, but also because it simply preserves availability of services. Accountability, clinical practice guidelines, and treatment expert consensus statements should, collectively, encourage and require practitioners to document the quality of care they administer, the outcomes of treatment, and, perhaps most important for long-term care availability to those who need it, the costs of helping patients (McLean & Woody, 2001). It is and will remain in the best interest of patients that clinical practice is anchored in science and scientific principles of evaluating progress, outcome, and cost-effectiveness. Realistic demands on the current model of health care dictates that this reality must be supported or a collapse is not just a possibility but instead a foreseeable, if not predictable, eventuality. Traditional fee-for-service models of care provision simply are not sustainable, nor are they necessarily desirable. Although under such a model of care, the decisions about care were made by the treatment provider and the patient (without a third party being involved), it fostered and perhaps even encouraged the provision of service *because more services created more income.* This, unfortunately, meant some unscrupulous (and some not so ill-intending) practitioners provided services for the sake of providing services, or earning more income, rather than providing services for the sake of necessarily alleviating suffering. Unchecked, this led to an endless need for psychotherapy, which is now broadly recognized as both absurd as well as undesirable (Sanderson, 2003). Although this ridiculous "endlessness" should not be a justification used by managed care for arbitrarily limiting number of sessions available to patients, it does suggest utilization and cost-containment efforts should focus on the quality or effectiveness of interventions made available to patients needing help. Cost containment (i.e., efficiency) must be balanced with providing effective clinical outcomes; length of care is not necessarily directly related to progress and outcome. Shorter is not necessarily better across psychopathology, even if there are some anxiety disorders that lend themselves to extremely rapid treatments (e.g., specific phobias).

Effective care provision now protects systems from later, heavier utilization by then more complex and complicated psychological problems that might worsen if previously provided with less than adequate care. "Less than adequate" could readily be defined as any intervention that does not address or focus on the central mechanism(s) of problems, because not focusing on such will likely leave their condition mostly intact to flare again through a reworsening of unresolved pathology. Following this logic, economics will be protected by effective care. In the end, systems monitoring utilization and costs of services will (and should) require practitioners to provide "optimal" care, or the least extensive, intensive, intrusive, and costly treatment that will successfully solve patients' specific presenting problems (Bennett, 1992). This is the current stance taken by many care organizations. This leads to the obvious question about what, then, exactly constitutes empirically supported treatments (EST) and evidence-based practice (EBP), because these are the zeitgeist of the industry.

EST, EMPIRICALLY VALIDATED PRACTICE, AND EBP

Empirical practice guidelines are based on the premise, first of all, that patient care can be enhanced by the acquisition and use of current scientific knowledge. Empirical treatments attempt to directly answer and address in treatment such common patient questions as: "What approaches to psychotherapy are beneficial? Is my psychotherapy helping me with my problems? Is the psychotherapy I am considering likely to be beneficial for me?" Specifically, empirical treatments are those that have been shown to be "beneficial" in scientific studies meeting several stringent criteria. What *beneficial* means and perhaps is can be argued, but from an empirical treatment perspective, it means that patients who participated in specific research of, for example, in vivo graduated exposure in the treatment of agoraphobia, achieved better results than patients who received *either* no treatment (commonly referred to as a "wait-control" group) *or* attained at least equal results to patients who underwent an alternative, perhaps competing, beneficial treatment. In addition, the research studies performed to evaluate one treatment's effect vis-à-vis another's used a particular type of study, namely a randomized controlled trial (RCT). RCTs are the accepted practice (scientific) standard for medical research trying to determine if treatments for specific disorders are beneficial. Treatments thought to be beneficial are also specifically only those that have been shown to be beneficial in more than one investigation and in which more than one team of researchers find the same or similar enough findings of support. The treatments investigated would also have to be manualized treatment, or be manual-based treatments, so that other practitioners replicate such treatments and specific methods of interventions with their own patients who have the problems described in the manuals. In a RCT, patients with, for example, obsessive-compulsive disorder (OCD) are randomly assigned to one of the treatment conditions being evaluated. For OCD, that might have been behavior therapy (probably exposure and response prevention, ERP), cognitive therapy, and perhaps medications only, and possibly also a delayed treatment condition (i.e., a wait-control). The treatment delivery is then controlled as much as possible. This typically means that therapists who are delivering the treatments follow a manual very closely, so that all treatment providers (at least within each condition) behave the same and do not deviate from an established treatment protocol. This ensures treatment (independent variable) accounts for any change (dependent variable), or so the reasoning goes. Other actions are often also taken to ensure that the independent variable is controlled as much as possible, so treatment duration is often kept the same and therapist experience is as balanced as can be had. All of these efforts at controlling the input variance are aimed at allowing the researchers to be reasonably sure that any results (output) can be attributed to differences between treatments, and, more explicitly, to specific treatment mechanisms. As can be easily imagined, RCTs can be expensive to conduct, so sometimes treatments are investigated, still with very stringent controls, in series of single-case studies.

The RCT's purpose is single-minded. It is to produce data. Scientific, carefully controlled data. Data that are as close to the "truth" as anything can be. Truth does not exist, really; truth, instead, is a position that is more or less supported or refuted by information. So something can be shown to be false or, in terms of treatments, to not work well (or perhaps not work at all), but something cannot be shown to be true. There is, instead, only variable amounts of support, which collectively might suggest or hint at what might be true, if truth were possible. Truth could always be adjusted by more or better data. This is where science gets murky, and where much criticism of empirical approaches stems from. At some point, researchers and statisticians (mathematicians) sat down and decided what would constitute small, medium, and large change. It was also decided what level of certainty (significance) would be "enough" to be "certain." The levels selected are somewhat arbitrary and, as such, open for much critique. For significance, for example, why are a 0.05 level significant and a 0.051 also significant, whereas 0.049 is not. Technically, it is not. Is it in reality? Why is $d = 0.3$ a small effect size, $d = 0.5$ a medium effect size, and $d = 0.8$ a large effect size? More rhetorical questions that relate to a healthy skepticism for science need answers. Exactly which cutoff points are selected is not truly relevant, so long as there is uniformity in what treatments are compared against and how those comparisons occur. Under uniformity, if treatments for agoraphobia are compared between graded exposure and insight-oriented treatment, and graded exposure is supported (Quality Assurance Project, 1982), it is difficult to make a solid argument for why the unsupported version should then be used with patients suffering with agoraphobia. If a treatment such as graded exposure is clearly robust, suggesting it should perhaps even be considered a first-line treatment for agoraphobia, why should other, less effective or ineffective approaches be used or offered? There are lots of opinions to be had about what treatments are helpful, but controlled trials are instead performed to discover the most objective data and information about what treatments are beneficial (for which conditions). RCTs are not about subjective opinions, whether they come from researchers, practitioners, politicians, or patients for that matter, but are instead about *what can be supported as beneficial*. Hence the term EST, a treatment that has been shown through empirical studies to be beneficial or as working in the treatment of a particular phenomenon.

In the 1990s it was becoming increasingly clear that even though the evidence existed for whether some treatment form was supported or not, there was a lack of utilization of that information in terms of informing practice in the everyday treatment settings. That is, the efficacy setting findings were not transporting down the effectiveness setting level in terms of what treatments were used. Indeed, even in light of the information about the efficacy of exposure for treating posttraumatic stress disorder (PTSD), exposure was not pervasively being used to treat PTSD in many effectiveness settings. Too often when practitioners were not using exposure, the consuming public did not know there was any problem with delivering treatment as usual. This is where Division 12 of the APA again stepped in to increase the dissemination of such findings in an effort to decrease the significant variability in treatments provided toward use of optimal approaches in which patients uniformly could receive the most effective treatments (and certainly not sham treatments). The Task Force on Promotion and Dissemination of Psychological Procedures (1993) produced a list of empirically validated treatments that were treatments that this task force could, using science and its accompanying principles for evaluation and decision-making, endorse as working for specific conditions. As research into what works, for whom, and when, this list is being continually updated with more psychological interventions that have been found to meet the criteria of empirically supported, empirically validated, and the like (e.g., Chambless, 1996; Chambless et al., 1998). The criteria by which some treatment is shown as efficacious (meaning it works) are stringent, but these reports are meant to promulgate only those treatments that indeed are considered well-established or probably efficacious in the treatment of specific psychological problems based on the strength of evidence (not subjective beliefs). The list does not suggest that just because something has not been evaluated for efficacy status that an untested treatment is ineffective. It does, however, put an onus on those who are using untested methods to show evidence or support for why they should be using the methods they are choosing to use. Some will say that they will not be able to put their intervention to the test of a RCT, but it should be clearly stated that tests can and should be performed through controlled single-case series. The lack of support, or evaluation, of untested approaches makes emphatic protests, usually against guidelines and consensus statements by those who use such unevaluated methods seem subjective (fear-based or ignorance-based) in foundation rather than based on some factual, data, or information-based objection. More disturbing, however, is the possibility that patients who are in nonvalidated treatments will stay in such treatments in hope (perhaps desperation) for positive change, or out of therapy relationship variables alone and thereby keep such unfortunates out of clearly effective treatments.

There are numerous guidelines available to help practitioners wisely decide among treatment options. For example, the Agency for Health Care Policy and Research guideline for treatment of depression (Depression Guideline Panel, 1993) suggests strongly that treatment should be time limited, focused on current problems, and aimed at symptom reduction rather than personality change. It goes on to suggest that long-term treatments are not indicated as first-line treatments, and that treatments that have not been studied in an RCT should not be used as a sole treatment for depression. CBT has, as another example, been identified by the Panic Consensus Statement (Wolfe & Maser, 1994) as an effective treatment for panic disorder. This statement is particularly interesting because it actually goes so far as to make clear that not using ESTs for the treatment of panic disorder may be considered, by some progressive and conscientious states, as malpractice (i.e., a practitioner who used a nonsupported form of treatment for panic disorder would not be acting in a prudent fashion). Understanding that there may not only be financial stability at stake, but also the possibility of lawsuits or other forms of litigation for not following recognized standards of practice, might speed up a broader circulation and use of proven methods. Indeed, acting professionally in accordance with such guidelines and consensus statements will protect practitioners against suits from poor quality of care. To make adaptation and clinical use easier for the everyday practitioner, there are now resource lists of treatment manuals and training opportunities for ESTs (Sanderson & Woody, 1995; Woody & Sanderson, 1998).

LOCAL CLINICAL SCIENTIST, EDUCATED ECLECTIC EMPIRICIST, AND SCIENTIFIC (EVIDENCE-BASED) PRACTICE

Local Clinical Scientist

The local clinical scientist model (Stricker & Trierweiler, 1995) presented a way of bridging science and practice through describing the practitioner as an active scientist who approaches each clinical interaction as a problem to be solved. In this fashion, every clinical interaction is similar to what might happen in a scientist's laboratory, where the practitioner must draw from a body of psychological knowledge and then apply such information as relevant and appropriate (i.e., locally, matching suitable modules to individual patients). In short, this model proposed critical knowledge about mechanisms of psychopathology and principles of change should be applied to clinical practice through an experimental case approach for individual patients in which scientifically derived clinical knowledge and information is applied to idiographic cases following the scientific method style of testing working hypotheses for support or refute. This model has had an important impact on treatment and psychotherapy training in that it has directed the field further in a direction of careful, systematic, and informed practice standards. Such standards for operation have translated into the many practice guidelines and consensus statements mentioned previously, but have also highlighted several critical issues for further practice. Practitioners will benefit from using a systematic model for how to assess, conceptualize, and treat patients; in addition, by using such a systematic, evidence-based model for treatment planning and delivery, the practitioner will enjoy certain protections by using guidelines and consensus to inform clinical decision making. The local clinical scientist provides such a model for psychotherapy and may be seen as a standard of care for the field.

The model is based on the scientific method. Science can be thought of as a careful, disciplined, logical search for knowledge. The search is specifically and necessarily conducted through an examination of the best available evidence. Findings are always subject to correction on discovery of better, more "true" or correct evidentiary explanations. The hallmark of the scientific method is *proof*, or evidence, which supports particular phenomenon. How one sets out to obtain such evidence is where the scientific method is especially powerful, because it does not (if adhered to in principle) rely on emotions or opinions; instead, it relies on facts and other forms of data, which can then be used to support or refute particular thoughts, beliefs, and assumptions about a phenomenon.

The scientific method sets out to obtain data through running carefully designed experiments and carefully examining results, which will lend insights into relationships such as cause and effect of phenomenon studied. The backbone, or strength, of the scientific method rests in its capacity for replication of experiments, which allows any and all (skeptics included) to reproduce the experiments and observe firsthand outcomes. Science is in its own foundation based in procedures for studying the natural process of Nature and its wonders. Such ways of systematic observation can readily be translated to clinical research and practice (Figure 3.1). Through repeated tests of hypotheses and consistent observations that support the forming understanding of clinical phenomena, a *theory* can be proposed that best explains them (given best available evidence).

It is important to point out that theories of psychopathology and associated mechanisms of change should not be accepted on the influence or convincing powers of their promoters, but should instead be viewed in light of what data have been obtained through careful (replicable) observation and experimentation. Practitioners should be extremely careful to not accept as factual or as "truth" assertions that are not well backed by evidence or data that are guarded closely enough to not allow replication, the cornerstone of science. A case in point would be eye movement desensitization and reprocessing (EMDR) therapy. Although the scientific method and EMDR's proponents have frequently been criticized for not being able to accommodate anything that is not supportable, there are many pseudosciences and pure charlatans who hope to take advantage of bending science for their own (typically financial) gain. For example, daytime and late-night television is filled with "infomercials" claiming the scientific solution for a variety of human malaise, ranging from low energy and low sexual desire to buying and selling real estate

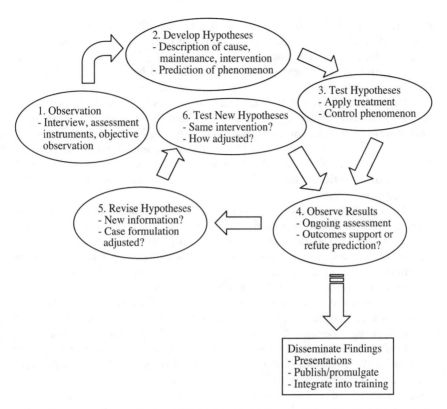

FIGURE 3.1 Scientific method in clinical practice. From: Truax, P. (2002). Behavioral case conceptualization for adults, in M. Hersen (Ed.), *Clinical behavior therapy: Adults and children* (pp. 3–36). New York: Wiley. Used by permission of John Wiley & Sons, Inc.

from the comforts of one's couch. All claim science backs their claims of instant results and success, but critical investigations have shown no active ingredients in various promoted supplements, whereas other research has shown some of the substances sold on easy payment plans have been directly harmful, and perhaps most interesting have been the illuminative facts that some proponents of such products have been convicted felons who have served prison terms for fraud and other charlatan acts.

EMDR is an example that has been strongly promoted as an important, alternative treatment approach to more conventional, proven anxiety treatment products such as standard CBT and exposure-based treatments. EMDR represented, to a large degree until its founder Francine Shapiro finally allowed dismantling studies in the late 1990s, a leap of faith. Faith can best be described as a belief that is not supported by logical proof or material evidence. By not allowing the rest of the field of psychology to critically evaluate her claims, Shapiro prevented a key component of any scientific theory, namely allowing it to be "falsifiable," meaning that theories of treatments must remain open to have other findings or theories prove the theory untrue, unfounded, or unsupported.

Interestingly, EMDR has received a listing of being "probably efficacious" for civilian PTSD by the Division 12 Task Force. This, frankly, is a travesty and misuse of science; nonetheless, EMDR is still listed as an EST. There are articles that do explore more fully the science and pseudoscience of EMDR (e.g., Herbert et al., 2000; Rosen, 1999), but a brief and critical analysis of EMDR for the understanding of how proper science can be misused is warranted.

The last decade or more has seen an explosion of interest in trauma and anxiety, and this trend is understandable given the fact that anxiety is the single most pervasive problem facing mental health today. Unfortunately, this trend has also brought with it the "Dodo-bird verdict," which in a nutshell suggests that all psychotherapies are equally effective (Luborsky, Singer, & Luborsky, 1975). Consequently, all sorts of "treatments" have gained respectability, and new treatments are exploding onto the market, often without careful efficacy research to first determine if and how they work (Lazarus, Beutler, & Norcross, 1992). This stance, however, has not been favored by empirically oriented researchers and practitioners (Beutler, 1991), who instead are favoring methodological rigor in validating intervention procedures (Fox, 1996). Most central to this position is that evaluation of new (and old) treatments must be based on substantive aspects of such approaches, rather than on appearance. If appearance is emphasized over substance, the process of inquiry runs significant risks of becoming pseudoscientific. Costs of adopting pseudoscience as science would be substantial and potentially dangerous. It is interesting that professional evaluation and promotion of EMDR has been characterized by pseudoscientific practices.

Although there are many treatments now clearly supported as working in the treatment of anxiety disorders, there are also many treatments being put forth through pseudoscientific means. Some examples are: thought field therapy (Callahan, 1995; Gallo, 1995), emotional freedom therapy (Craig, 1997), traumatic incident reduction (Gerbode, 1985, 1995), and visual-kinesthetic dissociation (Bandler & Grinder, 1979). Collectively, these "treatments" are referred to as power therapies, because they are supposed to be more effective than already available and proven methods for treating anxiety disorders. EMDR is the single most visible of these power therapies. According to Shapiro (1998), more than 25,000 practitioners have been trained in the controversial procedure, suggesting that the commercialization of EMDR has been incredibly successful, despite its apparent lack of scientific support. This should be alarming, but it becomes even more so when one considers all of the ailments for which EMDR is touted as an effective treatment (e.g., PTSD, attention deficit/hyperactivity disorder, dissociative disorders, self-esteem issues, personality pathology, spiritual development; EMDR Institute, Inc., 1995, 1997; Fensterheim, 1996; Parnell, 1996). It quickly begins to sound like a daytime or nighttime television infomercial, touting the latest snake oil for a myriad of human problems. Not only does the public desire the intervention (because of its trademarked, sensationalistic method), but some practitioners are incredulously even buying into the pyramid scheme-like training program.

EMDR's claims, when allowed true scientific scrutiny and evaluation, have not been upheld or been empirically supported (e.g., DeBell & Jones, 1997; Lohr, Tolin, & Lilienfeld, 1998; Muris & Merckelbach, 1999). Additionally, EMDR has been shown to rely on assumptions not supported by mainstream science (Lohr, 1996; O'Donohue & Thorpe, 1996; Shapiro, 1995). Most notably, the original claim that eye movement facilitates anxiety reduction has been found to be groundless (e.g., Pitman et al., 1996; Sanderson & Carpenter, 1992). This should be an important lesson to practitioners who are considering adding a new "skill" to their toolbox of therapeutic tricks; that is, be sure that it is not just a trick (or magic, which does not work) but that the therapeutic technique has some supportable merit as addressing some specific mechanism of pathology. Additionally, EMDR, as claimed, has not proven to be more effective or faster than traditional forms of exposure therapy (e.g., Devilly & Spence, 1999; Goldstein, deBeurs, Chambless, & Wilson, 2000; Muris, Merckelback, Holdrinet, & Sigsenaar, 1998). Overall, the empirical perspective and concerned critique of EMDR is supported by a 2001 (Davidson & Parker, 2001) meta-analysis, which found EMDR no more effective than existing exposure techniques and that eye movement is unnecessary for change. In short, the effective ingredients (i.e., exposure and cognitive therapy) in EMDR are not new, and what is (i.e., eye movement) is not effective (McNally, 1999). EMDR is simply repackaging recognized CBT techniques and adding a good dose of mystique, magic, and other pseudoscience for added, but irrelevant, effect.

So, because EMDR has been demonstrated to be more effective than no treatment on two occasions (i.e., Rothbaum, 1997; Wilson, Becker, & Tinker, 1995), it has met the necessary criteria for being "probably efficacious," lending it credibility that sometimes is touted to equal and surpass more conventional CBT. This is a disservice to the field of psychology and to prospective patients seeking help with, for example, PTSD. It is a strong affront to all because of what EMDR is known for, namely the trademarked eye movement technique that, truth be told, is

ineffectual and was most likely tossed in to make the approach sensa-
tional and different seeming. On a personal note, I will add that I cannot
accurately remember just how many patients have reported they tried
EMDR, but there are numerous; unfortunately, when asked what exactly
they did in treatment, they reported they got the eye movement component without the exposure or cognitive work that makes the approach
work. Not surprisingly, they reported EMDR "didn't work," which I find
both compelling and disturbing evidence for why practitioners would
be well advised to stay clear of finger-wagging approaches. If EMDR
is going to be incorporated, be sure to include the full treatment that
includes established effective exposure and proven cognitive techniques.
Eye movement alone is ineffective, and, arguably, possibly unethical.
When evaluating new approaches to treating psychological suffering,
it is the wise who will carefully examine what the principles of change
(empirically supported principles) are in the treatment, rather than looking
at what the trademark is (Rosen & Davison, 2003). Rosen and Davison
(2003; Tryon, 2005) have poignantly referred to EMDR as a "purple hat
therapy" (PHT), in which, in a "new" hypothetical treatment, patients
are asked to wear a purple hat while engaging in exposure therapy for
an anxiety disorder. PHT will, of course, be more effective than control
groups, because PHT contains exposure principles of change. However,
the proponents of PHT will attribute change to the wearing of the purple
hat. Additionally, these proponents will then create and offer proprietary
and trademarked PHT training seminars and products. This presents two
primary problems: (1) adding one or more functionally inert components
(e.g., eye movement) to an existing treatment of known efficacy can meet
"empirically supported" status and be perceived as a "new" approach and
(2) causal attributions or explanations of change are afforded to the inert
component, falsely attributing power to purple hats as containing some
curative principle of change. Implications can be profoundly costly!

Educated Eclectic Empiricist

Just because the Dodo-bird argument has produced a fieldwide slide
toward eclecticism (i.e., less adherence to specific positions, such as a
strict CBT, psychodynamic, or Gestalt), it does not mean that "eclectic"
has to be synonymous with aimless, poorly planned treatments that have
no foundation in research of theory (Fonagy & Target, 1996). Indeed,
done deliberately and conscientiously, eclecticism can be useful in clinical
practice. McLean and Woody (2001) have proposed and described a solid
model of clinical practice, on par with the local clinical scientist model,

which they have called the educated eclectic empiricist (E^3). In many ways the two models are similar, but the E^3 model contains many useful attractions for everyday practice.

The E^3 model argues that, regardless of what theoretical orientation a practitioner might subscribe to (or none), scientifically sound practice can still be used to inform and direct treatment in a meaningful, prudent, and ethical fashion. McLean and Woody suggest that such practice actually calls for an educated eclectic empiricist, but go on to illustrate that their elaboration on "eclectic" is tripartite. They report that their models require a practitioner to use a system of checks and balances between the scientific literature (educated), a variety of tested interventions (eclectic), and sound measurement (empiricist). It would be fair to suggest they are describing another model for using the scientific model on the local level. In their model, the practitioner is informed about and seeks out current information about a particular phenomenon he or she is treating, always updating the arsenal of information about issues in living. Practitioners also, in this model, seek out training and supervision in newly developing treatment approaches, but they still rely on established and supported intervention strategies to treat the clinical phenomena they encounter in everyday practice. As supported by the scientific method and Division 12 recommendations, the E^3 practitioner thus uses an ever-growing amount of knowledge to inform patient-treatment matching to ensure idiosyncratic patient needs are satisfied. The use of particular E^3 interventions are guided by ongoing assessment (as with the scientific model), which consists of practitioners relying on reliable and valid measures (instruments) that can gauge progress and outcome. Their model represents one of a few particularly compelling models for EVP.

Scientific or EBP

EBP, then, rests on three interlocking, interdependent components: knowledge of scientific findings to date and developing information, effective transfer of the information gleaned from the scientific literature to the everyday practice, and logical and astute progress and outcome measurement (McLean & Woody, 2001).

EBP relies on scientific knowledge for good reasons. For one, looking to such findings will help eliminate human subjectivity and human judgment errors. This is possible only because scientific knowledge comes primarily from outcome research, which has many checks and balances to safeguard against subjective beliefs or opinions. Remember that the scientific method will only forward theories that can be replicated and are falsifiable and, as such, protect against personal biases and opinions so often found within individual judgments. Ongoing education about the developing field of psychology is a necessary component for sound scientific practice. Many practitioners stop extensive learning after their formal education ends, either for theoretical reasons or purely pragmatic realities (e.g., the demands of an otherwise full practice makes it difficult to find the time to stay up with the latest developments in psychology, especially if practitioners see a variety of psychopathology in their practices). This is where manuals and treatment-oriented books come in to summarize outcome research and to provide direction in a fashion that by design will be evidence driven.

Although manuals will vary a great deal to what degree they offer concrete direction, they are nevertheless founded on research and, as such, might offer a shortcut toward using EBP, practice guidelines, and consensus statements to inform clinical treatment decisions. Some manuals offer more philosophical directions, whereas others might even offer explicitly what to say and do and in which order. For the range of anxiety disorders and other common, often comorbid conditions, there is now a range of manuals available (e.g., Sanderson & Woody, 1995; Woody & Sanderson, 1998). The Society for a Science of Clinical Psychology website (www.apa.org/divisions/div12/homepage.html) also lists many manuals available for practitioner use (a thorough listing of various manuals for specific phenomena can also be found in the Appendix of this book). Its website promotes the position that there is only one legitimate form of clinical psychology, that is, one that is grounded in science, practiced by scientists, and held accountable to the rigorous standards of scientific evidence. The Society strongly proposes that anything less is pseudoscience (EMDR being one demonstration). One of the site's aims is to bring to the foreground that much of "clinical psychology" is not scientifically valid, appropriate, or acceptable (because much of it does not adhere to scientific principles).

This lack of validity, appropriateness, and acceptability could be addressed through a broader adaptation of manuals, or at the very least practice guidelines and consensus statements. The largest influence as to whether such an acquisition happens is directly related to how well scientific clinical technology is transferred to the everyday practitioner. This is the common target of dissemination, which, unfortunately, has been all but ineffective. One way of circumventing this problem is not to disseminate trademarked treatments per se, but instead to promulgate the underlying, empirically supported principles of change (ESPs) that often make up such treatments (Rosen & Davison, 2003). If the practitioner understands why he or she is using a principle of change, it will far outweigh the benefit that might be had by being able to select a trademarked treatment because it might be associated with the treatment of a particular clinical phenomenon. Empirically supported amelioration of suffering is still about specifically targeting specific mechanisms of pathology with appropriately suitable and fitting interventions (principles); therefore, appreciating the *why* of intervention selection is more important than what brand-name protocol is applied. Certain branded protocols do contain the critical principles for treating a particular disorder (e.g., panic control treatment for panic disorder), but practitioners should have an appreciation of the disorder in question (i.e., understand the mechanisms of it) to inform their treatment planning from principles of change.

One of the single most consistent and perhaps best ways to form a thorough appreciation of what patients are presenting with comes from assessment. The shift toward ESTs (managed care and accountability are implicit therein) has also had important clinical implications for practitioners. Only through the process of assessment can practitioners thoroughly identify parameters of patients' problems, choose effective courses of treatments, and measure treatment outcome (Antony & Barlow, 2002). In short, assessment is a pivotal clinical activity that will be integrally related to later choosing among ESPs. From assessment information, practitioners can describe the phenomenon in question, and such descriptions form the foundation of case formulation. From case conceptualization and the information contained within flows the capacity to predict the occurrence of certain behavioral sets. It is from such predictions that the beginnings of control will flow. Assessment is the critical starting point from which every other clinical activity flows. I commonly advise graduate students that if there is any place in clinical practice they spend any "extra time," it ought to be in assessment, because it serves as a foundation for all clinical decision making that follows, and it might also protect against the delivery of what otherwise could seem like drive-through therapy. Although intake assessments are frequently conducted at the beginning of treatment, it is worthwhile noting that assessment is an ongoing process throughout treatment (progress measurement) and after formal treatment concludes (outcome and follow-up measurement). There are several broad-band and narrow-band strategies for achieving several goals, ranging from diagnosis to symptom monitoring. Chapter 4 contains discussions about assessment and measurement issues and descriptions of many of the common anxiety disorders (and related conditions) that will likely face practitioners who either specialize in anxiety or simply see anxiety in general practice.

Clinical Cases: Illustrations of Assessment, Formulation, and Treatment

The only man who behaved sensibly was my tailor;
he took my measurement anew every time he saw me,
while all the rest went on with their old measurements
and expected them to fit me.
—George Bernard Shaw

ASSESSMENT PROCEDURES FOR ANXIETY DISORDERS

Although general assessment strategies can be helpful in treatment planning and delivery, this book focuses on assessment that will gather the specific information necessary to plan for and deliver empirically supported treatments (ESTs). Evidence-based work requires specialized information to help ground the treatment in science and evidence. Based on a careful and thorough assessment, a practitioner should be able to derive a warranted diagnosis. Such a diagnostic workup will then also allow the practitioner to use practice guidelines and consensus statements to appropriately select a suitable treatment protocol that, through its principals of change, will specifically address relevant symptoms of a disorder detected during assessment. In an effort to make assessment and measurement the most meaningful, I will discuss combinations of broad-band and narrow-band instruments.

Broad-Band Options

The last 30 years have produced an explosion of structured and semi-structured interviews intended to reliably detect various psychological problems. This arose out of a rather embarrassing clinical assessment history of such low reliability and validity that diagnoses were not derived with any greater probability than chance itself (e.g., Beck, Ward, Mendelson, Mock, & Erbaugh, 1962; Spitzer & Fleiss, 1974). Structured and semistructured interviews are specifically designed to minimize the sources of variability that render diagnoses unreliable (Summerfeldt & Antony, 2002). In traditional, unstructured interviewing, the practitioner was solely responsible for determining which questions to ask and how obtained data will actually contribute to a diagnosis. Inconsistency, or low reliability and questionable validity, has been the net, undesirable result. Standardizing and structuring interviews provides standardization of content, format, and order that collectively will be part of an algorithm that derives the diagnosis. This allows the practitioner to remain more objective in clarifying diagnoses, which often serve as a foundation for which treatments to recommend to patients. Although several diagnostic interviews are available, I focus here on the two most commonly used in clinical practice (which also happen to be the two most commonly used in research settings).

Anxiety Disorders Interview Schedule for Diagnostic and Statistical Manual of Mental Disorders (DSM)-IV (ADIS-IV)

The ADIS-IV is a clinician administered, semistructured interview designed to derive DSM-IV anxiety disorder diagnosis and to screen for other common comorbid and relevant diagnoses (e.g., mood disorders, somatoform disorders, substance use disorders). This is the single most commonly used diagnostic instrument used by anxiety disorder researchers, and it is seeing increasing use in many clinical settings, including in evidence-driven private practice. One of the strongest advantages of this instrument, in comparison to many other diagnostic instruments but specifically in comparison to the Structured Clinical Interview for DSM-IV Axis I disorders (SCID-I), is that it not only uses dichotomous (presence-absence) questions, but also extensively uses dimensional questions. Dimensional questions add a number of benefits. Not only do dimensional questions add enough content to clarify and solidify diagnoses, they also allow the foundation of treatment planning to occur through the establishment of baseline severity ratings in many anxiety domains. Whether for the purposes of progress or outcome measurement, dimensional questions serve to provide many anchor points against which effectiveness of interventions can be gauged. Although dimensional measures are not entirely absent in the SCID-I, they are not as well done and fail to provide the detail that may be useful both for diagnostic clarification and treatment planning and delivery. That anxiety disorder researchers are predominantly using the ADIS-IV speaks volumes to its reliability, validity, and utility.

The ADIS-IV is available in two versions, the standard version (Brown, Di Nardo, & Barlow, 1994) and the lifetime version (ADIS-IV-L; Di Nardo, Brown, & Barlow, 1994). The standard version is the most commonly used version, because it provides information about current diagnoses. The lifetime version is more comprehensive (i.e., more labor-intensive) and provides information about current and lifetime diagnoses. A clinician manual and training tape are also available. The ADIS-IV is also available in a version for child (Silverman & Albano, 1996). In addition, the ADIS-IV is available in a range of language translations (e.g., Dutch, French, German, Portuguese, Spanish).

After demographic, presenting problem, and recent life stressor questions, the ADIS-IV flows into assessment questions directed at teasing out Axis I disorders. Because the ADIS-IV is focused on detecting and gauging anxiety, it begins with the anxiety disorders (i.e., panic disorder, agoraphobia, generalized anxiety disorder [GAD], obsessive-compulsive disorder [OCD], specific phobia, posttraumatic stress disorder [PTSD], and acute stress disorder). The ADIS-IV then follows with sections for mood disorders (i.e., major depressive disorder, dysthymic disorder, mania/cyclothymia), somatoform disorders (i.e., hypochondriasis, somatization disorder), mixed anxiety-depression, alcohol abuse and dependence, and substance abuse and dependence. There are also screening questions for psychotic disorders, conversion symptoms, and familial psychiatric history. Medical history and treatment history questions are included to flush out possibly important contributions. The Hamilton Anxiety Rating Scale (Hamilton, 1959) and the Hamilton Rating Scale for Depression (Hamilton, 1960) are combined in a way that allows both interviews to be conducted simultaneously, and produce separate severity scores for anxiety and depression. It should be pointed out that such information could also readily be obtained using common, self-administered severity measures (e.g., Beck Depression Inventory-Second Version [BDI-II]; Beck, Steer, & Brown, 1996).

Compared with other structured interviews, the semistructured nature of the ADIS-IV affords the practitioner to ask clarifying questions. Nevertheless, rudimentary knowledge of the DSM-IV is necessary for the appropriate administration of the interview, because some decisions rules are based on clinical judgment about certain symptoms. Additionally, in comparison with the SCID-I, the ADIS-IV obtains more detailed information about anxiety disorders, including the dimensional ratings of symptoms and information about symptom subtypes. It also obtains patient answers about possible etiology.

SCID

The SCID is also a clinician-administered, semistructured interview that derives psychiatric DSM-IV diagnoses. It is probably the single most recognizable and used interview of its kind in North America. It is available in two versions, serving two separate but related activities, namely the clinician version (SCID-CV; First, Spitzer, Gibbon, & Williams, 1997) and the research version (SCID-I; First, Spitzer, Gibbon, & Williams, 1996). Between these two, the SCID-CV is the most commonly used instrument among clinicians because it is significantly less cumbersome than the full research version. The SCID-CV is limited, however, to assessing only for those disorders commonly found in everyday practice, whereas the SCID-I more completely ascertains information necessary for research on subtypes, severity and course specifiers, and similarly full information about other disorders than anxiety disorders. Unlike the ADIS-IV, there is a separate and complementary interview for Axis II personality disorders (SCID-II). The SCID-I is also available in an abridged version that includes only a screen for psychosis (in place of the lengthy, complicated psychotic disorders module in the regular SCID-I). Additionally, the SCID-I is available in a nonpatient version, which is to be used with nonpsychiatric patients only, and is primarily used for research purposes (e.g., community surveys, family studies). Last, the SCID-I is available in a computerized version often used in telephone interviews and follow-up in research.

There are many similarities to the ADIS-IV. For example, the SCID begins with an open-ended overview of demographics information that leads into exploring the presenting complaint. In this respect, they both produce information in similar ways, but in some respects they go about eliciting and obtaining the information slightly differently. The SCID, for example, concludes the introduction section with an optional screen of 12 questions that will inform the interviewer which modules may be skipped. The ADIS-IV has these screening questions occur at the dichotomous module-entry questions.

In the end, whether one chooses to use the ADIS-IV or a version of the SCID (probably the SCID-CV), it will be important to ask which set of diagnoses are most likely and of special interest. If the primary focus and chief complaint is in the anxiety disorder spectrum, then it might be wise to select the ADIS-IV because it will provide more information about the anxiety disorders than the SCID for everyday practice.

Disorder-Specific and Other Narrow-Band Procedures

While accurately deciding with the ADIS-IV or a SCID which diagnosis, or diagnoses, is present before selecting among treatment options, narrow-band (disorder- or phenomenon-specific) instruments are central to measuring progress and outcome during treatment delivery. Ongoing measurement is one hallmark common to the scientific practice and clinical practice. Measurement informs practitioners whether what they are doing in treatment is effective and whether the course of treatment should change. Ongoing measurement is also the backbone to outcome research, because before and after differences can be analyzed with a variety of statistical methods that can evaluate the significance of change realized by patients. Although this might at first glance appear research oriented, it should be used in clinical practice to inform practitioners what is happening with their patients. Numbers will play an important role for practitioners who decide to take on an evidence-based practice stance, because scores on narrow-band instruments (e.g., BDI-II) will be related to how practitioners, for instance, will decide whether treatment can end or needs to continue. Basic analyses of changes in scores on progress measures can inform practitioners about whether the changes obtained are meaningful enough to begin fading or ending treatment.

Jacobson and Truax (1991) described a statistical method for defining meaningful change in psychotherapy. Although it has been established that many patients improve with psychotherapy treatments, it is less clear just how much patients improve and whether the size of change (i.e., effect size) is functionally meaningful. That is, what is the end-state like? Can patients be discerned from a normal population sample? How much change is enough change before practitioners can stop treatment or begin to fade? There are many questions that consider how much change is enough and when practitioners withdraw. These kinds of questions can be answered by Jacobson and Truax's concept of clinical significance. Jacobson, Follette, and Revenstorf (1984) introduced a beginning assumption of meaningful change when they suggested that clinical significance has something to do with returning to normal functioning. They operationally defined this return to normal functioning in three related ways. First, the functioning of patients should fall outside the range of a clinical population sample that would be descriptive of the clinical phenomenon in question. Specifically, they argued, the end-state functioning should fall outside two standard deviations from the mean of the clinical sample in the direction of functionality. Second, the functioning of patients should also fall within the range of a normal population sample, defined as two standard deviations of the normal mean of a normal population. Third, the end-state functioning is closer to the normal mean than it is to the clinical mean. In short, when the posttreatment score on a narrow-band instrument measuring severity of the clinical phenomenon of interest falls within the normal range (i.e., is closer to the normal mean than the clinical mean), it can be suggested the patient has achieved clinically significant change.

Without going through exactly how to calculate clinical significance (see Jacobson & Truax, 1991, for explicit instructions), it is useful to point out that all that is needed to calculate clinical significance are three pieces of information: (1) prescores and postscores on some instrument that measures the variable of interest, (2) clinical and normal means of the instrument in question, and (3) test-retest reliability of the instrument. Assuming prudent practitioners use progress measures to assess change in their patients, they would readily have pretest and posttest scores. Points two and three can readily be obtained from a variety of sources, but should at least be available in the original article that describes the development of the instrument and its psychometric properties. Nonetheless, many books that described clinical phenomenon also describe narrow-band, disorder-specific instruments that measure severity of such human problems. Collectively, these data can be used to calculate important and very useful information to be used not only for the benefit of the patient but conceivably also for managed care/insurance reasons.

The single most important calculation that can be made from the collective data is the *clinical cutoff point*, commonly referred to as "C," which represents the threshold point at which patients are right at the cusp of falling either into a clinical or normal population sample, depending on the score on the instrument in question (Jacobson & Truax, 1991). This is relevant to practitioners in that it provides a ballpark measure of what a treatment plan should aim for in goal setting. It also provides much bargaining power with insurance companies when practitioners can report whether a particular patient is within the clinical or normal population distributions and just how close to means of such distributions a patient might be (in terms of standard deviations).

Second, a *reliable change index*, or "RCI," can also be calculated. This measure allows practitioners to grasp whether any change realized during treatment is actually substantial enough to represent true change, or a large enough change that it could not be attributable to simply the passage of time or chance of some sort. In other words, reliable change is a measure that would show how much change is sufficient to show the treatment works. This is also an important index for practitioners to have when negotiating with insurance companies. It gives the capacity to argue, for example, that, although the patient is still in the clinical population distribution, a reliable change has been realized, suggesting the treatment is indeed working; therefore, given more time (i.e., more sessions), the patient will likely move into a normal range. From an insurance standpoint, moving patients into the normal functioning range is desirable because in that range, medical utilization is dramatically reduced. Thus when a patient appears to be moving in the direction of "normal," more sessions are more likely to be authorized than if the patient simply appears "clinical." Clinical significance can be a great bargaining tool for practitioners who are accountable within a managed care environment.

Third, clinical significance allows practitioners to calculate whether individual patients meet the more coveted status of "recovered." Patients would be considered recovered if three conditions are true: (1) they started in the clinical range and finished in the normal range, (2) they crossed the clinical cutoff point, and (3) they realized reliable change. Although "recovered" might sound mostly like semantics, it represents truly meaningful change to a degree that former patients could not readily be discerned from normal samples. This is important because it means former patients are functioning enough like "normals" that they are indistinguishable. Practitioners who can produce this status in their patients might also find themselves courted by managed care (i.e., get more referrals) because of the cost savings a recovered status means to insurance companies and other health care management companies.

So, what role do disorder-specific instruments play? For one, they inform practitioners how severe symptoms of presenting complaints might be, but they can also, with some basic calculations, serve as both tools for treatment planning and dealing effectively with managed health care organizations and other third-party payers. Narrow-band instruments are the foundation on which evidence-based practice is built, because they are one clear mean for reliable and valid transmission of clinical data from patients to practitioners. They inform the course of treatment. As a guideline, after patients reach clinical cutoffs, it signals that fading might be appropriate. Additionally, after patients are within one standard deviation of a normal sample mean score on the instrument in question, it would also be defensible to terminate treatment. Although ESTs are about efficacious and effective treatment, they are also about efficiency. Numbers derived from disorder-specific instruments allow conscientious and efficiency-oriented practitioners to be frugal and prudent with care delivery.

For all of the good things numbers can do for practitioners, they can also point out when treatment is not working as one might expect. Often, when treatment is not working or when it is working suboptimally, it is a matter of a faulty case formulation, which might have led to the application of incorrect treatments.

CENTRAL IMPORTANCE OF CASE FORMULATION AND CONCEPTUALIZATION

Case conceptualization, or case formulation, is the last step in the assessment process before treatment planning and treatment delivery begins. Case conceptualization is equivalent to the scientific method's working hypotheses, or an explanation of the nature of patients' problems (i.e., the what) and how (i.e., the why) they came to be that way (Bruch & Bond, 1998; Krug-Porzelius, 2002; Petermann & Müller, 2001; Woody, Detweiler-Bedell, Teachman, & O'Hearn, 2003). The formulation, which flows from information gathered during an intake interview or assessment, is, therefore, a description not only of what the patient is like, but also of the practitioner's theoretical hypotheses about why the patient demonstrates the problems at hand (Berman, 1997). Weerasekera (1996) described formulation as hypotheses about how patients come to present with the particular problems they bring to therapy at the particular time they decide to seek professional services. Weerasekera breaks down the "hows" into four major domains, which collectively produce the how: (1) predisposing factors, (2) precipitating factors, (3) perpetuating factors, and (4) protective factors. These four domains are then also further broken down into individual factors and systemic (environmental) factors that might influence the hows and whys of psychopathology. Individual factors are further broken down into biological, behavioral, cognitive, and psychodynamic components; systemic factors are also further broken down into couple, family, occupational/school, and social factors.

Predisposing factors are any antecedent or predating factors that might make people vulnerable to specific phenomenon. For instance, family history of psychological illness is broadly thought to predispose people or make them vulnerable for developing certain disorders. So, a family history of anxiety or depression would make a person vulnerable for developing anxiety or depression, either through biological transmission or familial modeling of maladaptive coping strategies.

Precipitating factors are any events or experiences that occur more immediately before developing a clinical problem. Latency differentiates precipitating from predisposing events; both occur before the development of a disorder, but precipitating experiences occur close to the time of onset of clinical problems, whereas predisposing life circumstances can simply be the setting in place of the historical conditions that contribute to maladaptive reactions to stressors. Experiencing a panic attack while traveling over a bridge might be the precipitating event that serves as the ignition for a specific phobia, whereas biological reactivity or familial modeling of fear might be the predisposing factors that serve as the fuel for the panic reaction that lead to developing specific phobia or panic disorder.

Perpetuating factors are any factors that serve to maintain, sustain, or make worse the condition or disorder in question. Commonly, these are chronic problems and may be difficult for practitioners to discern. Medical illnesses, difficult work conditions, and other longer standing conditions would be illustrative of perpetuating factors. In anxiety disorders, escape and avoidance are the two most classic perpetuating problems that have clearly been identified to maintain and make worse clinical anxiety. It is also possible that precipitating events, such as having a panic attack on a bridge, could become perpetuating events if the precipitating events take on a chronic course (e.g., patient begins to predictably have panic attacks when encountering bridges).

Protective factors are resiliency factors, or protection against developing clinical problems. Although an absence of protective factors predicts developing clinical disorders, their presence prevents the ignition (onset) of serious problems. Such factors may be used by practitioners to help guard against developing more serious problems and can also enhance recovery and speed up positive change. Protective factors can be constitutional factors or environmental factors, but are largely tied to how people react in circumstances. Recall that anxiety disorders are in exemplar demonstrative of inaccurate reactions or overreactions, so increasing protective factors (e.g., greater somatic tolerance, questioning emotional reasoning, improving problem-solving skills, increasing appropriate assertiveness) may well become a focus or highlight in treatment.

Case formulation generally draws patient information from several broad areas. Although various models might differ slightly, broad information domains usually include: modeling and learning, life events, genetics and temperament, physical conditions, drugs, and socioeconomic and cultural factors (Krug-Porzelius, 2002). All of these domains can be seen as predisposing, precipitating, or perpetuating, depending on specifics. There are additional models that might be useful to practitioners' understanding of what's and why's. In particular, Hays's (1996, 2001) ADDRESSING framework might be useful in elaborating contributions for presenting complaints and general functioning. Her acronym stands for: Age and generational influences, Developmental and acquired Disabilities, Religion and spiritual orientation, Ethnicity, Socioeconomic status, Sexual orientation, Indigenous heritage, National origin, and Gender. Collectively, the factors that make up the ADDRESSING acronym can serve in predisposing, precipitating, perpetuating, and protective ways. A thorough assessment interview should elicit informa-tion from domain areas such as these to most completely inform working hypotheses about how and why patients are the way they are at the time of presenting for services.

Practitioners' clear and thorough understanding of the presenting complaint is pivotal in affording selection of the best fitting or most suitable treatment for the described problem. Therefore, a complete assessment made up of both broad-band and narrow-band measurement instruments is pivotal. Without a clear appreciation of contingencies that control (i.e., predict) the condition of interest, practitioners might not optimally aid patients. A good formulation will summarize patient problem areas, including information about how the problems arose, were maintained, and possibly made worse, and recommend the order in which to address various aspects of the problems. Within a good description of the problem rests clues for how to undo the contingencies to produce a different outcome. From the description of what predicts the condition, recommendations for specific treatment interventions will emerge. Additionally, prognostic indicators will suggest what level of care is most suitable and appropriate. In short, case formulation is informed by the interviewing, assessment and testing process, and data and infor-mation of all sorts discovered during such activities and also serve to guide selection of interventions through the predictions made within the case conceptualization.

Immediately after the assessment and formulation (hypothesis creation), the working guesses are evaluated through testing the hypotheses with inter-ventions meant to address specific contingency variables of presenting complaints. The successfulness of the intervention can then be evaluated with narrow-band instruments and clinical significance. If the treatment intervention fails to produce the desired effect, then the hypotheses can be revised and retested with alternate case conceptualizations not originally considered or thought to play minor roles in the presenting complaint (Meier, 1999; Tomkins, 1999). Fortunately, there are a multitude of treatment options available for anxiety disorders, many organized into user-friendly manuals that capture treatment mechanisms.

MANUALS, THEIR MODULAR USE, AND MANUALIZED TREATMENT STRATEGIES

There are many compelling reasons for using manual-based treatments. Primarily, because manuals capture the active change ingredients in vari-ous ESTs, manuals are helpful in ensuring all practitioners will have a good chance at delivering effective treatment. After all, several treatment approaches have been manualized (see Appendix A for examples), and such approaches would be best used if practitioners consistently used the active ingredients that have been shown to directly affect some mechanism of pathology and change. Indeed, studies have found that the use of manuals decreases between-therapist differences in the outcome of patients (e.g., Crits-Christoph et al., 1991), suggesting that with stronger adherence to proven methods of treatment uniformity of better outcomes are strengthened.

Concretely, manuals provide a ready-made, but supported, conceptual understanding of theories of psychopathology and models for change of such conditions. Additionally, they point practitioners directly to both general and specific skills of how and when to do the supported treatment interventions that are proposed to potentiate therapeutic change. Perhaps most central to evaluating effectiveness of interventions, manuals also direct practitioners in how to assess or evaluate efficacy and when to consider whether to change intervention strategies (Moras, 1993).

As mentioned previously, manuals and ESTs are not without their controversy. In basis, by definition, ESTs have to be manualized (i.e., the treatment outcomes have to better than wait-list, placebo, or alternative groups, and treatment have to be manualized). Much of the focus on manualized treatments, when part of efficacy research, is to control therapist variables, to be able to isolate the active change ingredients. Further, this ensures greater replicability and refutability, which in the long run ensures a greater likelihood that everyday practitioners will be able to deliver (on an effectiveness level) what has been created in efficacy studies.

Although the current psychotherapy zeitgeist promotes manual-based treatments, it does not equate to practitioners having to deliver entire treatments inflexibly from cover to cover in various manuals. Still, there are a variety of negative attitudes and misconceptions toward manuals, such as concerns about freedom and flexibility in sessions and deleterious effects on relationship (Addis & Krasnow, 2000). Despite such attitudes and misconceptions, it is possible, despite popular critique and pragmatic evaluations (e.g., Abrahamson, 1999; Goldfried & Wolfe, 1998; Henggeler & Schoenwald, 2002), to "breathe life" into manuals. So instead, more realistic, modular use of manuals is common practice, where appropriate modules are assembled to fit individual patients, as directed and indicated by their idiosyncratic case formulations (Beutler, 2002; Kendall, Chu, Gifford, Hayes, & Nauta, 1998). Although some profess outright love for scientific research (e.g., Borkovec & Castonguay, 1998), most practitioners are left to figure out how to use the empirical literature and manuals to their patients' best advantage; at such decision points, flexibility and creativity ensure that meaningful matches of treatment principles and protocols are made.

The danger of not going with manual-based, empirically supported, and evidence-based ways and means is that it will leave practitioners to deliver a blend of "who-knows-what" products. Sometimes it might work, but often it might not. With the scientific method as a foundation for practice, which is at the core of most manuals, at least a common standard for evaluation and practice is possible. Whether desirable or not, manualized treatment strategies offer standardization to practitioners decision making and treatment delivery, which in the long run will serve patients more reliably (validity perhaps remaining questionable) than historical trends of treatment as usual or as fancied. If practitioners took it on themselves to conduct research on their own patients seen in private practice or in other effectiveness settings, more could be learned about delivering manual-based treatments, whether more formally along specific protocols or more flexibly along lines of therapeutic principles and modules, to patients seen outside efficacy settings. Warren and Thomas (2003) laments that few practitioners engage in systematic evaluation of their patients, with a possible exception being mostly found among cognitive-behavioral therapy (CBT)–oriented practitioners who accept principles of relying on research in all respects to inform and guide practice. However, without ample case illustrations of how transportable, adaptable, and flexible ESTs can be in private practice, few new practitioners are unlikely to just begin practice in an evidence-based fashion. After all, for almost every manual available, there are far more books pointing to more artistic (less science oriented) delivery of psychotherapy services. Case examples from private practice and other smaller settings are not just desirable, but required for more practitioners to adopt evidence-based practice standards.

CASE ILLUSTRATIONS

The following sections include numerous case illustrations of real patients who have all been treated in small (nonefficacy) settings by me or my colleagues. Results reported on the presented patients are not atypical or unusual, but are instead what the author and colleagues commonly experience as standard in everyday practice. Obviously, some cases do not fair as well as described, but provided the treatment principles are delivered in a way that they do address the central mechanisms of the disorders described, patients fare very well. Whenever possible, information will be provided about clinical significance to elucidate what is not only possible, but commonly achievable by following CBT principles and practices.

Panic Disorder and Agoraphobia

Panic disorder with (PDA) or without (PD) agoraphobia is often a disabling and expensive set of disorders that, left untreated or undertreated, will result in unsustainably high medical utilization; not only is PDA/PD systemically damaging, but it also carries enormous personal and interpersonal costs (Ballenger, 1998; Davidson, 1996). As impairing and painful as PDA/PD often is, there are clearly established treatments available for panic and related symptoms. Given the high social and personal costs often associated with this condition, prudent practitioners will offer symptomatic relief. According to the DSM-IV-TR (American Psychiatric Association, 2000), PDA is characterized by recurrent panic attacks. Such attacks are commonly perceived as uncontrollable, unpredictable, and dangerous. Such discrete, but intensely frightening, episodes are usually made up of a combination of such symptoms as a racing/pounding heart, sweating and having hot/cold flashes, trembling/shaking, shortness of breath or feelings of smothering or choking, extreme chest pain and numbness and tingling, nausea and abdominal distress, dizziness, and unsteadiness. Additionally, patients often report a feeling of unreality, fear of losing control, going crazy, or that they are dying. The hallmark of PDA/PD is that panic attacks occur seemingly out of the blue, without warning or apparent reason, often leading to fears that something is terribly wrong with the person (e.g., experiencing a heart attack, a stroke, "going crazy"). Sometimes patients can experience just one or two of the symptoms, in which case, ironically, it is referred to as "complex panic," or limited symptom attacks.

CBT is the accepted treatment of choice for PDA/PD and will most often focus on systematically facing feared situations, interoceptive cues, and on reducing or eliminating general avoidance commonly developed through experiencing panic in locations or circumstances (which then become avoided; e.g., Barlow, Gorman, Shear, & Woods, 2000). This biopsychosocial treatment is what is often referred to as "panic control treatment" (PCT; Barlow & Craske, 1989; Craske & Barlow, 2000), and has most recently even been adopted into an intensive 8-day treatment program (Heinrichs, Hofmann, & Spiegel, in press).

The following case illustration is provided by Ricks Warren, PhD, ABPP, and is illustrative of the transportability of PCT to a private practice setting. In treating this case, Dr. Warren was able to eliminate panic attacks and worry about future panic attacks. Comorbid depression was also reduced to minimal levels.

"Bill" was a 27-year-old, single Hispanic male referred to Dr. Warren through an acquaintance. Bill had experienced his first panic attack a year before seeking psychological services for the problem. At the time, he reported believing he was having a heart attack, for which he sought medical services (as anyone believing a heart attack was imminent or occurring would reasonably do). Between the onset of panic attacks and seeking professional help for the panic, he reported seeking out medical help through emergency rooms approximately 20 times. In usual fashion, the panic attacks began to debilitate Bill; although he had entered graduate school, he was forced to take a leave of absence and return home. A family doctor prescribed Bill both antianxiety (benzodiazepine) and antidepressant (selective serotonin reuptake inhibitor) medications.

Bill's panic attacks were exemplified by a racing heart, tingling in his extremities, hot flashes, nausea, lightheadedness, fear of fainting, and vomiting. During panic attacks, he most frequently felt and completely believed he was experiencing heart attacks. Ambulance and hospital personnel always denied these suspicions, but offered few tactics or recommendations for what to do when he experienced these types of sudden and intense discomforts. Dissatisfied, Bill went on to incur and endure multiple medical tests to check all sorts of physiological functioning that might explain the problems he experienced. These costly and nonreassuring tests all concluded there was "no clear evidence for pathology in any way." This left Bill further baffled and feeling further confused about what to do. He began to avoid friends and social activities, driving out of town by himself, going to restaurants and theaters, and a whole host of other situations on which he had either experienced a panic attack or feared he might again. He came to believe, despite the best medical tests and assurances from family and friends, that there was something terribly wrong with him. Because of various fears and physiological sensations that physical exercise would bring on, Bill also became more and more sedentary, going so far as to change his lying down position to induce the least chest sensations. In short, he was grossly affected by PDA.

The assessment conducted by Dr. Warren indicated Bill was suffering with panic disorder with agoraphobia (300.21) and major depression, single episode, severe, without psychotic features (296.23). Several self-report questionnaires were administered, such as the Fear Questionnaire (Marks & Mathews, 1979), the Mobility Inventory (Chambless, Caputo, Jasin, Gracely, & Williams, 1985), and the Body Sensations Questionnaire and the Agoraphobic Cognitions Questionnaire (both from Chambless, Caputo, Bright, & Gallagher, 1984). An expanded version of the latter was also included (Warren, Zgourides, & Jones, 1989).

The Fear Questionnaire was included to measure agoraphobic and social avoidance and overall disability from phobic symptoms. Because it is an instrument commonly used in clinical practice around the world, it would allow good comparisons against a variety of settings. The Mobility Inventory is one of the most commonly used measures of agoraphobic avoidance, and the Body Sensations Questionnaire and the Agoraphobic Cognitions Questionnaire both measure fear of physiological cues and related catastrophic thoughts. Fear of bodily sensations and associated catastrophic and fearful thoughts and thinking styles make up the focus of the PCT treatment. The BDI (Beck, Ward, Mendelson, Mock, & Erbaugh, 1961) was also used to track comorbid depression.

PCT was delivered to Bill by means of Barlow and Craske's (1989) client manual *Mastery of Your Anxiety and Panic (MAP)*. The MAP manuals have now gone through a series of updates, and are now delivering PCT in a third edition, aptly entitled MAP-3 (Barlow & Craske, 2000; Craske & Barlow, 2000; Craske, Barlow, & Meadows, 2000). The PCT delivered consisted of (1) education about the nature of panic and anxiety, (2) breathing retraining and progressive muscle relaxation, (3) cognitive interventions for probability overestimations and catastrophizing, (4) exposure to feared bodily sensations, (5) exposure to naturalistic activities that produce feared bodily sensations, and (6) exposure to avoided places. Other, typical CBT interventions were also used to combat specific symptoms; for example, Bill was taught how to challenge hopelessness and negative self-talk, and to increase activity levels.

In all, treatment totaled 21 sessions from start to finish, during which Bill's fears of panic and avoidance were all but eliminated. Additionally, Bill was able to discontinue use of medications originally prescribed for panic attacks. For practitioners who plan to use a benzodiazepine discontinuation module as part of the PCT to assist patients to stop relying on medications that only artificially diminish physical sensations (ironically, this often makes patients supervigilant or sensitized to any physical sensation), there are special adapted manuals available that combine PCT and medication discontinuation protocols (Otto, Jones, Craske, & Barlow, 1996; Otto, Pollack, & Barlow, 1995). Of course, any discontinuation should be done with the assistance of the prescribing agent (e.g., psychiatrist, psychiatric nurse practitioner) for ethical and pragmatic reasons. According to critical evaluation of pretreatment to posttreatment scores on the progress measures, Bill's improvement was clinically significant. This accomplishment did not look exactly like what might be available in the established treatment manuals; for instance, Bill's total treatment spanned 21 sessions, as opposed to the typical 16 sessions commonly specified in the PCT manuals of the time (Barlow, Craske, Cerny, & Klosko, 1989). Bill's comorbid depression appeared to have affected PCT treatment, as it is suspected to do when depression is comorbid with panic (Clum & Pendrey, 1987; Laberge, Gauthier, Cote, Plamondon, & Cormier, 1993). As is common to depressed patients, interoceptive work took longer than might otherwise be expected in a "cleaner" PD case, because habituation can be impaired or prevented by substantial depression. Recall that repeated habituation is necessary for true extinction to occur. Nonetheless, with spending more time in the critical exercises and simply spending more time helping Bill debunk his irrational fears through direct experimentation, he was able to finally realize significant change comparable to all efficacy samples, suggesting that private practice settings and comorbidity do not influence outcome in an overly negative manner.

Whether individual practitioners use a manual or simply deliver PCT component or suitable modules out of PCT is not important, so long as the active change ingredients are used in treating PDA/PD. It is one of two anxiety disorders (PTSD being the other) that requires formal treatment for a return of normal functioning. There are a variety of resources beyond the few listed in this case illustration already. Some additional manuals that practitioners who are interested in delivering evidence-based treatments for panic and associated avoidance might be interested in are Taylor's (2000) *Understanding and Treating Panic Disorder: Cognitive-Behavioural Approaches*, Zuercher-White's (1997) *Treating Panic Disorder and Agoraphobia: A Step by Step Clinical Guide*, and Zuercher-White's (1999a, 1999b) *Overcoming Panic Disorder and Agoraphobia: A Cognitive Restructuring and Exposure-Based Protocol for the Treatment of Panic and Agoraphobia (Therapist Protocol)* and *Overcoming Panic Disorder and Agoraphobia: A Cognitive Restructuring and Exposure-Based Protocol for the Treatment of Panic and Agoraphobia (Client Manual)*. More overarching texts that have exceptionally strong chapters on panic and its treatments are Andrews et al.'s (2003) *The Treatment of Anxiety Disorders: Clinician Guides and Patient Manuals*, Van Hasselt and Hersen's (1996) *Sourcebook of Psychological Treatment Manuals for Adult Disorders*, and Hersen's (2002) *Clinical Behavior Therapy: Adults and Children*. See Appendix A for other manuals.

Specific Phobia

Specific phobia is one of the most common anxiety disorders, with life-time prevalence rates reaching as high as 13% (Kamphuis, Emmelkamp, & Krijn, 2002). The DSM-IV-TR (2000) suggests that *specific* refers to the idea of persistent anxiety and fear being specifically triggered in specifically discernible situations or by specifically circumscribed stimuli (i.e., objects). Specific phobia was formerly known as "simple" phobia, but this name might have been changed when considering retrospectively that simple does not do justice to suffering and costs associated with this type of anxiety and fear. Specific phobia might take the form of situationally bound or situationally predisposed panic attacks, so PDA/PD will have to be ruled out through routine interview and investigation of primary causal variables. Indeed, specific phobia can cause such intense panic that extreme avoidance is all but assured to follow because of the power of negative reinforcement. Although many people might say they experience fear of specific situations or objects, clinical specific phobia necessitates the intense anxiety, fear, and avoidance behaviors must interfere significantly with the person's normal life. Nonetheless, specific phobia patients rarely seek formal (correct) treatment because they often become very good at avoiding what they fear. Fortunately, specific phobias usually only develop around a limited array of offending stimuli, so people suffering with this condition can function relatively well for many years. As with most anxiety conditions, however, specific phobias can also worsen to the point of disabling the patient. Specific phobias that do not spontaneously remit, such as animal (dog) phobias often can do, tend to continue into adulthood without treatment.

For example, recently I worked with a specific phobia patient who could not cross bridges (for fear of heights). If she had never needed to cross a bridge, this might not have represented a problem, but because Portland, Oregon, is split in half by the Columbia River and her livelihood depended on selling real estate, where mobility is pivotal to selling properties, this fear had become a significant problem. Additionally, she could not ride up in elevators unaccompanied, and then only with great distress; needless to say, this problem (acrophobia: fear of heights) was also not exactly conducive to the real estate business. She was also unable to visit her daughter who lived across the river, leaving her dependent on others to come to her. Slowly but surely her "comfort zone" had become curtailed to a small enough square encompassing only her bare necessities (e.g., grocery store, post office), and even then she felt compelled to stick to smaller back streets and other "safe" routes. As is often the case with specific phobias, her sense of safety (or lack thereof) was driven by situations and places she had experienced intense and frightening panic attacks. Luckily for her, specific phobias are especially responsive to exposure-based behavioral treatment (Antony, Craske, & Barlow, 1995; Bourne, 1998a, 1998b; Emmelkamp, 1994).

In an effort to continue to provide opportunities for practitioners and graduate students to hear voices and experiences of real patients, I will next offer the personal story of "Laura" and her reflections about her life before exposure-based treatment, what her experience of treatment was like, and what her life is like after treatment. Again, her real-life account is offered here in an attempt to provide a level of insight that practitioners, researchers, and helping professionals of all kinds can only guess at. At the time of referral, she was a 52-year-old, divorced Caucasian female living alone, who was trying to make life work in any way. She was referred by a colleague who was then treating Laura's daughter. Identifying details have been altered, but the details of her personal story remain unchanged.

As a small child, the open back stairs of the Portland Forestry Center's fire lookout station were torturous, no matter how many times I tried to climb them. How I would have been happy to see the Center in ashes! I was afraid of heights on tall wooden cherry picking ladders, too, but we loved going to local farms to eat our fill and get paid for the rest. My tree fort in the backyard was wonderful at only 10 ft off the ground. In the summer, I could usually sleep with my pillow by my open window of my second-story bedroom because I didn't want to miss the mysteries of the night. Summer camps were my most anticipated vacations, except for the hikes high above the waterfalls, with winding narrow trails and wet, fuzzy cliff walls to hug to keep from slipping over the edge. The canoe trips were always a favorite as long as we paddled within a quick swim of the lake banks. Life was full and fun, but unexpectedly scary at times, but I enjoyed all of the childhood activities my friends did.

At 22, my choice to cross the 100-foot canyon to get to our cabin in the woods was a necessity that often came with tears and angst, but jumping off the bridge to the swimming hole far below was not a right of passage I felt compelled to perform. There were the odd times of anxiety, usually tied to potential real and present dangers. Living in the isolated woods does have its challenges, but the tradeoff was an exquisite adventure.

As a young mother with a preschooler, a marriage that was tearing apart, and a job to juggle, I was suddenly dizzy every time I went grocery shopping, anxious at friends' houses, uncomfortable outside of my house, and depressed at staying home. I sought my first diagnosis with a doctor who diagnosed low blood sugar. I went on a low-carbohydrate, high-protein diet, took vitamin supplements, and worked on decreasing the stress in my life. As I took more control of my life, the anxiety decreased. The day that my husband moved out, my life felt back on track, and all things seemed possible again.

Five years later, with an up-and-down real estate income, 3 years of missing child support checks, and having bought my first house, I nearly screeched to a halt on the freeway for fear of heading onto the ramp of the biggest bridge in our city.

That shocking display of creating a potentially deadly accident with my child in the car told me that I was not to be trusted driving freeways and reinforced my growing discomfort with bridges. A few months later, I got stuck on my favorite bridge as it lifted for a river boat. It was the last bridge that I drove over for almost 20 years.

Fast forward to my ever-dwindling driving, living, and working radius: The theme of "I am not to be trusted" had spread to many places. I had become the neighborhood specialist in my real estate field because it represented the two-lane neighborhood streets that I could still get around on. Yet, that left out many sections of the greater metropolitan area, and soon across river/east-side buyers and sellers that I had worked with had to be referred to other agents. My income was suffering, financial stress was building, and I knew that my whole life was constricting.

Throughout the last 20 years, I had sought help with various doctors and support groups, neurolinguistic reprogramming, past life regression, hypnosis reprogramming, relaxation therapy, and eye movement desensitization and reprocessing. Each therapy gave me some knowledge helpful in understanding my personality and development, relaxation tools, interesting interpretations of childhood memories, and fascinating past life possibilities. **None of these therapies did anything to get me back on the roads and bridges that I had learned to drive on in my teens!** [Emphasis added.]

Desperation—financial, professional, and social—forced me to listen to yet another recommendation, this time to seek out a panic disorder doctor, for one more try. My daughter was then living in her first house across the river and I couldn't get there unless she picked me up and drove me over. My elevator fears were causing a lack of interest in an entirely new district of high-rise condominiums in my sales neighborhood. I had begun to look for a new job with more stable income and realized that I could not get to most interviews on my own, much less work there. My options had shrunk to a new low and by this time the stakes had become too high not to try and tackle this again.

With some hope and some expectations that it might only be a Band-Aid, I went to Dr. Rosqvist. I listened to him telling me the science of this disorder, realizing that unknowingly, but instinctively I had learned some normal, but nonetheless maladaptive coping skills directly related to what happens physiologically to a body in panic. These connections and recognitions made the science ring true. His explanations and teachings reeled me in and gave me hope. At once fascinated by the science of the problem, and comfortable with his calm, matter-of-fact approach, we started to work together on the staircase of his 14-story office building. Little by little, I huffed and hugged my way up to the top floor. The higher we climbed, the more the process seemed to slow gently into several sessions. Although I experienced some milder panic attacks, hyperventilation, and gripping fear, which was all supposed to happen, Dr. Rosqvist persisted with the patience of an expert so sure of his process. He taught me so many things. For instance, he taught me a breathing technique that has unlocked my diaphragm, allowing me to breathe more slowly, deeply, and with relaxation. I believe I will use this conscious, more relaxed breathing to enhance the rest of my life.

Quickly, after having spent a lot of time climbing stairs to previously unimaginable heights, we moved on to elevators and with the same process of "repetition until boredom." My fear was once again overcome by the thrill of taking that elevator eventually all alone, several floors at a time; each time it became more of a game to see what I could actually do, and dropping him off to wait for me while I went farther and higher. **These were my first real feelings of conquering the demon that had hounded me for 20 years!** [Emphasis added.] Now, it was fun to go to my therapy sessions. Even when the rest of my life felt like it was falling apart, I knew that if I made myself go to my treatment sessions, I would have something positive happening in my life. It seemed to be the highlight of many weeks I recall from that dismal time in my life.

Just as unexpectedly as we had moved from success with stairs to elevators, one day Dr. Rosqvist suggested that we hit the road and pick a bridge for our next session. So, I picked him up, somewhat nervously, in my car outside his office building. It was amazing; there he sat next to me in the passenger front seat, as calmly and sure of our success as he had been on every other appointment. I warned him that that this was not a "normal" appointment, and that he had better do a great job talking me into the task and that he better be ready to grab the wheel to save us both when the inevitable disaster would come along. Each time I painted some gruesome picture, Dr. Rosqvist would return to the science of probability, the actuarial tables, and the feet on the ground question of "Did that ever actually happen to you, to anyone you actually know, or to most of those other people out there?" We drove around the base of our first bridge several times until I gave up and asked him to take us across. Before doing so, we agreed on what I had to pay attention to and what I could not do, like avoiding looking out, and engaging in other safety behaviors. So, we switched seats and he drove onto the bridge. He did very well, too, going back and forth, in and out of traffic, virtually wearing a rut across our bridge route, until I became quite bored. After all, we both knew he could do it. So, finally, I asked to take the wheel. I made my first pass from the east side to the west. I was shocked with having done it without halting to a stop or screaming and crying the whole way. It was simply amazing! I think I was stunned that I could do it, and so readily too. That surprise encouraged me to try west to east, which was a little harder. But back and forth we drove. Dr. Rosqvist is quite the character because there were times when I wanted to poke him in the ribs to make sure he was ready to spring into action, and not half-asleep instead. Finally, after wearing my own virtual rut into that bridge, I was beginning to feel "more normal" and even a little thrilled with my accomplishment. I couldn't believe I had done, repeatedly at that, what I had not done in 20 years!

For our next session, I drove with him back and forth, still nervous, but with a feeling of increased competence. During that drive, he asked me to drive the bridge some without him. Wide-eyed in disbelief, I negotiated the alternative of first having him ride quietly in the back seat so I could pretend that he wasn't there. That worked well and was a good transition to build my confidence. For my big, independent trip, I picked an interesting spot to drop him off, a store called the "Booty Call" where I had seen leather- and chain-clad teens. I said that I was ready to try the bridge alone if I could drop him off there; that way, we could both be entertained and slightly out of our element! Always calm and unworried and probably a bit relieved at this break in monotony, he grinned and obliged my proposal. Within minutes of having dropped him off, I had made it across that bridge for the first time on my own in almost 20 years, so I waved to him on the corner and went for another round! Another round turned into several more and each time I waved to him as I passed. When I finally picked him up, I was jubilant. His story of adventure was disappointingly anticlimactic, however, because the Booty Call was a used clothing store, with only a few patrons. One thing that has occurred to me about Dr. Rosqvist is that he must have great patience and an active imagination to fill the "do it until you are bored" hours involved in this kind of therapy, and he also must just be quite desperate to get out of his office!

As I write this, I am aware of the many times in my life that I have stepped into my fear zone to experience fun and adventure; I want to remember that the payoffs have almost always made it worthwhile! I can hear Dr. Rosqvist saying to my scary stories, "And what happened? Did you drive off the bridge, fall from the cliff, cause an accident on the freeway, faint, run, or die?" To date, to my own surprise in recognizing this fact really, none of these bad things have actually happened in real life, which apparently is the law of averages that he impressed me with in our first meeting. It's almost funny how my mind didn't seem to grasp that fact for all those years.

Why did this therapy work? In part, I think it helped that I was finally desperate enough to be willing to try again to face my fears. I was also fortunate enough to find a program that *actually* works, and a doctor who had the knowledge to teach me the science that helped me understand what was happening with my brain, body, and behavior. The systematic and predictable process that Dr. Rosqvist taught me to help me challenge my fears and overcome them is surprisingly simple to remember and even relatively easy to do. With his guidance, I took it in manageable steps, practicing the steps until they became boring, and kept doing it even on days when it wasn't totally easy. With the help of my friends and my family, I will continue to ask for "ride alongs" when I take on new and especially hard challenges. I know now that Dr. Rosqvist is right when he said that riding one elevator *is* just like riding any other and soon one bridge and one freeway will become just like any other. I am so grateful to the ever earnest and calm Dr. Science Rosqvist, a brave soul who would walk every step and ride every mile with me, and for finally giving me the tools to expand my life to its fullest. I would encourage anyone with these kinds of issues to try this life-altering process. It means so much to begin to trust oneself again.

Laura is representative of many specific phobia patients I have worked with, in that she had "successfully" avoided situations until her freedom of movement had become so constricted she could no longer fulfill some of life's basics (e.g., working, seeing family when she wished to, engaging in basic travel around town). Her treatment began with an assessment to clearly distinguish among any present anxiety problems and other possible issues. My standard assessment practice, which serves as the intake interview, is to perform an ADIS-IV along with narrow-band instruments that appear appropriate after the diagnostic interview. She met a diagnosis of Specific Phobia (300.29), Natural Environment Type (heights), and Situational Type (driving), as well as Major Depressive Disorder, Single Episode, Moderate (296.22). Three narrow-band instruments were selected for Laura to specifically monitor progress in her symptomatology: the Acrophobia Questionnaire (Cohen, 1977), Attitudes Toward Heights Questionnaire (Abelson & Curtis, 1989), and the BDI-II (Beck et al., 1996). Her treatment spanned 20 sessions and focused on exposure to situations that produced fear and anxiety. The treatment consisted of a combination of in vivo exposure and in-imagination exposure, usually used to enhance in vivo work. Following is a "disaster script" that she recorded onto a loop-tape to use in conjunction with driving exposures, after driving in all kinds of settings and under all kinds of conditions became much easier.

> I'm starting to drive over the Burnside Bridge, but where are the cars that I can follow? I feel so alone, and I can't trust myself to stay on the bridge without cars to follow. My muscles are tightening, and my feet and hands are tingling and cold. I'm trying so hard to be me, to be sensible, and think clearly. Yet, I'm confused, distracted, and light-headed. I'm terrified that I'm being sucked into the void. I can't trust myself to stay on the bridge. I can't handle the bridge, and I'm being pulled toward the void. I'm helpless to stop it. I'm afraid. I couldn't stop it even if I tried. It's hopeless. Suddenly, the car crashes through the bridge and I'm all alone and it seems forever until I hit the water. And crash, I'm there, in the water. The car is sinking, and the cold, cold water engulfs me. I'm giving up. I'm letting go. I'm dying. I'm dead.

As with all exposure work, Laura's followed a collaboratively determined hierarchy designed to take her from easier to harder tasks. Each step was repeated, as she puts it, until she became "bored" with the task, or had habituated to the task and had experienced at least a 50% reduction in her Subjective Units of Distress scores. Because the literature on specific phobias is relatively unanimous that patients can experience excruciating panic attacks, I first taught her a variety of somatic stress management skills. By using diaphragmatic breathing, she would be able to keep exposures within a tolerable range that would make her less likely to escape from the exposure tasks before habituation, and progressive muscular relaxation would keep her daily stress levels lower. These relaxation skills were all taught preemptively to maximize the odds that she would remain in treatment after she began in vivo exposure work. Additionally, several worry management skills were taught to make her more effective in critically evaluating her subjective experiences. By being able to reasonably evaluate risk in exposure situations, she would be more inclined to attempt them in the beginning. Getting her to approach feared situations would be pivotal to treatment success, as is also common to most other anxiety disorders. To maximize odds she would complete the treatment, I took additional time in teaching her the natural science behind anxiety and how to use somatic and cognitive skills to combat fears systematically. During initial exposures in an office stairwell, she was never pushed further than she was willing to go, so she would not have to escape; although initial in vivo work was tentative, she progressed quickly after she came to see that her feared outcomes were not coming true, and her anxiety began to diminish more quickly. Before long she was combining in vivo with in-imagination exposure to obtain a desirable arousal from which habituation would be both possible and easy to achieve because of a lack of a floor effect common to poorly arousing tasks.

Although the statistical concept of "recovered" (Jacobson & Truax, 1991) might be somewhat misleading because patients often exhibit some residual symptoms, Laura met the three necessary components of recovery by (1) beginning in clinical distributions and finishing in normal distributions, (2) crossing clinical cutoffs, and (3) realizing reliable change. Follow-up measurements suggested minimal slippage, but well within the normal range of functioning. Interestingly, since treatment, she has worked extensively to bring this anxiety problem to the attention of news media sources (giving radio interviews, appearing in newspaper stories) and has appeared in public forums to bring attention to the problem and the solutions that successfully resolve this all-too-common plight.

There are some suggestions that specific phobias represent a basic preparatory response in reaction to fundamental threats, such as heights, deep water, lightning, and animals of various sorts with the capacity to harm (e.g., dogs, snakes). In this fashion, there would exist some primitive priming toward stimuli that are fundamentally dangerous. This notion might be supported by the fact that there are no known specific phobias known to exist for more modern, yet truly dangerous stimuli, such as handguns, for example.

It is worth noting that one particular kind of specific phobia requires a supplementary treatment approach. Blood-injection-injury type exhibits the "vasovagal syncope" response in which, after initially rising as is common to anxiety reactions, heart rate and blood pressure suddenly and rapidly fall and muscle tone is also dramatically reduced. This interesting response is presumably because of the vagus nerve, a parasympathetic nerve that innervates the chest and upper abdomen (Barlow, 2002). This phenomenon is also suspected to be part of a behavioral descriptor of the German term *platzschwindel*, referring to the sensation of dizziness in public places, or more simply *platzangst*, which describe fear of open spaces. Although Laura endorsed strong beliefs that she would faint, she reported that she had never done so in her lifetime in response to her anxiety and fear, ruling out this particular peculiarity. Should she, however, have reported a history of fainting, then a particular technique, applied tension (e.g., Öst & Sterner, 1987), would have been introduced to teach her to prevent the fainting response.

Although many anxiety-disordered patients are commonly taught various relaxation forms to decrease stress reactions such as increased blood pressure, applied tension teaches patients to increase blood pressure to prevent fainting. Öst and colleagues describe this technique as being especially important for patients who actually faint, rather than just believing they will. The method is made up of contracting the major muscle groups in the arms, torso, and legs for 10- to 15-second intervals or until the patient feels warmth spreading in the face. With daily practice, this increase in blood pressure can be brought on quickly and easily when needed, and effectively prevents the syncope response. I have found this technique most pertinent to specific phobia patients who have a difficult time with getting injections or having blood drawn.

Social Phobia

Social phobia is more often referred to as social anxiety disorder to make it more consistent with how other anxiety disorders are described (McNeil, 2000). According to DSM-IV-TR (2000), social anxiety disorder is indicated by marked and persistent fear and anxiety with exposure to social or performance situations (e.g., public speaking, writing or eating in public, meeting strangers or authority figures), in which the person believes he or she will be scrutinized, negatively judged, or thought of negatively by others, or that the person will do or say something to embarrass or humiliate himself or herself. This social anxiety can be found in both specific and circumscribed situations, such as for public speaking only and more broadly across many social situations. When anxiety reactions are found to be more pervasive and spanning most situations, it is often referred to as "generalized social phobia." This DSM-IV-TR specifier does seem to matter, possibly a great deal, because it carries important prognostic implications. The literature has clearly shown that circumscribed and generalized social anxiety respond differently to the stress of social situations (e.g., Boone et al., 1999; McNeil et al., 1995). Indeed, the suggestion has been made that avoidant personality disorder may be a particularly virulent form of generalized social phobia (Reich, 2000; Widiger, 2001).

Because of its nature, the preferred treatment modality for social anxiety is group (Heimburg & Becker, 2002); however, my own clinical experience suggests it might be difficult to get many social anxiety-disordered patients to agree to a group format (i.e., given social exposure is the core difficulty in social anxiety, going straight into a group format might represent too large of a step), so an individual format might be offered as a precursor to group or as a stand-alone treatment. Nonetheless, much of treatment will be focused on going into social situations (exposure) to evaluate more critically and objectively what actually happens and what evidence there exists for some of the beliefs and assumptions held by socially anxious patients (Schneier, 1999). Clark's model (Clark, 2001; Clark & Wells, 1995) of social anxiety offers the most compelling model for how to conceptualize social anxiety. In a nutshell, this model proposes that the socially anxious patient believes or thinks that others can see just how vulnerable, weak, or bad he or she feels, so the patient begins to use various safety behaviors to "cover up" his or her own perceived flaws and shortcomings. The problem with this behavioral response is that it makes patients even further aware of their flaws, and (perhaps most central to the model) it makes them into a "social object" that they believe they have to control to a degree that simply is not possible, nor healthy or human. Unfortunately, as long as patients engage in safety behaviors of various sorts (e.g., wearing light clothing to prevent sweating from getting hot or flushed, gripping utensils or glasses tightly to prevent shaking or dropping them, using body position to inhibit interactions), they cannot experience what actually happens when they do not protect themselves to such a degree (e.g., Johnstone & Page, 2004; Powers, Smits, & Telch, 2004; Sloan & Telch, 2002). Remarkably, catastrophic expectations do not typically occur when they set out to test overly negative expectations. Through repeated exposure, without using safety behaviors (i.e., response prevention rules are adhered to), they become more at ease and easygoing while around others, and actually begin to engage in interpersonal interactional patterns that signal social interest. Ironically, most socially anxious patients desire social connection and contact, but go about it in such a way as to inadvertently send off cues that suggest disinterest or discomfort, leading to isolation and (at times) confirmation of social fears (L. Alden, personal communication, June 9, 2002).

Following is a case I recently treated. "George" was a 45-year-old, never-married male who was referred to treatment by his primary care physician. His presenting concern was extreme discomfort in social

situations, which he tended to simply avoid because they were too discomforting. At the time of referral, he was unemployed and had been so
for almost a year after; surprisingly, he had tried to work as a landlord
in property management, which requires a high rate of interactions with
tenants who are delinquent and hostile. He reported that the property
management duties involved interventions that were too intense and that
he felt he simply was not able to handle. Additionally, he was cohabitating
with a girlfriend of approximately a year, and she was noting significant
concern about his withdrawal and avoidance and unwillingness to engage
in social activities with her. He also suffered with comorbid depression,
for which he had been hospitalized a few months before referral. His primary care physician recommended George get some "psychological help"
because medications prescribed appeared only marginally effective.

On presenting to my private practice, I conducted an ADIS-IV with
George, which confirmed the diagnosis of Social Phobia, Generalized
(300.23) and Major Depressive Disorder, Recurrent, Severe without Psychotic Features (296.33). Narrow-band instruments selected
were the Social Interaction Anxiety Scale and the Social Phobia Scale
(Mattick & Clarke, 1998) and the BDI-II (Beck et al., 1996). The Social
Interaction Anxiety Scale and the Social Phobia Scale were selected
because they are considered to measure two distinct social fears, namely
the fear of interacting in groups and the fear of being observed and scrutinized by others; the two instruments are commonly administered as a
pair, because they complement each other very well. At the beginning of
treatment, George scored in the severe range on all instruments.

The treatment began with a typical psychoeducational component,
which explained anxiety as a natural and normal response to real and
perceived stress, and models for understanding social anxiety specifically. This collective information served to make George feel better about
himself because he felt so different and strange in comparison to people
around him. Much of his depression stemmed from believing he was
somehow "lesser" or of lower worth or value than others, flawed in
some fundamental ways, and that he was a "loser" for not being able to
be more successful in life.

Because social anxiety is in foundation a disorder of misperception,
guided by faulty thinking and flawed reasoning, the first therapeutic
step involved cognitive interventions aimed at teaching George to better
evaluate just how he was thinking and reasoning. Not surprisingly, it
was quickly discovered he engaged in a variety of common thinking
errors, such as all-or-nothing thinking, fortune telling, catastrophizing,
emotional reasoning, labeling, and mind-reading. By teaching George
to use automatic thought records, he was able to begin to see why he
often felt so bad in social situations and why he was commonly inclined
to stay away from such uncomfortable scenarios. In this fashion, he

Situation	Fear
Giving an "open mic" musical gig for money	100
Giving practice musical gig for no money at an "open mic" tryout	90
Going to a social group, and introducing himself and meeting at least 3 people	80
Taking a walk along the river and saying "hello" to strangers, and meeting people who greet him back	70
Going to a coffee-shop and saying "hello" and introducing himself to at least 3 people	60
Calling an acquaintance and going to a coffee shop to "catch up"	50
Going with his girlfriend to a theatric show	40
Going with his girlfriend to a coffee-shop, and just sitting and watching people and writing in his journal	30
Standing outside his house on a not-so-busy time of day	20
Thinking about going outside where GF might encounter other people	10
Sleeping	0

FIGURE 4.1   Fear hierarchy for George (social anxiety disorder).

learned to not only identify faulty thinking and reasoning, but also how to begin to challenge problem thinking when it occurred. This stage in treatment helped George feel better about himself, but he remained significantly uncomfortable in social situations because of remaining high arousal and reactivity. That is when exposure exercises were discussed in terms of multiple values, such as providing a means of verifying his newfound cognitive skills and disproving lingering doubts he had about what would happen in particular situations, as well as reducing inaccurate physiological reactivity. George related well to this because he reported that his physiological anxiety made it difficult to stay clear in his reasoning, because anxiety made it feel bad no matter what the reality of a given situation might actually support.

The exposure work started with the systematic development of a fear hierarchy of real-life situations George found difficult (Figure 4.1). He was instructed in how important it was to remain in situations until his arousal had diminished by at least 50%, so a starting point was agreed on that fell in the bottom third of his hierarchy. Initially, he chose to go with family (individuals known well by him) to the beach for a weekend. His fear was that he would not know how to make small talk, and that the people who were part of the trip would think he was "weird" and ignore him. We developed a general scheme of how to conduct himself in the small (family) group to not inadvertently signal disinterest or discomfort (e.g., don't sit on the outside edge of a circle of people, but sit instead next to people away from the edge, or if standing square shoulders to people, and look into their eyes when speaking). After his return to the next session, he reported that he found the exercise discomforting at first, and he noted he was anxious, but then he noted that by following some of the basics for how to interact with people, they responded to him differently than they previously had. In fact, they did not dismiss or ignore him, or say mean-spirited things to him, but instead they were very friendly and excited to see George engage in the family activities as much as he was doing. He also discovered that his initial unease and anxiety quickly diminished after about an hour, especially when it dawned on him that what he was fearing would occur had not happened. He reported feeling very encouraged by this experience and was eager to try out other experiments to see if what he had believed for years would also buckle under actual test and scrutiny. He proceeded up his initial hierarchy, and after much success in staying in situations for longer periods without terrible things happening and anxiety all but dissipating, he modified his hierarchy to include many arenas he had historically had difficulties with. At the end of treatment, 16 sessions later, he had met all necessary criteria for "recovered" (Jacobson & Truax, 1991). Although he continued to exhibit some residual symptoms, he actively chose to pursue such symptoms and occasional troubles by purposely facing his remaining, residual fears. At 6-month follow-up, he was even further improved.

Obsessive-Compulsive Disorder

Obsessive-compulsive disorder (OCD) was, until the middle of the 1960s, thought to be treatment-refractory. It was also not unusual to mistake it or misclassify it as something much more serious, such as schizophrenia or psychosis. Fortunately, since then, the behavioral techniques of exposure and response prevention, a CBT approach with now-established efficacy for reducing OCD symptoms, was being developed by Victor Meyer (1966) and Meyer and Chesser (1970). Since then, this insidious condition has graduated from an intractable, refractory condition to a condition with multiple, efficacious treatment options available, including both psychotherapy and pharmacotherapy (Baer & Minichiello, 1998; Bejerot, 1999; Foa & Emmelkamp, 1983; Koran, 1999; Steketee & Tynes, 1991; Wadström, 1998).

OCD is now considered a commonly occurring anxiety disorder, with estimates in the general population ranging from 0.05% to between

2% and 3% (Bejerot, 1998; Jenike, Baer, & Minichiello, 1998; Koran, 1999; Kozak, Liebowitz, & Foa, 2000). In its more severe manifestations, it is often a debilitating and excruciating disorder, wherein the patient suffers tremendous difficulties in multiple life areas (e.g., occupational, social, interpersonal). Based on the DSM-IV-TR (American Psychiatric Association, 2000), obsessions are defined as: "recurrent and persistent thoughts, impulses, or images that are experienced, at some time during the disturbance, as intrusive and inappropriate and that cause marked anxiety or distress" (p. 457). For example, an obsession could be a parent having repeated thoughts about killing a child. Additionally, the thoughts, impulses, and images are not excessive worries about real-life problems; instead, they are ego-dystonic. The content may be viewed as foreign or alien and outside of the person's control; in other words, these signs, symptoms, or experiences are uncomfortable or unwanted (e.g., Lindkvist, 1999). Experiencing thoughts, for example, about personal finances may in fact be useful and be seen as adaptive and as self-generated; however, having thoughts of impulsively plunging a kitchen knife into another person would probably be unhelpful and unwanted.

Compulsions are defined as "repetitive behaviors or mental acts that the person feels driven to perform in response to an obsession, or according to rules that must be applied rigidly" (DSM-IV-TR; American Psychiatric Association, 2000, p. 457). Examples of compulsions may include, but are not limited to, hand washing, ordering and arranging, checking, praying, counting, or repeating words silently. These behaviors and mental acts are designed to neutralize, prevent, or reduce discomfort of some dreaded event or situation, but either the activity, whether overt or covert, is not connected in a realistic way with what it is designed to neutralize or prevent or it is clearly excessive. For example, a person washing his or her hands until they are raw and cracking would illustrate this excessive response to distress.

From the description of obsessions and compulsions, it may not be immediately clear how serious and incapacitating these problems can be. Rachman and Hodgson (1980a, 1980b) poignantly commented that without the experience of people who suffer with these difficulties, it might indeed be difficult to imagine how a persistent urge to check the security of one's home before leaving for work each day could grow to such a magnitude that it impaired the individual's entire life. Equally unimaginable might be how someone who is troubled by intrusive, unacceptable thoughts suffers, and how it can reach such proportions as to imprison the person and prevent him or her from carrying out constructive work, or maintaining interpersonal relationships. In its extreme forms—an intense fear of dirt and disease, for example—it could lead to moving to a new house every 6 months and eventually to even avoiding whole regions of the country. It would indeed be a mistake to underestimate the intensity and extent of suffering involved with OCD. On the one hand, it might not manifest itself in more ways than what to the onlooker appears to be idiosyncratic, curious eccentricities. On the other hand, in its more extreme forms, it can become truly incapacitating, in which the simplest chore, such as washing hands, might consume half a day or more (Hersen & Bellack, 1999).

It is not uncommon to find that OCD symptoms eventually spread, surreptitiously, to the patient's social, occupational, and family life (Jenike et al., 1998). In this fashion, extensive rituals and avoidance eventually interfere significantly with daily life (Salkovskis, Richards, & Forrester, 2000). Indeed, OCD patients do report substantial social and work dysfunction, and they are almost four times as likely to be unemployed than the general population (Franklin, Abramowitz, Kozak, Levitt, & Foa, 2000). They also appear to be more likely to never marry (Steketee & Pruyn, 1998).

The following case illustration is of "Herbert," a 20-year-old, gay male who was self-referred for treatment of severe OCD because he reported being "fed up" and "ready to deal with the problem." At the time of intake, his Yale-Brown Obsessive Compulsive Scale (Y-BOCS) score (32) suggested he was in the severe range. Herbert's main concern was reported as negative intrusive thoughts that were repetitive, excessive, and against his wishes. The main theme of thoughts was on the topic of (his own) death and dying, commonly by certain types of cancers or AIDS. He reported that he had experienced similar thoughts about loved ones (e.g., thinking and actually being [feeling] convinced that his mother had been killed whenever she was late in returning home). He reported that these thoughts of death were in his head, "every second of the day," and that this phenomenon translated into persistent fear that indeed he was going to die, that he would die soon, or that he did not know exactly how he would die. He reported feeling "trapped" by these thoughts, and he was reluctant to "move ahead in [his] life" while he felt impaired by them. He indeed reported not setting goals, not doing much, and allowing his life to "not go anywhere" so long as his thoughts were disturbing him.

> Although he reported having a high school degree, Herbert reported that he stopped attending community college because of interference from symptoms, and feeling like it would be a waste of his time anyway, because he reasoned he would be dead soon. These thoughts could often be fueled by subtle signals throughout his body. For example, whenever Herbert experienced a sore and tight chest while stretching, he would quickly and naturally interpret this as meaning that he had some sort

of cancerous tumor in his chest. Similarly, he reported that at one point he discovered a small amount of blood in his stools, and this had led him to fear that he had colon cancer. This belief and fear was so strong that he sought advice from his doctor, who ordered a medical test to determine if there was anything wrong. Although he obsessed extensively over whether the colonoscopy would be too painful to tolerate and whether he would die during the procedure, the results found nothing wrong. The doctors reported that most likely he was just tearing slightly, possibly from constipation and straining while defecating. Although he intellectually understood what they were telling him, and he felt somewhat relieved in the moment, he reported feeling very concerned that they may have missed something or that they misdiagnosed the problem, and he really did have colon cancer.

In response to these sorts of fears, Herbert often responded by trying to convince himself that the problem has a low probability of being true. He tried to reduce his fear by looking up medical research and trying to find information that would suggest that "it wasn't true." He also tried to distract himself by thinking of other things, which of course also inadvertently lent further support to how dangerous and threatening thoughts about death are. He also sought reassurance from his parents and, to a degree, from the medical community by undergoing numerous medical tests and exams. He also noted that he avoided activities that are likely to spark many of the aversive thoughts, such as having dinner with his parents and ice skating.

Although obsessions about death and dying represented the primary content, he also endorsed other kinds of obsessions. For example, he reported being afraid that he would fail to wake up in the morning for work, so he checked his alarm clock repeatedly to verify that it was set, and that it was set for the correct time. The way that he checked was to touch a particular button on the alarm clock, and thereby he "judged" whether it was all right by whether or not it felt "just right" on his thumb all the way up during the release of the button. He reported that he had never failed to wake up in time, yet he often believed that "this time it will happen!" He also frequently believed that his home would be burglarized (and that he would be killed), so he often went around the home to check locks around the house to ensure that it would be difficult to get in and that he would notice if someone tried. The house has never been broken into.

Herbert also engaged in other, magical types of thinking. For example, he often played video games, such as Tetris. While doing so, he would frequently think that the number of "lines" he got in the game had some special meaning for how old he would get; so, if he got 40 lines, it meant that he would die when he was 40 years old. He also endorsed that he used to have a lot of special rules and sequences for himself in earlier years, before the central theme became about death and dying. When he was younger, he reported that he used to save everything; however, at the time of presenting for treatment, he had gone in almost exactly the opposite direction, and had hardly anything at all as he was not expecting to live very long.

Rachman's formulation of intrusive thoughts as *aversive stimuli* was used as a basis for treatment, with exposure and response prevention being the primary mode of treatment. Abramowitz (2002) poignantly illustrated exposure and response prevention remains the treatment of choice for extinguishing obsessive thoughts and cognitive rituals. In this fashion, specific thoughts that bothered Herbert were identified along a fear hierarchy, and repeated exposure to these noxious messages began. During the exposures, Herbert was not to engage in any covert or overt behavior to diminish, distract, or delay what he was being exposed to. The exposures took both the form of disaster scripts and loop-tapes to make the noxious words and sentences inescapable (response prevention) and to facilitate repeated habituation and eventual extinction. In addition, he also ran a number of behavioral experiments to test a variety of assumptions and beliefs he had come to hold as true; historically, he had not dared test some of his disturbing thoughts and beliefs, so he had not collected any evidence that directly contradicted his fearful obsessions. Predictably, he initially worsened on all measures, but then quickly experienced significant reductions in the frequency of intrusions. He also reported a meaningful change in how such intrusions affected him. Although he still experienced some of the kinds of thoughts he initially had been very disturbed by, they ceased being able to change his mood or to change what he was doing in life. At the end of treatment, his Y-BOCS was a 10 (mild), and his BDI-II was a 9 (minimal). Both represented clinically significant and reliable changes when compared with baseline measures (Y-BOCS 32; BDI-II 27), supporting a "recovered" status. Although some residual symptoms remained, he was not affected by remaining thoughts (i.e., he did not become emotionally upset by them) and they did not affect his social and occupational responsibilities (e.g., he continued to work, and worked more, and enrolled in school).

To illustrate the universality of exposure-based treatment, I will include two additional case illustrations of the treatment of OCD using exposure and response prevention methods that were treated by a colleague in Uppsala, Sweden. Sandra Bates, PhD, is a licensed psychologist at the Institute for Cognitive-Behavior Therapy in Uppsala. She regularly used exposure methodology and commonly uses natural settings to maximize treatment effectiveness and outcome. Her two cases follow.

CASE I

A 25-year-old woman was admitted to a residential treatment facility after unsuccessful outpatient treatment for OCD. Her symptoms had gradually accelerated in the previous 5 years, leading up to being hospitalized after an unsuccessful suicide attempt. On admission to the treatment facility, she was diagnosed with OCD and secondary depression.

The primary focus of her obsessions was her fear of committing sexual acts with children or household pets. To cope with these fears she used direct avoidance in the form of physical distancing and indirectly in her choice of clothes and her physical appearance. Attributes such as body hair or revealing clothing increased her feeling of being a morally despicable person, and she spent large amounts of time choosing and caring for "dangerous" clothing.

Treatment was directed at gradually eliminating her avoidance while simultaneously participating in all activity at the treatment facility. Clothing was chosen arbitrarily (on the basis of activity and weather) rather than how contaminated it felt. After a month of treatment, ending with her using all clothing, she gradually exposed herself to pictures, films, and actual animals with special attention to directing her attention to sexual attributes. Thereafter, she exposed herself to pictures of preschool children, watching anonymous children at playgrounds, restaurants, and sporting events and then in normal activities with children of staff members while eating, building with blocks, and playing catch outside. All activities included exposure to the "risks" she was subjecting helpless animals and children to.

The final exposures took place in her home, where she was left alone with her family's pets and to babysit for her cousin's preschool children. After treatment, she was able to move to her own apartment, enroll in a junior college, and enjoy a normal relationship with a man her own age. The results of her scores on Y-BOCS (32 to 17), BDI (32 to 13), and Compulsive Activity Checklist (CAC; 21 to 10) were all significant and reliable.

CASE 2

A 28-year-old woman applied for outpatient treatment at a CBT clinic after 2 years of psychodynamic supportive therapy for her OCD. Her psychiatrist had diagnosed her as having both OCD and a personality disorder (avoidant personality). She received government reimbursement for treatment for a maximum of 40 hours, for which she paid 10% of the fee.

Her husband and mother were present for part of the assessment and for part of the exposure exercises in the second week of treatment. In addition, the therapist met with all three of them at the end of treatment to summarize the results and agree on written guidelines for continued exposure and response prevention.

The patient's primary obsession was of being contaminated by dog excrement, which she believed would make her repulsive to herself and to other people. Her compulsions consisted of protracted showering of up to

3 hours at a time. She also repeatedly washed her hands 10–20 times per day, for 15–90 minutes each. Because she felt compelled to be especially careful about contact between different parts of her body, she used a new towel for drying each of her hands and several towels after showering. This resulted in large amounts of laundry, with numerous secondary rituals designed to separate underwear from other clothing and her husband's clothing from her own.

Additionally, she monitored flies and other insects in the house because she felt they may have been in contact with dog excrement. When she walked outside, she was careful to keep her skirts and hems of her pants well above the pavement whenever she walked past dog excrement. If she walked across areas with dog excrement, she was careful to maintain at least a 1-m distance. Clothes that had come in contact with places with dogs were washed repeatedly, put away in plastic bags, or discarded.

Needless to say, she spent a great deal of time planning her movements so that she could avoid all contact with dogs and dog excrement. Often she stayed at home and asked her husband or parents to purchase her food and do other errands. She had tried numerous medications and was using clomipramine (200 mg/day) when she applied for treatment.

Treatment was directed at a hierarchy of places and activities and response prevention was instituted gradually rather than all at once. Exposure started initially at the clinic, with a plastic bag with dog excrement in a glass jar with lid. During the course of one extended session she was able to tolerate having the jar in her lap, with the lid off and the bag open. She then contaminated the clothing that she wore to the session and agreed to wear the clothes to her parents' home, thus also contaminating their living room and kitchen. She declined to contaminate her own apartment at that time. During the week that followed she was asked to contaminate herself with a dry wash cloth that had been used to wipe the outside of the contaminated jar and then to go for a 30-minute walk in an area seldom frequented by dog owners. On returning home, she sat outside on the patio and read the evening paper for 30 minutes, then leaving the paper for her husband to read when he came home. Hand washing during this first week was rehearsed at the clinic the first few times (see Figure 4.2 and Figure 4.3). Her "best" time was 5 minutes, which she was instructed to follow at home, with the help of a timer in the bathroom, and with 10 washes per day as maximum allowed.

To maximize the effects of treatment, the therapist went to the patient's home 3 days per week, 4 hours per visit for the next 2 weeks. During these home visits, the patient touched increasingly contaminated objects in her apartment and then continued to spread the contamination to chairs, tables, eating utensils, clothing, and shoes. After the first week of exposure, the patient felt that everything was "ruined," so there was no sense in avoiding anything indoors. Her greatest difficulty was reducing her washing rituals to manageable proportions. The alternative of not washing/showering at all for the week was declined.

FIGURE 4.2   Contamination exposure 1 (mock patient).

FIGURE 4.3   Contamination exposure 2 (mock patient).

The second week was directed to activities outside the home, walking close to dog excrement, standing and gazing at it, disposing of litter in dog latrines, and shuffling through wet leaves in the park where numerous owners walked their dogs. During all exposure exercises, she was asked to rate her anxiety. Initially she started at 8–9 of a possible 10. After prolonged exposure, her ratings were no lower than 4–5. Therefore, it was of utmost importance that she maintained 5-minute hand washes, followed by contact with a contaminated cloth to maximize the feeling of not being "clean." Showering was never reduced to less than 30 minutes, but she could complete it without help.

The remaining 8 hours of treatment were spread out over the course of 2 months, with weekly visits directed at monitoring progress, troubleshooting specific incidents, and encouraging the patient to engage in normal, pleasurable activities. At the end of 3 months of exposure treatment, she was able to go out in the evening, in a long skirt, to walk through dog parks, and eat a meal with her husband and his family without compulsive behaviors. Time spent in compulsions was reduced from 38 hours/week at baseline to 9 hours/week after 3 months. Although her Y-BOCS scores only dropped from 32 to 18, her BDI dropped from 29 to 14, which reflected an improved quality of life in many areas. Follow-up at 1 year showed a further slight drop on the Y-BOCS (16), but an increase in the BDI to 16. She had started going to night school and reported improved relations with her husband and family. She stayed on clomipramine for the course of treatment, but had managed to reduce her dose to 100 mg/day.

Posttraumatic Stress Disorder

PTSD is one of the most serious and disabling anxiety disorders, and is one of the most unique in that it necessarily has an identifiable etiology, namely exposure to a traumatic event or events. PTSD, along with panic disorder, is the most disabling condition within the anxiety spectrum of psychological conditions. Caustic events that commonly spark PTSD are combat, natural or manmade disasters, and physical or sexual assaults; regardless of the nature of the event, it is either actually life-threatening or it is perceived as such. Although the syndrome has been recognized and recorded since the Civil War, trauma-related sequelae have only been officially recognized by professional psychology with the introduction of the *Diagnostic and Statistical Manual of Mental Disorders-Third Edition* (DSM-III; American Psychiatric Association, 1980).

Although PTSD prevalence rates are not without controversy, it appears that approximately 61% of men and 51% of women report having experienced at least one such event in their lives (Kessler, Sonnega, Bromet, Hughes, & Nelson, 1995). Although the 1980 version of the

DSM suggested that these traumatic events are outside of normal human experience, actual (and unfortunate) prevalence rates suggest otherwise. PTSD is an all-too-common condition. Such surveys indicate that fully one-third of those with PTSD never fully recover, and 88% of men and 79% of women with a lifetime experience of PTSD have also experienced at least one other recognized mental disorder (McLean & Woody, 2001). Because of common efforts to avoid reminders of traumas, PTSD patients often withdraw socially and may turn disproportionately to alcohol or drugs (Kilpatrick, Acierno, Resnick, Saunders, & Best, 1997). Collectively, this suggests effective and adequate treatment of PTSD is paramount.

People exposed to traumatic events and who experience PTSD are highly likely to activate physiological and psychological resources designed to assist them in responding to the threat in such a way that maximizes their odds of survival. Unfortunately, this extreme activation also occurs after the actual trauma experience is but a memory. In addition to the necessary traumatic event experience, people with PTSD also commonly display three symptom clusters: (1) reliving or reexperiencing the event through intrusive memories, nightmares, flashbacks, or physiological or psychological reactivity to reminders of the events; (2) pervasive avoidance of reminders of the events, or of situations, circumstances, or people that might serve as reminders, or emotional numbing; and (3) persistent symptoms of arousal and hypervigilance, such as sleeping problems, anger or irritability, exaggerated startle responses, and significant difficulties in concentration or impaired decision making (Gray & Acierno, 2002). These symptoms often disrupt all domains of human functioning (i.e., personal, social, occupational).

Two illustrations will be offered. Deborah Wise, PhD, is an assistant professor at Pacific University, and her case of motor vehicle accident-induced PTSD will be provided first. Case 2 describes a case I recently treated, in which a female patient had survived a natural disaster in which her companion had been killed.

CASE I

Ms. X was a young woman who was referred for treatment to address symptoms of anxiety subsequent to a car accident in which a pedestrian died. At intake, she reported the following symptoms: recurrent and intrusive recollections of the accident, anxiety while riding in a car, anxiety that prevented her from driving, feeling distressed when reminded of the accident, trying to avoid thoughts about the accident, difficulty remembering parts of the accident, feeling detached from others, loss of interest in leaving the house or engaging in tasks of daily living, difficulty working or getting out of bed, sleep difficulties, being fearful of being alone, irritability, hypervigilance, bouts of crying, and feeling sad and guilty. At the time of intake, she had the following test scores: BDI 8 (mild) and PTSD Symptom Scale 19 (moderate). Because of seeking treatment within a month after the accident, she met criteria for Acute Stress Disorder.

Ms. X was seen for 18 sessions of CBT to address her anxiety symptoms. Although she initially avoided distressing thoughts and did not complete homework assignments, her avoidance was eventually addressed through cognitive challenging, in-session experiences of habituation to negative affect, and in-session completion of missed homework assignments. As Ms. X began to address her distressing thoughts, she was encouraged to engage in in vivo exposure exercises. She was taught breathing retraining and encouraged to identify adaptive coping mechanisms. She collaboratively developed a fear hierarchy, ranging from sitting with the therapist in a parked car while reading an account of the accident to driving alone at night past the site of the accident while singing along with the song that was playing at the time of the accident. Through increasingly "facing her fears" by working through each step of this hierarchy, she experienced a significant decrease in anxiety.

Additionally, she was taught to challenge cognitive distortions. In particular, her thoughts that the world is a dangerous place, that she could not tolerate this type of event again, and that she could have prevented this incident from occurring were challenged.

At the end of 18 sessions, all treatment goals had been met. Ms. X's anxiety was minimal, and her depression was absent. At termination, she received the following test scores: BDI 0 and PTSD Symptom Scale 2 (minimal). Additionally, she was able to drive alone at night past the site of the accident while listening to the song that played at the time of the accident with minimal anxiety. She was also able to successfully and independently challenge cognitive distortions that had been identified throughout the course of the therapy. At the last session, she described feeling "very well."

CASE 2

"Lisa" was a 26-year-old, Caucasian, college-educated female. She was self-referred because of great difficulties in daily functioning. At the time of initial assessments, she was employed part-time but had great difficulties sustaining work for more than a few weeks at a time. Before the trauma she experienced and approximately a year before seeking services, she had sustained stable, full-time employment without any difficulties within marketing. Her chief complaints were difficulties sleeping because of horrific nightmares, difficulties eating because of a lack of appetite, intrusive memories throughout the day, going to great lengths to avoid reminders of the event and various stimuli that would serve as reminders, and significant "edginess," irritability, difficulties concentrating, and making basic decisions. She also reported feeling very uncomfortable around people and experienced episodes of profound sadness. PTSD was affecting her personally, socially, occupationally, and in every way she could report.

Her traumatic experience had occurred almost a year before seeking treatment. She had been traveling in Vietnam with a friend, using a motorcycle to access less-traveled areas. Their traveling might best fit under the rubric of adventure traveling. Toward the end of their trip, during monsoon season, they were traveling on a narrow mountain road when they were hit by a naturally occurring landslide. The statistical odds of such an event alone were slim, but nevertheless happened to catch them as they passed by. The landslide absorbed both Lisa and her male traveling partner and brought them to fall over a 60-foot-high cliff through brush, jungle, and rocks. Although it is not clear, this landslide may have shielded them from such a fall (as they were inside of it through the fall), but the slide pushed both of them into a raging river, swollen from monsoon rains. Although her memory of the whole accident was fuzzy, she reported being repeatedly pushed under water and being bashed against giant boulders. Her injuries were extensive. Her lungs were punctured, her ribs were broken, several other bones were cracked and broken, one of her feet was almost crushed, and she was covered in cuts, scrapes, and bruises. She was bleeding from head to toe. Somehow, she emerged onto the riverbank after almost drowning several times. She managed to scramble back to the road, where she went into shock. Local villagers found her, brought her into their homes, and cared for her until she could be brought to a regional "hospital" for emergency care. At the primitive hospital, no one spoke English and Lisa could not speak Vietnamese. There, she was "patched" as best could be, and surgery was even performed on her foot without the benefit of anesthesia. She reported that even though the surgery was tough, it was not nearly as distressing as the accident itself. She spent about a week in this primitive hospital when, by chance, an American traveler "discovered" her; after that, she was transported to Bangkok, where she remained in a hospital for a couple of months. During this time, she learned that her traveling partner had been found dead.

After returning to the United States, she began to notice some problems. She was becoming very nervous about small things and would jump at the slamming of a door. She did not like the sounds of motorcycles, the sound of running water, she began having flashbacks when she encountered Southeast Asian people, and she began to feel incredibly guilty that she was alive while her partner had been killed. These symptoms slowly grew, morphed, and developed over approximately 9 months, until she concluded that she was unable to live in any semblance of normalcy. She called The Anxiety Disorders Clinic in Lake Oswego, Oregon, after coming to the conclusion herself that she must be suffering with some kind of significant anxiety problem, if not outright PTSD.

When I initially spoke with her by phone, it was clear she was suffering with PTSD (with delayed onset), so I explained what the phenomenon is and how it is effectively treated using CBT with exposure. At that first conversation, she was unnerved by the idea of exposure, so she asked for referrals for "less difficult" treatments. She tried both supportive psychotherapy and EMDR, but called back a couple of months later reporting that neither worked and that her symptoms were worsening. She agreed to come in for at least an assessment session. The assessment consisted of the ADIS-IV and the Clinician Administered PTSD Scale – Second Revision (CAPS-2), which confirmed the primary diagnosis of PTSD, with secondary depression and significant social anxiety.

The treatment started with preparatory exercises (e.g., sleeping schedule, eating schedule, relaxation, exercise, cognitive work), but shifted to exposure work at session five. Her exposures started with writing about the accident and producing disaster scripts that she later used for imaginal exposures. These exercises progressed at a pace and intensity she could tolerate and agreed to. A few sessions later, she was accompanied to a very green and lush city park that had trails and running water to replicate a jungle environment. At that location (Audubon Society of Portland Bird Sanctuary), she walked along dirt trails and next to small streams. She was initially very uncomfortable with this exposure exercise, because it looked much like the jungle in which her accident had occurred, but with repeated exposures, she was able to not become aroused in that setting. More challenging imaginal exposure work was also conducted, focusing on very specific aspects of the accident, such as being nearly suffocated in the landslide, nearly drowning, and so on.

During the active treatment phase, a fortunate event happened. The 1-year anniversary of the accident occurred. Anniversaries and other important dates (e.g., birthdays of people who died) are prospective points of lapses and relapses, so treatment was able to focus on relapse prevention and processing the anniversary "flair" that predictably happened. After 18 sessions, she was quite a different person. She had accomplished clinically significant and reliable change and met all of the criteria of "recovered." Further, she was well below even normal means on all of the progress and outcome measures given, which included the Posttraumatic Cognitions Inventory (Foa, Ehlers, Clark, Tolin, & Orsillo, 1999), Anxiety Sensitivity Inventory, Social Interaction Anxiety Scale, and Social Phobia Scale (Mattick & Clark, 1998), BDI-II, and Beck Anxiety Inventory (BAI).

Generalized Anxiety Disorder

The central and defining feature of GAD is chronic, excessive, and uncontrollable worry and anxiety about a number of events or activities of life. Even though GAD has a lifetime prevalence rate of approximately 5% (Kessler et al., 1994), making it one of the more common anxiety disorders, it has not been until recent years that effective treatments have been developed and promoted for this condition (e.g., Borkovec & Costello, 1993; Dugas & Ladouceur, 2000; Heimburg, Turk, & Mennin, 2004; Rygh & Sanderson, 2004). This lag in both theory and treatment might be due to a lack of patients seeking help for GAD; in fact, people with GAD often do not seek help unless they develop some other, more immediately distressing problem (e.g., they become depressed). On average, when GAD patients seek help, they have suffered with the condition for decades or more (e.g., Yonkers, Warshaw, Massion, & Keller, 1996). Why do so few GAD patients seek help? The most common explanation is that GAD is akin to a low-grade fever, in which patients can actually function quite well without help, until something else happens to make it more like a high-grade fever that is incapacitating. Indeed, of GAD patients, 75% meet diagnosis for another anxiety or mood disorder (Brawman-Mintzer et al., 1993; Brown & Barlow, 1992). As a comparison, panic disorder and PTSD are both like high-grade fevers that require formal treatment to be able to function in basic ways (Hersen, personal communication, June 9, 2004).

Although GAD patients also often worry about similar things most people worry, or at least think about (e.g., interpersonal relationships, family, home, finances, work, illness), clinical "worriers" additionally worry excessively and uncontrollably about many minor items ("Will I get stuck in traffic?" or "Will I make it on time?") and unlikely future events ("Will I someday have to declare bankruptcy?" or "Will I someday be homeless?"). Indeed, pathological or problem worriers often believe worry is useful, and consequently use worrying as a prime coping mechanism (Wells & Carter, 1999). Another principal feature always seemingly present in GAD patients is their distinct tendency to live in the future. They have an exceedingly difficult time focusing on the here and now to the degree that even when things are going well for them, they often worry that things will change. Ironically, by being future-oriented, they often do not do in the present what would assist in preventing future-oriented fears from coming true. Dugas, Gagnon, Ladouceur, and Freeston (1998) suggested many GAD patients exhibit extremely poor problem-solving orientations because they are so future-oriented, in that they are not sufficiently here-and-now focused on real-life problems that can be fixed. Unfortunately, when current problems are not solved, they tend to compound, and perhaps even turn into what GAD patients fear most (e.g., by not paying the mortgage, or calling the bank if unable to do so, bank representatives will be calling, and if that is not responded to, then perhaps there would eventually be a foreclosure, whereas speaking with the bank immediately begins to address the problem). However, long-term follow-up illustrates that with a shift toward effective problem-solving, among other interpersonal changes, GAD treatment gains can be sustained and patients treated with a model that emphasizes intolerance for uncertainty through targeting worry and problem solving, and uses exposure significantly better than those who remain untreated (Dugas et al., 2003).

The following case is of "Trish," a 27-year-old, Caucasian, single female who came to treatment initially because of a depressive episode. On assessment and investigation, however, it quickly became clear that GAD was a better fitting primary diagnosis and principal problem area, because she professed to "always having been a worrier" and many of the problems she needed help for were worry-based. Chronic and then severe pathological worry had finally left her feeling exhausted and down about herself, the world, and the future.

Trish described herself as a perfectionist, and as always having been concerned with "getting things right." She did not care for situations that were spontaneous or ambiguous, and she all but despised surprises. This desire for control and certainty about situations and outcome led to many problem behaviors; for instance, while she would worry about prospective future financial problems, she was so future-oriented she often "forgot" or simply did not deal with her current financial situations, which was largely being driven by being a graduate student. She did not wish to incur large student loans, so she had decided to work while being a student. Although this was partially effective, she always struggled to meet her tuition payments and had been assessed some additional fees for late payment. In addition, because she was so concerned with her academic performance, she called in sick with some regularity to spend more time studying or preparing projects; however, she had not looked into additional, other sources of funding for education that were free or carried liberal payback terms. A lack of dealing with current problems led many of them to compound and get worse than if she would have dealt with them earlier. Although she worried a lot about finances (among a slew of other topics of concern), she tended to not implement any potential solutions to her dilemmas. She finally sought treatment after losing her job (because of excessive tardiness) and realizing she would not be able to make her tuition payment.

Having Trish fill out worry diaries for a couple of weeks suggested her topics included, but were not limited to, finances, housing, public transportation and her car, grades, class performance, friendships, relationships with key people in her life (e.g., her boyfriend, her best friend, her parents, her grandparents), her part-time job, her pet snake, and her cat. For instance, even though her car was new, she feared it would break down or that she would crash it, so she frequently took public transportation. Taking buses and light rail, however, often made her worry about getting to her place of employment and to classes on time. Being a graduate student working on a masters of business administration fed into her perfectionistic tendencies. Having been a perfect A student in high school and college made her feel that she had to obtain perfect grades to excel after graduation. This meant she had to spend an inordinate amount of time studying and preparing for projects. Many of her peers prepared adequately enough to earn them As and high Bs, but none of them spent nearly as much time as Trish. She believed by worrying about her performance she could ward off negative outcomes, and even if those eventually happened she would be better off because she had been concerned about it. She looked at worry behavior as a positive personality aspect, which she thought meant she cared about herself, other people, her education, and her pets. She also believed worry would motivate her to take steps in the world that would protect her from many of the "bad" things she was envisioning.

Treatment started with a focus on helping her understand how worry breeds anxiety, exhaustion, and real-life problems. Through diary keeping, she was able to recognize the sheer extent of her worry, and she was also able to track behaviors she engaged in that would resolve or ease many of her problems. Although she worried a great deal, she did not engage in behaviors that would directly address her concerns (e.g., look for a higher paying job so she would have to work less, look for grants and scholarships that would not have to be paid back on graduation). She also learned relaxation skills to reduce how tight, tense, and spiraling out of control she felt at any one moment (i.e., diaphragmatic breathing and progressive muscular relaxation). She was also taught how to reevaluate the value of benefit she saw in worry. This was perhaps one of the most valuable preparatory exercises she performed, because it helped her realize that although she appeared very concerned about very many important things in life, she was not equally effective in actually positively dealing with them. This disturbed her a great deal and led her to have a firm commitment to changing how she conducted her life. After all, she wished to be "perfect," and in her behaviors she recognized, slowly at first, but then more bluntly, that she was ineffective. Because or her perfectionistic tendencies, her criteria for success had to be toned down. Exposure started around her intolerance for uncertainty by having her perform activities that she was not already certain about the outcome, such as going to movies to which she did not know the ending and going to restaurants she did not know whether she liked or not. Additionally, she started preparing less for exams and projects, something that was incredibly difficult for her. She feared by doing so she would fail exams, be reprimanded by her professors, and be thrown out of school in a matter of months. On scrutiny, she agreed this would be extremely unlikely because she had not experienced a B ever in the graduate program, or ever for that matter, and her "failure" of receiving Bs (the lowest grade she could envision herself getting if she did not prepare at all) was actually unlikely to be career ending. She noted several friends, who were then working in the field, had many Bs on their transcripts, and she regarded them as extremely competent in their work, confident in their abilities, and financially successful.

As always occurs in exposure treatment, she developed a fear hierarchy collaboratively with items such as "see a movie I don't know the ending to" toward the bottom, items such as "look at and fill out grant and scholarship applications" in the middle, and "not studying or preparing at all for an exam" and "putting in a small effort into a graded project" as being toward the top of the hierarchy. Within 16 sessions, she was able to progress up her hierarchy and perform many of the tasks repeatedly. Unforeseen consequences included obtaining federal grants and extremely low-rate loans she believed she would never be able to get and being hired into a marketing firm at a significantly better salary than she had ever made part-time while she was still obtaining her MBA, with opportunities for upward mobility when she graduated. She did graduate, and with honors, with two Bs nonetheless, and went on to successfully move up in the company that had hired her during the last year of her studies.

Perhaps more interestingly, she found she did not need to prepare as much as she had been, and she was still able to obtain grades she wanted. Only when she purposely "bombed" exams was she able to produce Bs, which she purposely did to find out what it would feel like and how it would affect her personal and professional life. She found that she had much more time to be with friends and acquaintances, and she got married 6 months after graduation (not to her boyfriend of 5 years). Although she and her mother planned most of the wedding, she let her husband surprise her with the honeymoon destination. Many "problems" stopped happening because she affected change and took care of real-life, here-and-now issues (e.g., balancing her finances and paying bills the week before they were due) that otherwise had recycled and blossomed into large problems (e.g., having been previously reported for multiple late payments on a variety of bills). Not surprisingly, when she took a better problem-solving approach to living and performed exposure around future-oriented fears, she not only worried less, but she stopped feeling depressed and instead gained a happier outlook on life.

Health Anxiety

Hypochondriasis, or health anxiety (HA), can be conceptualized as a specific variation of GAD. That is, HA is hallmarked by chronic and pathological worry and anxiety, but focused more exclusively on health concerns as opposed to on a variety of topics. HA, as with GAD, can fluctuate, can be highly debilitating, and in 50% of people with HA the problems persist for years (Taylor & Asmundson, 2004). As with GAD, HA has until more recently remained a conundrum for practitioners and researchers alike, in part because of most patients worried about health do not seek out mental health treatment. Instead, HA cases first show up in emergency rooms and general medical practice, and there is often some resistance by patients to conceive that the illnesses they are imagining are just that, a figment of their imagination based on misinterpreting bodily signs and symptoms as "proof" of serious disease or disability (Furer, Walker, & Freeston, 2001). Only through repeated medical tests that show there is *nothing* wrong with the patient, and then only usually with significant persuasion of medical professionals, do patients begin to entertain the idea that perhaps they are catastrophizing normal bodily events as indicative of impending doom. Of course, a key to CBT approaches is to shift patients away from a disease model of explanation for their symptoms and toward other, alternative (more normal) explanations for their experiences (Wells, 2004). This is necessary for patients to believe symptoms do not always signal serious disease or illness; however, outside of a willingness to entertain other explanations, treatment cannot succeed. A willingness to accept a referral to a mental health specialist is perhaps the first move in accepting such alternative explanations.

What does HA look like, and why does it seem to be such a pervasive problem for those who suffer with its effect? In short, HA patients engage in a number of safety behaviors, exemplified by the classic escape and avoidance style of coping. For example, many HA patients repeatedly check bodily symptoms (e.g., a fluttering heart) or signs of possible illness (e.g., pulse rate). They also seek more conventional reassurance from medical tests and medical professionals, rely on information from medical encyclopedias, websites (e.g., WebMD), and also extensively use health aids (e.g., vitamins and supplements) to maximize health status (e.g., using only health foods, organic foods). Rachman (personal communication, June 1, 2002) suggested that all checking behaviors ironically result in the exact opposite of their intended effect; that is, the more a person checks, the less certain he or she becomes. In this fashion, HA is very similar to GAD, in which intolerance for uncertainty plays a central role in the etiology and maintenance of symptoms and impairment. Fortunately, this similarity means HA can be treated using similar principles to what is used in treating GAD (i.e., cognitive restructuring to help the patient become a more critical, creative, and meaningful observer of their experience; relaxation to help moderate basic arousal; and exposure to burn out excessive and unwarranted biophysiological reactivity).

In fact, when treating HA, exposure is always used together with response prevention. Patients are systematically exposed to imaginal, in vivo, and interoceptive cues for fears, whereas they are asked to not check, ask for reassurance, or rely on other forms of safety behaviors. Because fear of illness and disease is often connected to fears of dying, extensive work is often conducted to help patients cope with such fears more effectively. Exposure work about death often includes reading obituaries, reading stories about people who died, visiting funeral parlors and cemeteries, creating one's own will, and writing one's own obituary. Much emphasis is placed on the notion that death is a natural and normal part of life and that all people do have health problems that eventually will lead to death. Teaching patients to cope with the uncertainty about how and when they will die is central to the overall treatment package. Recent outcome data (Furer, Walker, & Vincent, 1999) suggest that this is not only possible, but 83% of patients treated in this manner no longer meet diagnosis of HA at end of treatment. Because of the central concern about somatic problems, HA patients are less inclined to use medications to treat their symptoms, and (once informed of the benefits of psychotherapy vis-à-vis medications) often prefer CBT approaches. In this sense, after patients acknowledge at any level that symptoms might be representative of a flawed way of reasoning, and not signs of impending disease, they are often willing to work quite hard at positively affecting their experience. They do, nonetheless, need to be at a stage of acceptance that alternative explanations for what feels to be true are possible, if not even plausible. Without such acceptance, they may be outright resistant to treatment.

Following is a case illustration of "Oliver," a 36-year-old, Caucasian, single male who presented to treatment after a history of 15 years of health and illness worry. He finally presented because he had run out of health insurance coverage and was evaluating just how much money and time he had spent obtaining medical tests and medical opinions over the years, all suggesting there was nothing wrong with him.

Oliver's main concern was reported as a preoccupation with fears of having a disease, contracting a disease, or becoming sick with a major medical disorder. Typically, these fears centered around concerns of dying from medical issues related to cancer and tumors (e.g., colon, brain), heart attack and heart disease, stroke, or choking on foods. These fears arose from misinterpreting bodily symptoms (e.g., stomach distress, hemorrhoids, headaches, heartburn, feeling tired). As is common to HA cases, this preoccupation caused Oliver significant distress and also interfered significantly in his personal and professional life (e.g., he was reluctant to exercise because of fear of causing a heart attack, he frequently left early from work because of feeling ill). These fears of disease and, ultimately, of death had led to significant avoidance and other safety behaviors. For example, if he believed that he was experiencing a heart attack, perhaps from misinterpretation of the meaning of heartburn, he had historically gone to emergency rooms to get "checked out," and more recently he had called medical doctors for reassurance about his health. Information that he had obtained from various medical professionals never permanently relieved his fears, however, and he was commonly struck with the same or similar fears within a few days or a week of seeking professional reassurance. Additionally, he was highly avoidant of physical exercise because it produced sensations (e.g., an accelerated heart rate, chest pain, feeling hot and clammy) that he equated with danger signals. Ironically, this had likely contributed to becoming overweight, which in itself was causal in producing the very sensations he reported fearing.

In response to these health anxieties, he would become ruminative, self-focused, and avoidant. He would also engage extensively in checking behaviors and reassurance seeking. At times, avoidant behavior became preventive in nature, and when he could not avoid completely he would, for example, slow the pace of walking if he had to walk greater distances, or reduce distance walked, if possible, and he would take prescriptions and over-the-counter medications to reduce sensations when he had to engage in challenging activities, such as flying (i.e., he did not fear plane crashes, but instead that the "canned air" would make him sick).

Treatment started with common preparatory exercises, such as re-laxation training to moderate wildly fluctuating anxiety, some cognitive restructuring to teach him how to be a more objective observer during exposure work, and developing a fear hierarchy of situations and circum-stances that produce the physiological cues and signals he historically had interpreted as impending death. These ranged from seeing news-paper or magazine advertisements or billboards for cholesterol and stroke medications to walking or performing other tasks that would produce an increased heart rate and eating spicy foods that commonly produced stomach aches or diarrhea.

His exposures began with an in vivo physiological focus and ended with an in-imagination death focus. His physiological exposures included stair climbing, walking and biking, and eating "offensive" foods (i.e., foods that were likely to give him stomach problems and heartburn). Initially, as is common to the first few times a patient engages in exposure work, he was very careful with himself during exposure work (e.g., walking only a half flight of stairs). Eventually, as he realized the symptoms were not indicative of impending death, he pushed himself much harder (e.g., walking 14 flights of stairs without my presence). Multiple measures of progress and outcome were used to monitor progress and change, such as the Intolerance for Uncertainty Scale, and at the end of treat-ment, only 13 sessions later, he had accomplished both significant and reliable change and he met the stringent criteria of "recovered" status. At a 6-month follow-up, he had further improved from his posttreat-ment end-state functioning by an additional 30%, suggesting further that completely independent change was realized by continuing to use what he had learned during the active treatment phase.

Trichotillomania

Trichotillomania is a little studied, yet often profoundly debilitating con-dition hallmarked by repetitive hair pulling, commonly from the scalp or facial region, but such compulsive/impulsive behaviors can also target the genital area or any area with hair. Because hair is most often pulled from the scalp, many trichotillomania patients present to treatment with clearly bald spots. Many patients hide these side effects through "camouflaging," or wearing hats, scarfs, or other means of covering areas negatively affected by pulling behavior (Mansueto, 1991). Hair pulling shares common etiology with other impulse control disorders, such as skin picking and nail biting. All are nervous habits, which are clearly excessive or occur too often, but may also have significant overlap with normal self-grooming behaviors (e.g., Stanley, Borden, Bell, & Wagner, 1994; Stanley, Swann, Bowers, Davis, & Taylor, 1992; Swedo & Leonard, 1992). Additionally, as with Tourette's disorder, another hallmark, besides pulling hair until noticeable loss occurs, is the building tension that occurs before pulling. This is similar to a premonitory urge commonly occurring in Tourette's disorder, which refers to somatic, sensory, and ideational symptoms that preceded tics; premonitory urges are often experienced as needs, urges, prickly feelings, and tension that build before and are relieved by tic movements (Leckman, Walker, & Cohen, 1993). Indeed, at least 50% of trichotillomania patients report experiencing some sensory stimuli (e.g., itching, burning, and sensitivity in the scalp) just before pulling it. Some of this sensory information may in part be produced by other behaviors, such as touching or playing with the hair before pulling.

The treatment of choice is called Habit Reversal Training and was developed by Azrin and colleagues (e.g., Azrin, Nunn, & Frantz, 1980). It includes six components: (1) self-monitoring, (2) habit control motivation, (3) awareness training, (4) competing response training, (5) relaxation training, and (6) generalization training. Although the components work together, two deserve special focus; competing response training is very similar, if not identical to, response prevention, and generalization training is similar to in vivo exposure to potential situations or circumstances that contribute to urges to pull. The other components are all very important and are commonly found as standard components to many complete anxiety-disorder treatment packages. The active ingredient in Habit Reversal Training is exposure and response prevention, because they, in combination, serve to expose patients to circumstances that historically have been able to produce the pulling behavior and force a deconditioning of that response (through competing response training/response prevention).

"Robert" was a 26-year-old, Caucasian, single male seeking treatment for virtually nonstop hair pulling from his chin line. This repetitive and clearly excessive behavior left Robert with an often extremely red and irritated face, and with lots of ingrown hairs that often became infected and turned into blemishes. Besides Trichotillomania (312.39), he also met diagnoses for Tourette's Disorder (307.23), Obsessive-Compulsive Disorder (300.3), Alcohol Abuse (305.00), and Cannabis Abuse (305.20). Within the complexity of his presentation, Robert's principal complaint was the excessive hair pulling, which he felt he did not have control over. Although he exhibited significant motor tics at intake and throughout treatment, this aspect of his presentation was not of concern to Robert. The OCD was closely related to the hair pulling behavior, because the OCD was of a version commonly associated with Tourette's disorder, namely sensation-focused or "just so" OCD (e.g., touching, tapping, rubbing, ordering, arranging, and deciding most things based on whether they feel just so). Robert participated in a substance treatment program concurrently with Habit Reversal Training treatment, so polysubstance abuse was also not a primary treatment focus. Instead, the treatment focused more exclusively on hair pulling and just-so feelings.

Robert noted early that he had little awareness of his virtually automatic (unconscious) pulling behaviors, and reported significant annoyance at only being able to notice pulling after commonly having been pulling for 10 or 15 minutes. Of course, after Robert was pulling, it was almost impossible to stop until the episode naturally stopped (i.e., he *felt* it was complete). Helping Robert identify which variables contributed to pulling episodes was accomplished through self-monitoring and awareness training. This helped him identify that times of inter-personal stress and tiredness and moments of more automatic mode (e.g., listening to music, reading, driving) all made it much more likely that a pulling episode would start. Problem solving was used to address such issues as best as could be done (e.g., establishing a regular sleep schedule, exercise schedule, covering basics of assertiveness training, and general problem-solving skills).

When it was clearer under what circumstances the undesirable behavior occurred, Robert was taught a number of competing responses to use when he felt the urge to pull. For example, he was taught to put his hands into his pockets, clench his fists, and rub a piece of rough material he was instructed to keep in his pocket. Although Robert found that making sure he obtained enough sleep and exercised regularly dramatically reduced his stress levels (and by default, his pulling behaviors), we also purposely put him into situations we knew would be very challenging to him, so that he could experience the urges to pull while practicing the competing responses. He initially found this difficult to do, but found that with repeated practice, fewer and fewer circumstances were able to stress him to the point that he began to pull hair. The results were visually obvious; at the beginning of treatment his skin was often red and irritated, but toward the end of treatment (10 sessions total) his skin showed no signs of picking or pulling, and he was able to let stubble grow on his face in a way that is fashionable these days among men. Part of his provocation exercises was to let his stubble grow and to not shave it, so that he would have actual hair to focus on for exposure exercises. At the end of treatment, he was also able to increase his work and he had re-enrolled in university classes. Although his hair pulling behavior was under significant voluntary control at the end of treatment, he did still exhibit remaining OCD symptoms, and such symptoms were incorporated into a formal relapse prevention plan, in terms of monitoring for certain types of stressors and whether he would become "feeling-focused" in their presence. Follow-up suggested that although he encountered some short episodes of resurgence now and then, Robert was mostly symptom free (i.e., reported a lack of hair pulling) 6 months after treatment.

Compulsive Hoarding

Compulsive hoarding is defined as the acquisition of and failure to discard possessions that are useless or of limited value, resulting in clutter that renders living spaces unusable for their intended purpose, and causing significant distress and impairment (e.g., Frost & Gross, 1993; Frost & Hartl, 1996; Frost, Krause, & Steketee, 1996). Despite its close connection to OCD, compulsive hoarding has until more recently only received relatively little clinical and research attention, but it is becoming increasingly clear that hoarders exhibit specific, strongly held beliefs about their possessions, whether valuable or genuinely not (e.g., trash), which are similar to obsessions (Steketee, Frost, & Kyrios, 2003).

Indeed, compulsive hoarding occurs as a principal symptom in about 20% to 30% of OCD patients, even though compulsive saving does not show up under OCD in the DSM-IV-TR, but is instead listed as a subsymptom of obsessive-compulsive personality disorder ("is unable to discard worn-out or worthless objects even when they have no sentimental value"; DSM-IV-TR, p. 729). This classification of compulsive saving as a personality disorder symptom lends clinical insight into how challenging it can be to adequately treat compulsive hoarding and that it not only requires a commitment on the part of the patient but on the part of treating practitioners as well. The only available (experimental) treatment protocol available (Frost & Steketee, personal communication, July 2004) estimates treatment will last at least 6 months. My own, anecdotal experience of treatment of compulsive hoarding suggests it commonly lasts 6 to 12 months, with 18 months being the longest I have spent treating this complex, challenging, but predictable condition.

Many practitioners are quite shocked by what they encounter when they initially begin to work with hoarding patients, because what they often observe they have no preparation for or ways of relating to. Unfortunately, many uninitiated practitioners experience a "knee-jerk" response of feeling obligated to report their patients for health or fire hazard violations. When such reports are made and they are actually acted on by either county or city agencies, the typical responses are to completely (and forcibly) clean out the patient's place of living and hoarding and to possibly even hospitalize the patient. For what should be obvious reasons, this degrading and dehumanizing experience is often perceived as incredibly stressful to hoarders and it tends to leave them very distrustful of mental health "professionals." If practitioners are to work with compulsive hoarders, they may have to seek consultation about being flexible with reporting mandates. Simply put, if all hoarders who represented a health or fire hazard were reported, there would be very few left to actually treat. Ironically, without treatment, compulsive hoarding does not remit on its own, and after hoarders have been "cleaned out," they usually only require a year or two to arrive back at the point where they were reported, only then to be more secretive about their behaviors and distrustful of helping professionals.

This represents a potentially significant problem for hoarders, because they may be realistically concerned that they will be reported if they seek treatment and for many practitioners as well, because they may be unprepared to provide adequate treatment for a vexing condition they may not fully understand. See Figures 4.4 and 4.5 for two fairly benign pictures of a hoarder's home to provide a small but useful insight into what practitioners might expect to see should they decide to take on treatment with such patients.

Approximately every 6 months I get a referral for a patient who exhibits the hoarding phenomenon. Given that hoarders are generally unlikely to seek out help (at least voluntarily), this small number represents a gross underestimation of their true numbers. The first dilemma facing any practitioner looking at such a referral is to determine why the patient is coming. Often these patients are not coming on their own accord, but instead at the insistence of a significant other or because they have "been discovered" and are under threat of being cleaned out by a local agency. These aspects are important prognostically, because they may lend clues to the level of true preparation for change or individual desire for change. As a standard practice, I ask prospective patients to convince me why they need help and why I should help them. Although this may sound somewhat uncaring, I would argue that it helps explore prospective patients' motivation for change and differentiates between the "visitor effect" and a genuine desire for change. The visitor effect refers to a tendency for some patients to only work at their predicament when someone is coming to visit (e.g., practitioner visiting for a home visit), but not when no one will be checking on them and their progress; the difference speaks to whether patients would be likely to engage in

FIGURE 4.4   Compulsive hoarding example 1.

FIGURE 4.5   Compulsive hoarding example 2.

structured homework because they see its inherent value or whether they might only clean when it matters to others (Steketee, Frost, Wincze, Greene, & Douglass, 2000).

"Tom" was a 58-year-old, Caucasian, never-married male living alone in his birth home. He had inherited this home from his parents who had built it themselves. He self-identified as a hoarder and that he had engaged in saving behaviors for most of his life. He was seeking help with the problem because he had recently retired and he was therefore spending a lot more time at home. While employed in a manufacturing job, he spent the majority of his waking life at work, only being home for short stretches overnight and to prepare meals. During the last 10 years of working, he had slept in his kitchen, because most all other spaces of his three-bedroom house (three bedrooms, a living room, two bathrooms, a full basement and garage) were filled with personal belongings ranging from newspaper to clothing and odds and ends. There was even a considerable amount of trash and garbage in his home that were in various stages of decay. When he was no longer working, but lived instead at home, he found that his constricted space was far insufficient for him.

After an initial office-based assessment, an in-home assessment was conducted during which measurements and "before pictures" were taken. A useful gauge for change over time with hoarding is repeated pictures and physical measurements. The two-session visit to his home revealed that the kitchen was the only area of the home that was usable in any way. From the kitchen led little corridors to a couple of areas of the home necessary for everyday use (e.g., one bathroom, the front door where mail was dropped into a mail slot). Bedrooms could be peered into, but could not be entered because they were blocked with boxes and a blend of various obstacles. The living room contained a 5-foot depth of newspapers, on top of which boxes were stacked to the ceiling. The most profound realization was to observe the stairwell that went down into the basement. When the door was opened, it revealed a solid mass of bags, boxes, old clothing, and other objects and belongings. It was not possible to see into the basement at all. When asked, Tom confessed it had not been possible to enter the basement for 20 years, and that the basement was much like the living room, stacked from floor to ceiling with boxes, bags, and newspapers. Judging from the musty smell that emerged from the basement, there must also have been organic materials there at some point that were in various forms of decay and decomposition.

Treatment started with twice-weekly sessions, which were consumed with beginning to sort belongings into broad categories and deciding what to do with various items (e.g., display, discard, store). The first 6 months were spent in this fashion, systematically sorting through belongings and making decisions about what to do with them. Several storage systems were designed to appropriately store belongings that were going to be kept. After 4 months, Tom slept in one of his bedrooms for the first time in 10 years. Going was slow at times, and at times there were even setbacks, as Tom would get an urge to pick up something "free" at neighborhood garage sales. However, by monitoring the balance between what entered his home and what left, he was able to ensure a greater outflow than what came in. After 6 months, only necessities came into the house, and much more material left at a greater rate.

Although he was able to throw much of the trash away that littered his home, some items (e.g., old newspapers) he felt compelled to donate to a local library. Other items, which he felt were "too good" to be simply thrown away, he donated to St. Vincent de Paul's. After a year, his whole top floor was clear and was appropriately being used. The last 6 months were spent excavating his basement and garage. When he finally was able to pull in his car into his garage, he poignantly observed that he had only ever been able to pull the first car he ever owned into the garage, suggesting that some of the cluttering had been familial and had even predated his own struggles. For the past 5 years of follow-up, he has been able to keep his home clutter-free, although he readily admits he continues to have a hard time with garage sales and other "near-free" opportunities; "still," he observes, "I have kept a balance between what comes in and what leaves." Exposure to decision making and actually letting extraneous belongings go played a necessary role in his recovery.

CHAPTER 5

Complicating Factors in Anxiety Treatment: Obstacles and Solutions

> Do the thing you fear and death of fear is certain.
> —Ralph Waldo Emerson

Empirically supported treatments for anxiety disorders should work, and should work well at that, or so the literature suggests. However, anxiety treatment only works if the treatment is delivered and performed as it was designed and intended. In short, if patients do not do what they fear, then the death of that fear is very uncertain! There may be many reasons why what should work does not. When treatment is not progressing as anticipated, it behooves practitioners to carefully consider what complicating factors might serve as obstacles to optimal outcome. There are a multitude of reasons, both patient- and practitioner-based. When exploring reasons, it is important for practitioners to not fall into the trap of thinking of patients as resisting treatment per se, because such a stance might readily lead to committing the fundamental attribution error (i.e., the patient [not the circumstances] is construed to be at fault or as a bad person). If these obstacles can be met and understood, then perhaps those challenges can be turned into opportunities for successful outcomes (Freeman & McCloskey, 2003). Without critically examining the challenges, improvement is unlikely, and, if treatment fails, it is relatively clear that patients will just continue to seek treatment elsewhere; thus, in an effort to reduce overall medical utilization, effective treatments need to be delivered, and obstacles to such interventions need to be surmounted. Indeed, overcoming such challenges collaboratively can enhance ultimate outcome. What follows are discussions of various, common challenges that have been documented in the history of psychotherapy as sometimes representing roadblocks to successful treatment outcomes.

MEDICAL AND SUBSTANCE-INDUCED ANXIETY

There are a number of medical conditions and substances that may contribute to common anxiety and comorbid conditions (e.g., depression), and these variables need to be understood because the treatment approach might be altered depending on what condition or substance is present.

For instance, hyperthyroidism, or an overactive thyroid gland, is one medical condition that can cause panic attacks. Controlling the over-activity of this gland can eliminate panic attacks; unfortunately, the standard panic control treatment protocol is unlikely to be able to affect this underlying etiology. Medical disorders often need medical interventions, even if they might be assisted by psychological methods. Panic might therefore remain unchanged, unless the thyroid function is controlled. Likewise, pheochromocytoma, a rarely occurring tumor on the adrenal gland, can also cause panic attacks.

Certain substances can also cause panic attacks, such as the use of amphetamines (including prescription versions). Benzedrine is often considered to be a culprit for panic attacks, but is commonly prescribed for asthma or weight loss. Similarly, excessive caffeine use may serve as a source of panic attacks. As it turns out, caffeine is the single most commonly overused/abused psychogenic substance in the world (Paterson, 1997b); therefore, a medical/physical examination could determine whether panic attacks are caused by these kinds of medical problems or substances or whether they are actually part of a "legitimate" panic disorder (i.e., recall that a diagnostic exclusionary criteria is that panic attacks cannot be a direct physiological effect of a substance or medical condition).

Caffeine deserves a moment of scrutiny. It is a stimulant (a xanthine), and its effect is to accelerate heart rate, respiration rate, and metabolic rate, and it acts as a diuretic. Individuals who are anxious would be well advised to limit caffeine intake, because it otherwise might trigger the kinds of physiological reactions common to panic attacks. Addiction to caffeine occurs at such low levels of consumption as 450 mg/day. Although 450 mg might sound like a lot, it can be acquired rather quickly. Standard drop coffee contains 130 mg per 5-oz cup. Five ounces is less than the smallest cup Starbucks Coffee advertises; its "Short" cup (available only by request, from under the counter) is 8 oz, which would contain approximately 208 mg caffeine. The first size that shows up on Starbucks' menu board is "Tall," containing 12 oz, or 312 mg caffeine. The second size is "Grande," containing 16 oz, or 416 mg caffeine. The last size is "Venti," containing an astonishing 520 mg caffeine in 20 oz. It has also become clear that Starbucks coffee also contains more caffeine than most of their competitors' drip coffee, making these likely underestimates. Although this might initially sound like a vendetta for Starbucks, it is not; it is simply an attempt at pointing out how simple it is to consume enough caffeine in today's busy world that physiological changes will occur that mimic or cause panic attacks. A thorough interview, with attention to all substances used, should adequately screen for problematic substances that induce anxiety-like physiological responses.

Additional medical conditions may be present and may contribute to anxiety experiences. For instance, hypoglycemia, or low blood sugar, can cause people to feel shaky and weak, and to panic. Mitral valve problems, or fluttering of the heart, might produce the same problems. Asthma, allergies, and gastrointestinal problems may also contribute to these kinds of reactions. It would be necessary to control these variables to find out whether a person still continues to experience panic attacks. It may turn out that these conditions exacerbate panic, but their removal does not remove panic disorder. Although correcting for hyperthyroidism usually corrects or stops panic attacks, correcting conditions such as allergies might not stop panic attacks. It is therefore often recommended that patients who are presenting with significant anxiety disorders who have not had a complete physical and medical examination in the past year should do so to rule out any underlying physiological cause that can be otherwise controlled.

AXIS II PRESENTATIONS

Although the topic of personality disorders is not without controversy (e.g., often perceived as patient blaming), it is worth noting this may be an area of consideration when treatment is especially problematic. Negative, often derogatory, terms used to describe especially challenging patients might include "resistant," "unmotivated," "oppositional," "uncooperative and noncollaborative," "stuck," or "have not hit bottom" (Foertsch, Manning, & Dimeff, 2003). Although these ways of conceptualizing patients are not especially helpful, it might point to more obvious problems. For example, some have argued that personality disordered patients have never gained the skills necessary for more adaptive functioning and their inability to change is therefore a reflection of lack of skills rather than active resistance (Beck, Freeman, Davis, & Associates, 2004).

Given that anxiety disorders often need very specific treatment interventions, "personality disorder" labels might also be reflective of patients' negative cognitions stemming from previous, unsuccessful therapy. I have worked with patients who have been in long-term treatment formats for many years, sometimes decades. When they finally, for whatever reasons, seek out cognitive-behaviorally oriented therapy, they are often bitter about the lost years, the money they have spent (for no apparent gain), and how "treatment" has not worked to date. Often, they want to know, up front, how you will be any different; this somewhat cross position can be unnerving to the uninitiated or naive practitioner because the stance, on the surface, seems rather challenging (if not oppositional). I find that a thorough explanation of the phenomenon in question (i.e., learning theory explanations for how they work, how they are maintained, and how they remit), and why "treatment" has apparently not worked yet puts many patients at ease. Additionally, I share openly with them treatment planning and treatment target selection criteria, as well as progress measures after treatment commences, which often leaves patients feeling like I am not engaged in something magical but instead something very systematic, which they are, by design, an active part of.

Another factor that I quickly consider when treatment is not going well or when it is even "failing" is what will happen if patients improve. Fundamentally, I believe people only engage in behaviors that either get them something desirable or get them out of something undesirable. It is pretty straightforward, in a functional analytic perspective, to consider why people are doing what they are doing. Sometimes, when treatment is not moving, and it should be, I consider that the patient might face undesirable outcomes if he or she improves. Sometimes patients are aware of this, and sometimes they are not. I can still vividly recall a patient having a rather frank discussion with me about what it would mean to him if he "recovered." He had spent the last 20 years trapped in severe obsessive-compulsive disorder. He explained that, at 30-something, he would have to think about what he would do for work, an education, dating, and a variety of other potential stressors, all stacked on top of each other. Because he was disabled by his condition, he had not been required to engage in things such as education, working, or dating. If he improved, he would have to face them all. It was too much. Instead of focusing directly on symptoms, the treatment instead shifted toward work skill acquisition and socializing. After a few years of developing skills necessary to live an everyday life, he reengaged therapy and improved tremendously.

Instead of ignoring the pink elephant in the room, I find that open conversations about "observations" (based on data typically) serve to open communication about "resistance" and similar conceptions about nonresponse or poor response to established treatments. Ignoring such factors usually only serves to frustrate the practitioner and further alienate patients from effective treatment options.

POOR INSIGHT, DELUSIONAL BELIEFS, AND OVERVALUED IDEATION

Level of insight varies broadly from complete insight and appreciation of one's problems to total denial of illness. This, of course, suggests that judgment can be either very good or completely lacking depending on the level of insight. Insight can be defined as an understanding or the motivations behind one's thoughts or behaviors, but it can also be defined as a recognition (appreciation) of the sources of one's emotional or mental problems (Neziroglu & Stevens, 2002). Kaplan and Saddock (1993) suggested that "insight" refers to a person's capacity to appreciate causes and meanings of situations.

There may be many reasons why patients do not have sufficient insight into their problem situations, ranging from intellectual functioning to sophistication and desire. Many aspects of the mental status exam will predict well what level of insight any given patient might have for his or her circumstances. Neziroglu and Stevens (2002) proposed four different levels of insight: true emotional insight, intellectual insight, partial internally based and externally based insight, and denial of illness.

True emotional insight is representative of the highest level of insight possible; that is, patients' awareness and understanding of their own thoughts, feelings, and motives can be used to change behavior. This highest level of insight is characterized by sound judgment and knowledge that can be used for thoughtful and purposeful planning and execution of targeted behavioral sets. This level's exemplar is the critical, creative, and meaningful thinker who can purposely shape his or her experience through control of life's circumstances.

Intellectual insight is commonly seen in psychotherapy practice, in patients who grasp that their level of maladaption is due to their own thoughts, feelings, and behaviors. What lacks in this type of insight is the failure to generate appropriate problem-solving solutions. Patients at this level of insight tend to make the same mistakes repeatedly, without enough insight into why and how these mistakes occur, and they therefore tend to be incapable of stopping such cycles unassisted. Because they are not naturally able to use sound judgment, without training, they do not learn from previous mistakes and experiences.

Partial internally and externally based insight is representative of patients whose awareness misguidedly attributes problems either to unknown factors within the person or external factors outside of the personal control or influence of the sufferer. Exemplars of this level of insight are character/personality disorders, anger control problems, and alcohol and drug abuse. Often, patients exhibiting this level of insight are only vaguely aware that there are problems and that they may need help and commonly deny there are any problems, maybe even actively resisting any efforts of help.

Denial of illness is demonstrative of the very lowest level of insight, as demonstrated by complete lack of insight. Fortunately, this is not common, and is predominantly confined to such problems as pervasive and severe mental illness or chemical or organic deficits. Patients in this category might be in a full manic episode, floridly psychotic, or experiencing some kind of dementing process. The lower levels of insight are not appropriate levels of functioning for highly structured and directive exposure-based therapy, because the patient would not be able to understand sufficiently what he or she is being asked to engage in or to provide full consent to treatment.

Delusional beliefs are similar to this lowest level of insight and are problematic when encountered, because the patient holding the pervasive, immovable belief is commonly not open to testing evidence that goes counter to his or her beliefs or assumptions held to represent "truth." Delusional patients often believe so strongly that any attempt to dissuade them about their beliefs is met with great distrust or suspicion. Attempts to provide contrary evidence are usually met with a paranoid position toward the provider, who is seen as either crazy or as being out to somehow harm or cheat the patient. For obvious reasons, delusional patients do not make good candidates for directive cognitive-behavioral interventions. Such approaches are based on the premise that patients will be able to act as scientists with their treatment provider to test out beliefs and assumptions as if they were scientific hypotheses that deserve testing before they are accepted and incorporated into emotional functioning.

Overvalued ideation is similar to low levels of insight, or semidelusional thinking, in which overvalued ideas are on a continuum between rational and delusional thoughts. In short, overvalued ideation is a pathological thought process with poor insight (Kozak & Foa, 1994). Because beliefs tend to have fixity, they are only open to modification through direct challenge. Therefore, only those patients who can accept working with a practitioner to challenge their beliefs may be suitable for cognitive and behavioral interventions. Some level of willingness to consider alternatives is necessary for such interventions to work. Overvalued ideation can be defined as a belief a person feels justified in holding and that strongly determines the person's behaviors. Overvalued ideas involve strong personal identification and sometimes intense affective reactions to any challenge of such ideation (Clark, 2004). Overvalued ideas can be distinguished from delusions by just how firmly the belief is held and by how important the value of the belief is to the self, as well as the rigidity (inflexibility) of the idealized value (Veale, 2002).

Patients who demonstrate overvalued ideation may demonstrate lower levels of outcome, because such ideation may interfere with such processes as habituation and extinction (Foa, Abramowitz, Franklin, & Kozak, 1999). When treatment response is especially poor, practitioners would be wise to question whether the patient could be demonstrating a delusional level of ideation. Fortunately, delusional beliefs are readily identified without too much difficulty, because delusions are unresponsive to clearly contradictory evidence and tend to take on bizarre, implausible qualities, and delusional patients do not appear overly distressed by their strange beliefs (Insel & Akiskal, 1986; Kozak & Foa, 1994). Overvalued ideation and delusions provide obvious prognostic concerns and should not be taken lightly when considering treatment.

BIPOLAR DISORDER AND MAJOR DEPRESSIVE DISORDER

Bipolar disorder is hallmarked by extreme affective dysregulation, from extremely low (depression) to extremely high (mania). The second primary hallmark is that psychosocial functioning (marital, occupational, or social) is disrupted sufficiently enough that hospitalization is required (Miklowitz, 2001). Sometimes these swings also occur with psychotic features. Unmanaged bipolar disorder is inappropriate for exposure-based treatments. First, there would be a problem with habituation and extinction processes so the treatment would likely fail. Second, such patients may be unable to comply with regular homework and other structured tasks and instructions. When bipolar disorder is adequately managed by medications, exposure-based treatment can proceed. I have frequently worked with psychiatrists in delivering collaborative treatment components that address the multiple issues facing the bipolar/anxiety-disordered patient. When followed closely by a prescriber familiar with bipolar disorder, exposure-based treatment usually goes very well. The key factor is to keep the mood stable throughout the active treatment phase.

Clinical depression presents its own unique challenges to successful anxiety treatment. Many anxiety-disordered patients are at least mildly to moderately depressed (Foa & Rothbaum, 1998). Significant depression can inhibit emotional processing, which is a necessary component of exposure-based therapy; therefore, when significant depression is detected, it may be wise to treat depression before proceeding with specific anxiety interventions (McLean & Woody, 2001), if such interventions are to be based in exposure exercises. Minimal depression should not interfere with habituation, but moderate levels might. The best test is to see whether within-session and between-session habituation will occur. Often, with mild to moderate depression, within-session habituation will occur, but with moderate to severe depression, between-session habituation will fail even when within-session habituation occurs. Between-session habituation is necessary for repeated habituation to lead to extinction, because reactivity must be reduced for extinction to be possible.

Additionally, when patients are depressed, it becomes important to monitor for suicidal ideation and intent. Hopelessness is a better predictor of completed suicide than is suicidal ideation; unfortunately, depression and anxiety both load heavily on hopelessness factors, making comorbid depression a risk variable when treating anxiety disorders. Because comorbidity with anxiety should be expected and depression can easily exacerbate anxiety symptoms, I commonly assess for depression when I conduct intake interviews with anxiety-disordered patients. When I find it present, I usually use a depression outcome/progress measure (e.g., Beck Depression Inventory–Second Version) to closely follow any negative mood fluctuations. Typically, comorbidity will increase severity, and this will commonly lead to careful pacing, ordering of interventions (e.g., depression before anxiety, pharmacotherapy), and prognostic adjustments. Collaborating closely with patients and other treatment providers (e.g., primary care physicians, nurse practitioners, social workers) who might be part of an overall treatment team (whether in a multidisciplinary setting or not) will become even more important to success than it might normally be. Other concerns often come with depression and comorbidity, such as lower motivation and desire for change.

MOTIVATIONAL INTERVIEWING AND MOTIVATION ENHANCEMENT TREATMENT

Motivational problems in anxiety-disorder treatment are often connected with an unwillingness to experience high levels of anxiety; in fact, many anxiety-disordered patients appear hypersensitive. Because of hedonistic principles (see chapter 7), they can be quite unhappy, if not outright unwilling to do what is necessary for fear to subside, namely repeatedly facing exactly what they fear. Again, the premise behind exposure therapy is by repeatedly facing what one fears, unwarranted reactivity is deconditioned. Facing one's fears is paramount and absolutely necessary for anxiety to remit. Motivation to face challenging experiences is required for successfully treating anxiety with exposure-based techniques.

A patient's motivation for engaging in treatment might not be very high, especially if he or she does not grasp the rationale for the treatment procedures. In the worst-case scenario, a patient with overvalued ideation believes there may be some real cause for concern (i.e., his or her fears are correct) and may exhibit a low tolerance for increased anxiety levels, as would have to be experienced during exposure-based treatment. In such a case, therapy would not have a good chance of working, because the patient would be highly unlikely to actually engage the treatment. If he or she were to do it at all, the patient might simply disconnect from his or her emotions and just go through the motions of performing the tasks, but not really allow the critical, reparative emotional processing to take place. Avoidance of any sort should be self-evident after nonresponsiveness is investigated; escape and avoidance behaviors should be carefully screened for when treatment appears stagnant or slow.

Motivational interviewing and motivation enhancement treatment are increasingly used to help patients discover their own reasons and rationales for positive personal change, and can be especially useful when working with patients who exhibit lower motivation levels for facing challenging emotions, anxiety, and fear. Although motivation enhancement treatment is complex, it surrounds such traditional activities as consciousness raising, decision making, and exploring options for change. It is already being used with anxiety disorders in which patients demonstrate stage of change resistance (e.g., are resistant to action-oriented interventions because they are either in precontemplative, contemplative, or preparatory stages of change). Through matching interventions specifically to level of stage of change, patients can be moved into action stages, where they can improve as do other patients after they have initially failed to respond. Some researchers are finding that motivation enhancement treatment can be used to maximize efficacy for empirically supported treatments for anxiety by including stage of change analysis and integrating stage of change appropriate interventions (e.g., Foa, 2000; Miller & Rollnick, 2002; Prochaska, 2000; Westra & Phoenix, 2003).

GENERALIZABILITY, TRANSPORTATION OF GAINS, AND ECOLOGICAL RELEVANCE

Practitioners need to be mindful of whether the treatment provided in analog settings will generalize, or transport back to natural environments in which patients have to function after the treatment ends. This is usually more of a concern when treatment is delivered in a more restrictive setting, such as a residential treatment setting. It may be that the natural cues will be awaiting patients' return when they come home from restrictive settings. If nothing special has been done to prepare them for how to face or deal with such naturally occurring (i.e., ecologically relevant) cues, this may be a significant risk factor for relapse. Therefore, it may be important to incorporate ecologically relevant variables into active treatment to prevent the recurrence of major symptoms after patients return to natural locations (Rosqvist, Thomas, & Egan, 2002; Tharp & Wetzel, 1969). See chapter 2 for a more complete discussion of the role of natural environmental settings for optimizing impact of empirically supported treatments and exposure-based treatments.

ENHANCING COLLABORATION: USE OF PARAPROFESSIONALS AND MENTORS

While the mentoring program will be described in chapter 6, the role of significant others has not yet been thoroughly elaborated. Most patients spend a small amount of time with their providers; there are other people in patients' lives who spend far more time with them. These people may be able to play important roles for patients who are undergoing exposure-based treatments. However one presents it, exposure treatment involves some discomfort and, as such, this type of intervention can be an aversive experience. If left entirely on their own to perform challenging homework, some patients may follow their hedonistic tendencies and not engage the work or they might not do so fully or as completely. However, public commitments to significant others seems to diminish this avoidance or escape tendency. Therefore, it can be important to integrate significant others into treatment to ensure patients are more likely to more fully engage and completely carry out therapy tasks.

So, who are significant others? The most obvious answer would be spouses and partners and other direct family members. But significant others can be employers, teachers, and anyone else patients feel comfortable in involving in their treatment. Cautions need to be taken by considering what effect disclosing someone's psychological illness might have on, for example, employment status. Involving a significant other can be immensely helpful, but also requires that such a person then becomes aware of what the patient is struggling with. If a potential significant other does not understand mental illness, it could lead to adverse responses. Patients need to carefully consider who might serve well in the role of a significant other before disclosing to that person their desire to integrate him or her into a formal treatment package. I would highly recommend choosing less "critical" people to serve in this role, because picking centrally important persons (e.g., employers) could have unintended, negative effects. Nonetheless, I have found that most people who have been identified as potential significant others are more than willing to help, because they usually tend to be (by selection) people who are already at least partially aware of the patient's difficulties and who have some kind of investment (emotional, professional, or otherwise) in seeing the patient recover. For confidentiality reasons, patients need to broach the subject with such people, but commonly do so with greater confidence when backed up concretely by their provider (e.g., calling a potential significant other during session, where practitioners can also speak with the person to clarify any questions or concerns that might arise). I work frequently with integrating family members into treatment, and also find that employers are willing and capable of helping as well. I would recommend practitioners consider this option if they find their patients have a difficult time completing homework or performing challenging tasks initially without some more formal support.

LEGAL ISSUES: POSTTRAUMATIC STRESS DISORDER, LITIGATION, AND TREATMENT RESPONSE

Posttraumatic stress disorder (PTSD) is an unusual syndrome in that, unlike other anxiety diagnostic categories, an etiological event is often specified: exposure to a traumatic stressor (McNally, 2003). Some of these traumatic events have led to physical injuries, prolonged pain, and suffering, which are all material for litigation and lawsuits. Such legal actions may only represent pragmatic issues for psychotherapy, in that during such a process, there are commonly hundreds of appointments for legal questioning, discovery, and assessment, which then typically are also replicated by opposing teams. Patients who also have current legal disputes stemming from injuries may not be regularly available for exposure-based interventions, which in large part depend on regularity to produce repeated habituation and extinction. If there are significant amounts of pain as a result of injuries, that can be a poor prognostic indicator because it is thought to interfere with some kinds of emotional processing and, therefore, can directly interfere with the habituation and extinction process. If significant pain is present, it should be monitored and managed, and close attention should be paid to within- and between-session habituation patterns. It is also not unusual to find many litigants frustrated and angered by the legal process, and, unfortunately, significant anger is also a poor indicator for exposure therapy because it also interferes with habituation processes. If patients in exposure-based treatment are in litigation, it may be important to integrate stress management techniques and training into the overall treatment package (e.g., Gottlieb, 1997; Lazarus, 1971; Meichenbaum, 1977; Meichenbaum & Novaco, 1977; Suinn, 1990).

The often thorny issue of compensation may directly affect progress and outcome. Payment for pain and suffering is based on the premise of damage or illness; by default, this means patients do not (potentially) receive compensation for injuries if they are not "sick" (e.g., Rosen, 1995). Motor vehicle accident and combat PTSD are the two most commonly problematic patient sets. In my clinical experience, I have found consistently that motor vehicle accident PTSD patients do not recover in any meaningful way until they have settled their legal claims, after which they seem to proceed through treatment just fine. This is not necessarily akin to malingering or feigning symptoms, but appears to be some common process to stress related with being involved in litigation, where (often) the patient's integrity and honesty are questioned and accusations of "faking" are often leveled by attorneys representing insurance companies seeking to minimize their losses. There may be some outright malingering people, but they behave in such a way that makes them relatively easy to spot (e.g., claims of inability to perform the easiest of tasks, which only a profoundly disturbed individual could not do, while being able to do other, much more complex tasks, such as following complex instructions for dropping off material at another office). The majority of motor vehicle accident victims I have worked with have genuinely been injured and would sorely wish to be better, but somehow the legal process stands in their way of recovery. Because of this, I recommend practitioners consider waiting to commence exposure-based treatment until after legal disputes are completed; time and money may be wasted if treatment proceeds before legal dispute completion.

Combat-induced PTSD presents another sort of specter. McGrath and Frueh (2002) reported that as many as 94% of veterans with PTSD apply for financial compensation for their illnesses. This becomes especially relevant when one considers that often it is financial incentives that draw people to military service in the first place; consequently, seeking financial compensation may be more common among people who have otherwise limited occupational skills (Mossman, 1994). Burkett and Whitley (1998) reported that veterans who obtain a service-connected disability rating of 100% for PTSD can earn in excess of $36,000 per year, tax free and indexed for inflation, for life. Implications are substantial in terms of financial loss, should such veterans recover from PTSD. Again, this does not necessarily mean veterans are malingering, but it does put some serious prognostic cautions on outcome expectations if combat PTSD patients are receiving financial compensation for PTSD. Considerations for treatment should be made.

MANAGED CARE CONSIDERATIONS: FRIEND OR FOE?

Too often, practitioners are left with a sinking feeling at the mention of the word "managed care." Managed care, of course, is synonymous with utilization reviews, cost-containment policies and practices, and broad-based accountability in multiple ways. Practitioners who bill third-party insurance are probably all too familiar with having to submit elaborate and sophisticated treatment plans in exchange for fewer sessions than will be needed to adequately treat the presenting concern. One way to deal with this predicament, if not outright hassle, is to go to an all cash-only basis practice and to let patients try to recover their expenditures from their insurance carriers. This approach may not be very realistic, however, because few patients can afford to pay $100–$150 per hour for specialized services. Some masters-level–prepared practitioners are able to offer these specialized services at $75–$100 per hour, but even at $50 per hour, few anxiety-disordered patients (because of the occupational and financial impacts of the illness) can afford a complete treatment package of 15–25 sessions. Insurance is almost by default of economic circumstances going to be the payer of cognitive-behavioral interventions for anxiety disorders.

Given that this is probably going to be true for most practitioners, the news is good. Empirically supported treatments are desirable treatment products in the eyes of managed health care companies, because products such as exposure-based treatments often lead to lower medical utilization and health care access later. For every dollar spent on evidence-based practice interventions, far fewer dollars will be spent in the long run; insurance companies and managed care organizations are well aware that anxiety disorders commonly take chronic courses, and that without adequate treatment they tend to worsen to the point of needing more intensive/restrictive levels of care (read as more expensive). Because exposure therapy has such a strong research base and much scientific literature exists supporting its potency, managed care should be viewed in a friendlier light; managed care will want to contract with practitioners who use these scientifically supported methods to treat anxiety disorders. As a result, care organizations will be very responsive to treatment session requests and accommodations needed to adequately treat anxiety-disordered patients. Granted, proper administrative procedures will have to be followed, in terms of filling out forms and other recurring requirements, but there is a deficit of practitioners who can deliver empirically supported and manual-based exposure therapy for a variety of anxiety disorders. For instance, Marcks, Woods, Teng, and Twohig (2004) reported that, although some practitioners have heard of habit reversal training (Stanley & Mouton, 1996), the established treatment of choice for trichotillomania and other habit control disorders (e.g., skin picking, nail biting), far fewer (0%–9.7%) knew how to actually implement this basic but highly effective treatment strategy. Knowing how to properly implement specialized treatments for anxiety disorders, spectrum conditions, and comorbid conditions makes solid financial sense; however, it does necessitate practitioners orient themselves to empirical treatment models and means of interventions.

IMPLICATIONS FOR SOLUTIONS: SYSTEMATIC USE OF SINGLE-CASE RESEARCH, ENHANCED CASE FORMULATION, FUNCTIONAL ANALYSIS, AND FAILURE ANALYSIS IN TRAINING AND PRACTICE

Using empirical treatments does not equate to being pedantic and rigid in delivery and connection with patients. In fact, practitioners who employ these methods have to be mindful of what makes therapy work, for whom, under what circumstances, and delivered by which treatment provider. Indeed, practitioners have to scrutinize each new individual case to a degree that it is considered as an entirely unique case, unlike anything else that has ever been encountered. Practitioners need to understand thoroughly what makes certain conditions occur in certain individuals, because such professional insight is what guides the most effective interventions on a case-by-case basis. Practitioners, almost by default, if they wish to be as effective as they can be, have to be single-case researchers. They have to study their individual patients carefully and propose idiosyncratically meaningful models for observed pathology (whether dimensional or categorical). Only when useful (i.e., cause and effect) relationships are detected or proposed can tests of relevant hypotheses be tested through careful interventions. Understanding single-subject design becomes important to adequately understanding how to interpret progress and effectiveness.

Educating oneself to become a better single-subject researcher is as easy as picking up readily available literature (e.g., Barlow & Hersen, 1984; Campbell, 2004; Hersen, 1982; Parker & Brossart, 2003) and deciding how individual assessment, intervention, and progress measure will be conducted. Some universities are even offering specialized, single-subject design courses, which may also be apt ways of preparing oneself to act as a researcher might, but in relation to single patients (as opposed to with large samples).

Single-case design necessitates clear hypotheses about causal agents of observed pathology, and there is no better hypotheses generator than a thorough case conceptualization or formulation. Case formulation can be thought of as the parsimonious understanding of patients and their problems that effectively guides treatment (e.g., Berman, 1997; Eels, 1997; Eels, Kendjelic, & Lucas, 1998; Needleman, 1999; Nezu, Nezu, & Lombardo, 2004; Persons, 1989; Sacco & Beck, 1995; Turkat, 1985) through producing testable, stage of change sensitive hypotheses.

Case conceptualization becomes most important when treatment does not work, because within the formulation rests ideas for why proven interventions are failing to produce the desired effects. Case formulation is then often combined with functional analysis and failure analysis to establish what the obstacles to progress might be. As with conceptualization, functional analysis and failure analysis carefully examine variables that influence problem behaviors, or other targets of change. Indeed, such analyses are often integral to achieving the best possible design. Petroski (1992) argues that success is predicated on foreseeing failure, and Reason (1990) suggests that one should expect errors (failures) in humans and that such realities make errors a proper study in themselves.

In this day and age of accountability and managed care, it could easily be argued that practitioners should be better prepared to carefully analyze treatment nonresponse and less than optimal outcomes. It may be paramount to be especially adept at case conceptualization and to gather variables that through functional analytic or failure analytic analyses might reveal sources of low or no response. This activity would require more practitioners to be willing to look at their "failures," or cases in which treatment did not work as well as predicted. This might inherently be somewhat threatening, because the implication might be that the practitioner did not do a good enough job, or that he or she was not good enough. Many such discomforts and fears may be irrational or without basis, but hedonism will usually dictate that people will avoid what makes them uncomfortable, unless they actively are aware of this tendency and see some immediate benefit for going with the discomfort (rather than away from it). Failure analysis also often necessitates consulting with colleagues and peers for brainstorming sessions to derive possible explanations for such phenomenon, so it would entail a willingness to evaluate one's own effectiveness among peers. This willingness usually comes from professional maturity and is perhaps best promoted by setting up peer consultation groups that meet on a regular basis to discuss and explore challenging cases. The reality of practice suggests all practitioners will have their share of what in the clinical field often has become referred to as "head scratchers." Being willing to look carefully and systematically at such difficult patient presentations is the first step toward finding solutions for otherwise recalcitrant cases. Graduate students are strongly advised to seek out training in failure analysis, functional analysis, and to enhance their case formulation skills. Most of all, practitioners are advised to view failure in a different light, where it is not necessarily something to be feared and avoided, but instead something to embrace and learn from. Other careers capitalize on failure analysis as standard practice, which suggests psychology should follow suit. Bridge engineers, for example, learn how to become better bridge builders by studying bridges that actually fell down. Likewise, practitioners could similarly improve by studying "failure."

CHAPTER 6

Maintenance and Follow-Up Strategies: Preparing for Future and Continued Progress

People have a hard time letting go of their suffering.
Out of a fear of the unknown,
they prefer a suffering which is familiar.
—Thich Nhat Hanh

WHEN TO STOP TREATMENT?
ISSUES OF PROGRESS, TIMING, AND ACQUIRED SKILLS

Issues of treatment termination are all too familiar to the seasoned practitioner and bring a special concern for novice practitioners. How does one know when it is all right to stop treatment? It is the quintessential question that practitioners of all experience levels might debate, and in the current managed and controlled health care environment, it has also become a pragmatic question. Evidence-based practice can provide some systematic guidelines for how to make the decision to fade or terminate treatment.

Presumably, termination will occur when symptoms have abated sufficiently that patient functioning is considered "normal." However, what determines what is "good enough" progress will vary depending on which variables one incorporates into a decision to end treatment. If treatment was oriented toward self-actualization, it could conceivably go on for forever; indeed, some, more long-term theoretical orientations seem to carry out treatment far too long (sometimes decades!). Evidence-based and manual-based practices, however, do not unnecessarily prolong therapy, because they are symptom-driven. After symptoms fall within an acceptable range, typically specified to be within one or two standard deviations of the normal mean on a narrow-band instrument, treatment termination should be considered. This is where data become pivotal determinants of active continuation, fading, and termination.

Progress is perhaps best measured by clinical significance and reliable change. An empirically oriented practice values knowing just how effective treatment is, so evidence-based practitioners continually engage in progress assessment (Clement, 1996; Warren & Thomas, 2003). This allows such practitioners to know exactly when a patient has made enough progress to just pass clinical cutoffs, and such a marker is a good gauge for when treatment termination should be brought up. Some patients may be alarmed by discussions surrounding termination, especially when they are just beginning to feel substantially better (which is usually true of patients at or around the clinical cutoffs), so I find it most useful to include a discussion of the how, when, and what variables that influence termination during consent to treatment. Overall, I help patients understand that progress is what will determine when treatment ends, but that treatment does not end abruptly. Instead, treatment usually goes into a systematic fading process after reliable change is realized *and* the patient passes clinical cutoffs on central instruments measuring the phenomenon in question. The fade process then usually takes up to several months. This appreciation that treatment will continue, albeit less intensively (for in-session work), commonly serves to alleviate most patients' concerns (e.g., abandonment, fears of uncontrollable backsliding). Generalization training is a common focus during fading, because patients have already acquired the necessary skill sets and no new behavioral sets need to be taught per se. What is needed toward the end of treatment is a consolidation of therapy gains and a further push into domains in which new behavioral repertoires have not been fully tested.

HOW TO STOP TREATMENT: GENERALIZATION TRAINING

After treatment moves into a fading stage, generalization training is typically used to assist patients to become more comfortable with their newly acquired skills and to encourage and support them in becoming increasingly independent in continuing their own treatment and recovery process. After all, evidence-based practice typically uses a short-term intervention model and actively tries to not foster dependence on treatment providers. Autonomy and personal choice are values paramount to evidence-based practice.

After a patient crosses the clinical cutoff on an instrument measuring the severity of the phenomenon I have collaboratively been treating with the patient and they have also accomplished reliable change, I typically have a discussion about *generalization training*. My standard discussion highlights the idea that up to the point where we are in treatment has been a "pretraining" stage in which the patient has learned a lot about anxiety, how it works, its effects, and how to undo it and make it better. In the pretraining stage, patients have even completed a lot of exercises in which they have experimented with becoming more critical observers of their own experiences, how to make anxiety reactions diminish naturally by themselves, and how to effectively fix various problems that might have arisen because of anxiety. However, I explain, to date, the progress has been closely followed and supervised, something that will not be possible forever, and nor would that be desirable. Most patients readily acknowledge the problem that too much "hand holding" can cause, namely that the patient will not be able to enact the change strategies independently of the practitioner. Then I explain that the next stage of treatment (i.e., generalization stage) will involve a shift in roles and how treatment works. The foundation of the remaining treatment will be aimed at helping the patient become his or her own therapist in which the practitioner switches roles from being a treatment provider to being a supervisor. In this role shift, the patient switches from being patient to being the therapist and takes on responsibilities commonly administered by the treating practitioner, such as setting agendas, designing experiments, collecting and analyzing data, and problem solving less successful experiences.

Some patients might be skeptical at first about their capacity to act in the therapist role, because they likely had unsuccessfully tried to solve their own problems before coming to formal treatment. Such concerns can usually be addressed by having a discussion about how patients know when to stop treatment. Most patients report that they have gotten to a stage where they know what their therapist will say, and, in fact, the patients are already saying those things to themselves. They do not actually need the therapist anymore, because the patients are in many ways already saying and doing the very things a therapist would suggest they do and say. In short, the patients report that it is not that they have stopped treatment, but that they have learned to do the "method" of treatment themselves (Otto, Jones, Craske, & Barlow, 1996; Otto, Pollack, & Barlow, 1995). Generalization training is designed to formalize this otherwise informal tendency for patients to become paraprofessionals. To formalize this switch, sessions are stretched out in frequency, beginning usually with meeting every other week rather than weekly, as is standard in much of the active treatment phase. During their increased time away from practitioner oversight, the patients run their own therapy sessions; design, implement, and monitor their own experiments and exposures; and proceed to correct life problems. Their "supervisor" is available between sessions should something unforeseen or insurmountable come up, but only in terms of providing supervisory feedback instead of teaching new skills per se.

Many patients, especially after they have realized reliable change and have crossed clinical cutoffs—as they have then typically integrated many new skills and learned from other, more fully supported experiences—find that they are very successful in independently running their own treatment. With increased time between sessions, they also have sufficient amounts of time to more independently evaluate their newfound autonomy. With decreased pairings of their continued success and their treatment provider, the practitioner becomes increasingly superfluous. In this sense, "need" for the practitioner will be deconditioned, and self-reliance will instead be reinforced. This self-reliance is still backed up by the "supervising" practitioner, but there is literature that shows that availability during fading and posttreatment leads to decreased (inappropriate) patient contact. Although some practitioners might be concerned that making themselves available by phone between sessions and after treatment will lead to inappropriate levels of continued, patient-initiated contact, there is no support for this kind of understandable concern; instead, availability appears to foster a sense of increased self-confidence and self-reliance (Reitzel et al., 2004).

STOP REGRESSION TOWARD MEAN: RELAPSE PREVENTION TRAINING AND POSSIBLE RETURN OF FEAR

Relapse prevention is a necessary component of any complete treatment package, and good arguments could be made for requiring it as a last treatment component before discharge or termination. Despite the efficacy of cognitive and behavioral treatments for anxiety and fear, these phenomena are susceptible to at least partial recovery, meaning that a reemergence of anxiety and fear may occur after extinction. This phenomenon has often been referred to as a "return of fear" (e.g., Craske, 1999). Rachman (1979, 1989) has defined this concept as "reappearance of fear that was earlier present but had undergone a decline," and "the renewal of a previously weakened or extinguished fear." This resurgence or reappearance of anxiety and fear is not a newly discovered concept; rather, it has long been recognized (e.g., Agras, 1965; Wolpe, 1961). This collective knowledge makes it of outmost importance to prepare patients for the potential reexperience or recurrence of fear and anxiety. This is what relapse prevention sets out to accomplish.

Although a return of fear is not necessarily synonymous with clinical relapse, it may be a precursor, or a necessary precondition, for an eventual relapse. Because some anxiety is a normal and natural phenomenon, patients are likely to experience some anxiety and fear after treatment ends. In fact, therapy does not extinguish the patient's capacity for those emotions, but should instead reduce inaccurate reactivity and make patients better able to critically evaluate their experiences. Some instances of spontaneous recovery (of anxiety and fear) might still occur. Those moments is what relapse prevention targets by confining those moments to being only short episodes of "recovered fear" and preventing them from becoming a full, clinical relapse.

To more completely understand relapse, it becomes necessary to distinguish between relapses, lapses, and the concept of return of fear. In the formal relapse prevention training stage of treatment, conventionally delivered toward the very end of treatment, information is provided to patients so that they can be less likely to catastrophize any lapses or returns of fear experiences (which commonly occur after treatment). A lapse is a momentary regression toward a former level of maladaptive functioning style, but not usually all the way back and also not on a permanent basis (Marlatt & Gordon, 1985). Relapse prevention training prepares patients for how to best anticipate and deal with lapses to prevent patients from being overly alarmed and affected by them. Lapses are virtually bound to happen, so any full-treatment package will prepare patients for how to recognize a lapse, how to accept it without catastrophizing it, and what to do about it to ensure that it is not long-lived. It prepares patients to adaptively cope with problems as they arise after treatment has formally ended. All people will at some time have a bad day or a bad week. Bad things happen from time to time; statistically, this is normal and should be expected. Most people do not cherish these experiences, of course, but they still tend to work at correcting them and they try to learn from them in efforts to not repeat particular or general mistakes. Anxiety-disordered patients may have to be formally taught how to do this because their historical coping strategies have mostly consisted of escape and avoidance and therefore may not have lent themselves to learning effectively how to problem solve and cope with difficulties. Therefore, they may be less prepared for how to face a bad day or a bad week when it happens after treatment ends. They must be formally prepared to expect that "speed bumps" happen and what to do about them.

Relapse, in the clinical sense, means that symptoms of a disease are present after improvement; however, a complete relapse means patients are back at their pretreatment level of functioning. A relapse typically does not happen instantaneously. It usually starts as a lapse, or as a return of fear. It becomes a relapse only after patients do not cope with the slide or recurrence of symptoms in a proactive and adaptive fashion, but instead fall back on old (pretreatment) ways of coping. Because poor coping behaviors typically worsen anxiety, this might be enough for a relapse to occur. This necessitates preparing patients to know what to do when that day, week, or symptom does occur. The two predominant ways in which this is accomplished is through formal relapse prevention and booster sessions.

Relapse prevention training usually starts by informing patients about what to expect after treatment formally ends. It does so in part by reminding patients about what exactly it was that created the positive change they had experienced during their treatment, namely their work. They are then informed that their end-state functioning is supported by that work and that they should not expect to be able to maintain that level of change without some continued work. Three outcomes are possible after treatment: (1) patients could maintain their level of change and simply remain at that level, (2) they could continue to improve, or (3) they could decline. Most patients are somewhat distressed by the idea of worsening, because many of them are quite happy with their improvements. They do not want to regress and are often most interested in understanding how to prevent sliding from happening. This desire to at least maintain the current gains is a good avenue through which to discuss relapse prevention. They are then taught that to maintain what they have, they have to at least continue what they are doing to prevent slippage. In this fashion, as in generalization training, they are encouraged to continue to run their own therapy sessions to maintain the exercises that support the accomplished change. They are also told that if they wish to improve further, they will likely at least have to continue to do the current level of work and more. It is explained that improvement really does not follow a dose-effect curve (i.e., for one unit of dose [treatment], one unit of improvement is realized). Instead, lots of improvement is accomplished relatively early, whereas less improvement is possible later. Indeed, there does appear to be a diminishing returns phenomenon that governs therapeutic improvement. After formal treatment is over, patients will have to maintain their gains through continued work, but may have to work harder for additional improvements than they had to early in treatment. It may also not be possible to be "cured," but instead to achieve management and coping as realistic end-products. Management and coping implies continued work, and relapse prevention prepares patients for how to, for example, problem solve effectively enough so that maintenance is sustained and promoted.

REAFFIRMATION OF PROGRESS AND REMINDER OF PRINCIPLES: BOOSTER SESSIONS

Booster sessions are the other way in which maintenance is facilitated. I typically offer patients the availability of three or four booster sessions in a 6- to 12-month period after formally ending treatment. This offer helps in several ways. It makes it clear that additional help is available, if needed, and it lets patients feel, at least conceptually, supported in anything they may believe they will be unable to handle independently. It is clear that support networks are important predictors for the development of psychopathology, and support will also be crucial in staving off more permanent returns of problems. Less support, or no support at all, is a risk variable for developing psychological problems (e.g., McNally, 2003) and should be integrated into any aftercare plans to ensure that patients are well-prepared to face problems of living when treatment is no longer ongoing. Although support may not be solely capable of entirely preventing relapse, when patients know they can meet with their practitioner to process and resolve particularly challenging posttreatment challenges (and are perhaps even encouraged to do so in the face of particularly vexing problems), booster sessions may go a far way toward facilitating resilience in the face of posttreatment life difficulties.

Additionally, it may not be possible to encounter every kind of life challenge during the formal treatment phase (and this is thankfully not actually necessary because of generalization effects), so it may even be necessary or desirable to structure into the complete treatment package sessions on how to deal with future, known, and unknown circumstances. I do not find patients continuing to contact me much past formal terminations when we have agreed that a few sessions are available, and this seems to be what the best research literature seems to suggest about patient-initiated contact (e.g., Reitzel et al., 2004). Instead, what I have found is that when former patients have contacted me, they often do so to share how well they are continuing to do, often years after formal treatment ended. Occasionally, people do contact me for a true booster session, either because they have encountered something so different they just do not quite know what to do or because they have forgotten how to completely carry out some kind of exercise and want a reminder. Either way, I always make myself available for agreed-on booster sessions, and, typically, such sessions constitute providing support for how the former patient had considered handling new issues in the first place.

When I do meet with former patients, it predominantly turns out that they do indeed know what to do, or how to analyze situations and implement plans of action, yet just want that "sounding board" I had once been for them. The level of unconditional relationship inherent in the psychotherapeutic relationship might still mean at times that former patients wish to run something past their former provider for input and reflection; after all, the intimacy, trust, and support in therapeutic relationships is almost unlike anything else people experience in life. Very close and special relationships are often established with patients, who come to trust in their provider's support and guidance unlike ways in which people normally might use others to evaluate potentially challenging life circumstances. I strongly suggest practitioners continue to offer this to former patients, within reason.

CONTINUED INVOLVEMENT: MENTORING PROGRAM

A common way in which some patients maintain some level of contact with me as a former treatment provider is through a mentoring program I make available to patients who have successfully "graduated" therapy. This aftercare option serves both former and future patients well.

In the mentoring program, former patients, all of whom are willing participants, serve as "mentors" for patients who are just beginning treatment and are willing to be mentored during the treatment process. Because exposure treatments require patients to experience some discomfort, I find it especially helpful for a mentor to provide his or her own perspective on just how tolerable treatment will be and to serve as an example that patients will not be pushed faster or harder than they are willing or are capable of. Additionally, when new patients see former patients and hear their stories of success and change, it automatically boosts new patients' hope and expectancy that treatment will work. Although I offer outcome findings from the literature and often provide written materials about disorders in question and the efficacy of exposure-based treatments for such problems, there seems to be something additional that former patients can offer. Often they can serve to instill a level of hope that otherwise might not have been possible. Because I know there are multiple domains (i.e., extratherapeutic variables, therapeutic variables, placebo [expectancy and hope] variables, and specific intervention variables) that influence optimal outcome (e.g., Lambert, 1992), part of my task during treatment is to ensure that I try to affect each domain directly and indirectly. The mentoring program is one way in which hope and expectancy can be bolstered.

Those former patients who agree to serve as mentors also seem to benefit from this arrangement, in that they appear to stay current with their therapy skills. In fact, those who agree to be mentors also agree to continue using their skills in life more broadly on an ongoing basis and to not stop using what they learned in treatment. On an anecdotal level at least, this seems to serve as a protective factor against relapse, which can probably be attributed to former patients continuing to use skills learned during treatment. Indeed, many mentors go on to improve further than their end-state functioning (Jacobson & Truax, 1991) as assessed at termination. Öst (1989a, 1997) describes a formal maintenance program that has been associated with larger improvements during follow-up, lower proportions of patients needing further treatment, and fewer relapses. This program emphasizes that anxiety is a normal reaction, and that fear can be manipulated with simple skills to decrease inaccurate anxiety and fear reactions. It also clarifies the difference between setbacks (lapses) and relapses and provides a formal contract for how to deal with setbacks through further practice of therapy skills. In short, it is a formal relapse prevention program. The central component is maintenance of skills learned during formal treatment and applying them both when faced with stressors and on a regular basis (i.e., when not faced with new challenges). The key aspect of success of this program is continued use of skills. The mentoring program achieves a similar outcome, if not the same, in that it asks former patients to continue practicing and using their new skills and to share their experiences with new or prospective patients.

These findings, whether more formal or more anecdotal, suggest that relapse prevention and therapeutically prudent behavior after treatment termination will enhance long-term outcome. Practitioners may wish to consider making a maintenance or mentoring program part of their aftercare plans. Most patients who successfully complete cognitive and behavioral treatments would most likely be appreciative and willing to participate in such programs, especially if these options are presented in light of what will protect and enhance maintenance and further improvements.

CHAPTER 7

Professional and Public Persona: Conclusions and Future Directions for Disseminating and Increasing Use of Exposure Treatments

The goal of education is the advancement of knowledge
and the dissemination of truth.
—John F. Kennedy

PROFESSIONAL AND PUBLIC PERCEPTIONS

Behavior therapy, and especially exposure treatment, has the unwarranted professional and public image and reputation as being especially demanding, challenging, and perhaps even cruel. This kind of reputation is actually common to many, if not most, evidence-based treatments and empirically supported treatments, as the methodology and their structured nature is steeped in controversy (e.g., Addis, 2002; Andrews et al., 2003; Garfield, 1996; Henry, 1998; Kendall, 1998b; Kettlewell, 2004; Persons & Silberschatz, 1998). Although this type of reaction may be common and, at times, zealous, it is understandable and explainable; indeed, exposure treatment can inherently make the helping professional question whether he or she is aiding the patient well, and it often naturally will violate the normal hedonistic nature common to all people. There are a multitude of reasons why evidence-based practice is negatively questioned to the extent it is, but as will be demonstrated, these strong reactions are not scientifically well-supported and tend to be predominantly subjective in nature.

For example, when a behavior therapist applies exposure methodology, clinical symptom presentations will typically worsen initially. The patient will appear to become worse, not better. To some helping professionals, especially if uninitiated or naive to the learning theories behind fears (i.e., how they start, how they are maintained, how they worsen, and how they remit), this paradoxical but normal reaction may appear counter to the overarching, guiding principle of "do no harm" (Ethical Principles of Psychologists and Code of Conduct: Principle A—Beneficence and Nonmaleficence; American Psychological Association, 2002; Canter, Bennett, Jones, & Nagy, 1994; Koocher & Keith-Spiegel, 1998). This increase in symptoms, of course, is due in large degree to reducing or stopping avoidance and escape behaviors surrounding the feared stimulus or stimuli. In fact, because the patient will be asked to purposely and systematically face thoughts and other conditions and circumstances that they historically have coped with through avoidance and escape, this predictable and worsening phenomenon *should* happen. Avoidance and escape is what has sustained—and, in many cases, worsened—their symptoms, and, with time, this all too typical maladaptive coping stance will inevitably make it increasingly difficult to challenge or tolerate the fear (e.g., Andrews et al., 2003; Barlow, 2002; Emmelkamp, Bouman, & Scholing, 1992; McLean & Woody, 2001). Fear has a natural, insidious undertow that will predictably make it worse if it is not confronted; when left alone and fueled by safety behaviors, fear will fester as readily as any other wound.

Instead, when many patients initially appear worse, it is a positive sign that the exposure treatment is working as it should; that is, symptoms need to get worse before they can improve. This initial, temporary worsening is a positive indicator because it means patients are not continually relying on their standard, maladaptive coping mechanisms; in fact, normal patient symptom fluctuations can serve as good indicators for whether or not they may be continuing to engage in safety behaviors, whether overt or covert. Such counterproductive behaviors are known to interfere with within-session and between-session habituation, and therefore play a critical role in the extinction of inaccurate reactivity and, ultimately, in the recovery from the clinical phenomenon that bring them to treatment (e.g., Johnstone & Page, 2004; Powers, Smits, & Telch, 2004; Sloan & Telch, 2002; Wells, 1997; Wells et al., 1995).

Nonetheless, if a helping professional does not understand or appreciate why this is the predictable, *normal* recovery curve, then he or she may be justifiably (albeit erroneously) alarmed by the worsening development. Indeed, a vast majority of prudent practitioners would be alarmed by a worsening symptom presentation when the treatment approach does not support such developments. After all, treating clinicians desire positive symptom change in their patients, not the opposite. Therefore, awareness of the rationale for what they observe in their patients, especially when they initially appear to regress, will be central to keeping the exposure treatment on track, and effective. Should they instead be alarmed by increasing symptoms and patient distress, no matter how normal or predictable, they may prematurely stop exposure treatment. Ironically, terminating exposure exercises before habituation is achieved will only serve to further reinforce the misperceived value of escape, through the process of negative reinforcement and the resulting net effect that prevents extinction (e.g., Antony & Swinson, 2000; Hazlett-Stevens & Craske, 2003).

This sense of relief in the moment (of stopping) will be true not only for the patient but also for the naive clinician. An experienced behavior therapist, on the other hand, will more likely be frustrated by premature termination because he or she knows the experience will negatively contribute to the patient's symptoms and likely only serve to unnecessarily prolong treatment. Because of what escape teaches people, both the unsavvy clinician and the uninformed or ill-informed patient will be less likely to reengage the exercise (i.e., more likely to avoid it), as both experienced some slight relief when they disengaged (i.e., escaped before habituation).

Thus it is *pivotal* that the treating clinician understands, or at least appreciates, the learning theories that explain habituation and extinction (chapter 2), because this will allow him or her to predict the normal course of exposure treatment, including any early regressive patterns. Additionally, the clinician may feel more at ease professionally with purposely producing increasing discomfort in the patient, instead of always feeling like he or she has to strive to reduce it. Because exposure treatment is firmly grounded in learning theory, practitioners who grasp its powerful mechanisms of change also clearly and firmly know that they are not wavering from the core ethical preamble of "do good" (beneficence) toward violating "do no harm" (nonmaleficence) by engaging patients in exposure-based treatments. Rather, they see that the effective amelioration of anxiety disorders comes through the exposure paradigm *because* it leads to extinction of inaccurate reactivity and irrational reasoning; in fact, these methods afford the practitioner to genuinely strive to benefit those with whom they work.

Yet, this technical knowledge also has to be balanced against insight into their own natural, more subjective hedonistic tendency. In the knowledge of hedonism rests understanding and insight into why delivering an exposure product may still *feel* difficult or challenging to do. Many treatment providers who choose to use these methods are well-advised to anticipate an increase in personal duress when initially delivering such products, because their sense of delivering something that clinically feels "good" may be challenged. Even after adequate training in behavior therapy, they may still feel quite uncomfortable or at least uneasy with making another person, and especially their patients, feel "bad." This phenomenon is something that many behavior therapists face, seek supervision and consultation about, and, ultimately, have to reconcile (Hembree, Rauch, & Foa, 2003). However, with a reasonable, humanely graded hierarchy of exposure exercises, there is really no sensible reason why the experiences should *not* be tolerable, both for the patient and treatment provider; nonetheless, many professionals, even with knowledge about the efficacy of exposure therapy, avoid using exposure treatments even when they are strongly indicated (e.g., Astin & Rothbaum, 2000; Becker & Zayfert, 2001; Becker, Zayfert, & Anderson, 2004; Feeny, Hembree, & Zoellner, 2003; Rothbaum, 2004; Zayfert, Becker, & Gillock, 2002).

HEDONISM 101: DESIRE AND DRIVE TO FEEL GOOD, NOT BAD

Basic human nature, on an evolutionary level, will dictate a distinct and overarching desire and drive to maximize what feels good and minimize what feels bad, which begins to explain why the public reputation might be what it is (i.e., "how could something that feels/looks/sounds *that* bad possibly be 'good'?"). It also explains, in part at least, why helping professionals may not favor delivering exposure treatments: people generally do not like feeling uncomfortable!

In the modern world, people have a difficult time overriding this basic mechanism of survival. Survival is now hard-programmed at a deep, basic level of human functioning. Through eons of evolution, this basic modus operandi increased sheer odds of survival—if it felt bad, people escaped or avoided it. On an organism level, this approach has furthered the species. In the "cave days" of human evolution, genes were passed on at a greater rate among people who were more careful and cautious with experiences that felt bad (e.g., no shelter or interacting with predators or poisonous animals) or things that tasted bad (e.g., rotten or poisonous foods). At an earlier time in human history, paying close attention and adhering to hedonistic principles made great sense, and this biological survival system served to selectively find solutions that ultimately furthered the species. In a Darwinian way, things that felt bad used to disproportionately kill people. Reasoning based on how things felt made sense because doing so served a primitive, protective factor; over time, this reasoning has followed the species into modern day (Barlow, 2002).

In the modern world, however, where people are now mostly at the top of the food chain, have much more actual control over their own destinies, and their basic needs for survival are commonly met, these old ways and primitive alarm systems make less sense than critical, creative, and meaningful thinking, planning, and behaving (Paterson, 1997a, 1997b). Although modern-world survival depends increasingly on being more thoughtful than reactive, the basic hedonistic core programming still comes with people through the eons of genetic transmittal. Now, in modern times, what feels bad or uncomfortable might actually hold much more inherent value than what necessarily makes people feel at ease, at least in the moment. This is especially true for exposure treatments, which often are described by patients as somewhat uncomfortable and mildly to moderately distressing. Yet, exposure treatments are "good" for the patients who engage in them. Furthermore, untreated anxiety disorders produce incredible intrapersonal, interpersonal, and social burdens, and costs (Greenberg et al., 1999). Certainly, it is true, both from a learning theory and sociocultural perspective, that what feels good is not always good for people. Indeed, all too often what feels good is now commonly associated with less than desirable outcomes (e.g., eating high-fat, high-sugar, high-carbohydrate diets leads to alarming rates of clinical obesity and the associated health-risk variables and problems, such as diabetes; see Newman, 2004; "Overcoming obesity in America," 2004). Conversely, what feels bad (e.g., checking blood sugar levels and injecting insulin) can be good for survival. Besides preventing real health problems, what feels uncomfortable also appears especially adept at dispelling irrational and unreasonable fears; therefore, wholesale dismissal of negative feelings and experiences is a mistake.

Although these antiquated and often unhelpful tendencies may still be prevalent in most people naturally, exposure treatments aimed at correcting inaccurate reactivity and reasoning are not—and do not have to be—sadistic per se. In fact, they are much more palatable and humane than they are sometimes pictured or fabled to be (see patient perspectives and experiences in chapter 1). This notwithstanding, exposure methods *can* truly be torturous in the hands of the uninitiated, naive, and pedantic. Professor Gallagher (Figure 7.1) illustrates this point beautifully, with a comical, absurd twist that really brings home a critical point for helping professionals who are considering using exposure methodologies.

THE FAR SIDE®   BY GARY LARSON

Professor Gallagher and his controversial technique of simultaneously confronting the fear of heights, snakes, and the dark.

FIGURE 7.1

That is, exposure tactics needs an informed, intelligent tactician (not just technician!) who can apply a variety of empirically supported procedures, such as exposure, with finesse, common sense, and measurement with an eye toward the modular assembly of a meaningful treatment for idiosyncratic patients (Hayes, Kaholokula, & Nelson, 1999; Kendall, Chu, Gifford, Hayes, & Nauta, 1998; McLean & Woody, 2001).

Professor Gallagher may indeed be applying exposure methods, but he appears to be lacking the finesse for making it useful and effective for the poor patient who may not know any better. In either case, his patient, should he survive the "treatment," is highly unlikely to return, because most anything truly traumatic will dictate a future reluctance to reexperience it (hedonism 101). Unfortunately, Professor Gallagher may even be consulting one of the many empirically based manuals available for treating anxiety disorders; only his choice of *how* he is applying the treatment appears inhumane enough that it becomes both ridiculous and comical. In the real treatment world (i.e., not research settings), manuals are often viewed to possess qualities of inhumanity, if not at least as being cold and void of warm, human relationships and connection (e.g., Addis & Krasnow, 2000; Bohart, O'Hara, & Leitner, 1998; Elliott, 1998; Lambert, 1998). The clinical relevance of manuals has also enjoyed healthy debate and their utility has often been questioned as part of the efficacy–effectiveness debate (e.g., Castonguay, Schut, Constantino, & Halperin, 1999; Fonagy, 1999; Fonagy & Target, 1996; Henry, 1998; Smith, 1995). Manuals, and those who deliver manualized treatments, may be seen and experienced as punishing agents. In the hands of a Professor Gallagher, it may indeed be punishing because the treatment may be delivered in an unimaginative, pedantic, and unempathetic fashion (i.e., cookie-cutter/cookbook style manner). Many studies have examined practitioner attitudes and practices toward manuals and generally find the field of opinions of treatment providers divided between those who understand how to use manual-based and evidence-based approaches effectively and those who feel threatened by structured, empirically based methods (e.g., Addis, 1997; Addis, Hatgis, Soysa, Zaslavsky, & Bourne, 1999; Addis & Krasnow, 2000; Addis, Wade, & Hatgis, 1999; Craighead & Craighead, 1998; Hayes, Kaholokula, & Nelso, 1999; Kendall, 1998b; Najavits, Weiss, Shaw, & Dierberger, 2000; Silverman, 1996).

Indeed, what Professor Gallagher appears to be using is *flooding*, which is an established exposure technique; however, it is broadly recognized and accepted as less effective than systematic hierarchical exposure (e.g., Craske, 1999). Most behavior therapists would not use the flooding method of exposure as a first-line or preferred treatment because the long-term maintenance of gains made during flooding is not nearly as good as that made with gradual, hierarchical exposure. Flooding also has the distinct disadvantage of being substantially more difficult to endure, and could easily be viewed or construed as cruel and sadistic, especially if it were ever delivered without fully informed consent. A pivotal part of the consent to treatment is a transparent and thorough explanation of the rationale for the procedure so the patient appreciates why he or she will be asked to engage in the anxiety-provoking exercises (Miller, in press). Without a clear rationale and directions for why and how to properly engage exposure, experiencing something distressing makes as much sense as jumping into the deep end of a pool when one cannot swim to overcome a fear of water.

Unfortunately, the public, and some professionals, too, commonly mistake gradual, hierarchical exposure, which is eminently doable and absolutely tolerable, for flooding, which for many people, for reasons blatantly obvious in the Professor Gallagher cartoon, seem too challenging, demanding, and even cruel. In fact, helping professionals who deliver the flooding procedure may be seen as cruel and inhumane, or, in short, as sadists. Delivering flooding without a rationale or purpose could easily be construed as terrorizing the patient. The problem really is, because flooding is not used much, that the consuming public erroneously has construed exposure methods broadly as being similar to—or, in fact, the same as—flooding.

Most patients have serious doubts about—and often do—decline flooding treatment, understandably; there is little wonder why so many view exposure methods with great suspicion and distrust, when flooding is held out as the public persona or exemplar of exposure. It would only be natural to view something extremely challenging with caution and to really wonder what kind of person would wish to deliver such methods to another. Under such circumstances, the public and professionals alike can readily deduce exposure and those who deliver it as at least mean-spirited, if not worse; however, without adequate information about how systematic, hierarchical and gradual exposure truly works, the information used to reason with in the inferential process is primarily based on how it feels. Unfortunately, around fears and other unpleasant experiences, many people automatically reason with how it feels. That is, if it feels bad, it becomes bad; bidirectional reasoning, or emotional reasoning, thus reifies the belief into a "truth" or absolute that too often is not questioned (Arntz, Rauner, & Van den Hout, 1995).

So, why is exposure treatment often viewed so poorly, even in light of the commonly profound changes such methods can produce? In short, there are probably a few Professor Gallaghers in the world (i.e., a few practitioners truly do not know what they are doing and are unduly torturous in their misguided approaches to exposure work), information about evidence-based practice has not been adequately disseminated to helping professionals and the public, and people reason with how it feels when they think about facing their worst fears (flooding). In sum, the reputation is understandable and explainable, but not deserved. Much could be done to alleviate these problems, however.

RESEARCH-PRACTICE GAP

As the psychotherapy industry moves increasingly toward empirically supported treatments and procedures, one fact has remained true since the conception of structured, directive, manual-based, and now even evidence-based treatments. These established efficacious, powerful treatments are grossly underused, despite their proven effective nature. The research and practice gaps still exist, and such an antagonistic relationship unfortunately continues to contribute to the less than optimal reputation exposure methods still endure. This astonishing fact does not only influence the reputation associated with exposure but more poignantly continues to closely shape what it brings up for the helping professional exploring the use of such methods (i.e., beyond fundamental theoretical orientation debates, controversy, and suspicion).

If certain methods have been shown to work better and more consistently for certain types of psychological problems, why is there resistance among so many helping professionals to using these established treatments? If barriers to the adequate dissemination and usage of treatment protocols and specific procedures are to be sufficiently overcome, then it behooves academicians, researchers, clinicians, and practitioners to stop debating the merits of the treatments (i.e., the content) and shift their focus to addressing the objections (i.e., the process). When at an impasse, which outcome researchers and practitioners are irrefutably at, then shifting tactics may be in order. Instead of continuing to ask *why* practitioners are not adopting and using these methods (after all, the procedures in question clearly work, and typically work very well at that), let those invested in the outcome instead focus on *how* it is practitioners are choosing not to do so. There must be reasons, because there always are in two sides of an argument, for what is important enough to the everyday practitioner that he or she decides to resist something that clearly has been illustrated to help patients' specific problems.

Addis, Wade, and Hatgis (1999) put forth that the arguments and resistance centrally surround six main areas, or themes: (1) negative effects on the therapy relationship, (2) unmet client needs, (3) poor competence and job satisfaction, (4) low treatment credibility, (5) gross restriction of clinical innovation, and (6) low feasibility of manual-based treatments. In examining each of these areas carefully, it will be important to set the stage for a critical discussion; thus, it is important to point out that real-world treatment settings where the everyday practitioner delivers his or her treatment products are not the same as the academic or research settings in that the efficacy of various methodologies are established in large, randomized, controlled trials. The way in which a protocol or a manual is used can look very different between settings, but then again not. Having used protocols in both kinds of worlds and in managed care settings, I will lend my own experience of differences and similarities as case in point illustrations and make a strong argument for increasing the innovative use and adoption of protocols and procedures in everyday treatment settings.

From a critical perspective of what works in therapy, and being mindful of the current state of health care's (appropriate) demand for accountability and cost-containment, it would seem that science and practice should fit together like a hand and glove. Alas, the truth is far from such a perfect match; research and practice have enjoyed a very uncomfortable, almost dichotomous relationship. This is largely because of, as in many couples and dyads of all sorts, differing communication styles and difficulties in hearing one another. Nonetheless, research on what works should be able to offer practitioners many worthwhile products, which should make them feel effective, productive, and cost-conscientious when they choose to use them. Because most practitioners do not use manual-based treatments in their everyday practice, the next commonsense (process-oriented) step is to examine the typical objections. This exploration should not be performed in an effort to necessarily refute concerns and prove practitioners wrong, but should instead aim at seeing what some of the common misconceptions are about protocol-driven treatment products. Such misconceptions and concerns are largely responsible for the transportability problem facing research in disseminating highly efficacious products; ultimately, issues of transportability are why many patients are faced with less than optimally effective treatments (treatment as usual), and have a difficult time finding practitioners using such products as standard practice.

First, there is often the suggestion made that protocols are cold, calculating, and void of any human connection, when compared with treatment as usual. From the practitioner perspective, it is feared that rapport building will have to be abandoned in favor of delivering lock-step, authoritarian products, or that it will be impossible to develop and maintain a therapeutic relationship if a manual is used. Several authors (e.g., Raue, Goldfried, & Barkham, 1997) point to the important contribution relationship makes in producing positive change, so it would be foolhardy to try to suggest that relationship is irrelevant. Neither do manualized-driven or protocol-driven products actually suggest this to be true, however. Therapeutic relationship matters a great deal, in fact. In many psychology graduate training programs, students are often taught rapport building *before* actual intervention skills. This is done for good reason: relationship is paramount for optimal outcome.

For example, the literature on the comparative effectiveness of computer-assisted and therapist-directed treatment is quite clear: Patients need a human therapist to be best helped (e.g., Ackerman & Hilsenroth, 2003). Therefore, the more like a cold computer the practitioner becomes in trying to deliver a standard product, the greater the threat to the therapeutic alliance and outcome. It should be mentioned, of course, that there is no requirement for "therapeutic coldness" in delivering a protocol-driven product or procedure. Pedantically delivering a manualized product makes no sense at all, in fact, because rigid adherence to rules is likely to disturb the therapy relationship; however, it makes equally little sense to suggest one would have to be an unfeeling pedant to deliver a standardized product. In fact, in my own years in efficacy research settings and managed care settings, I have yet to meet such a pedant or anyone else void of human feeling and without desire for connection. If anything, what my experience in such settings does suggest it is that researchers are extremely vested in enhancing every aspect of the products they develop to increase the odds of ameliorating human suffering. Rapport and therapeutic relationship is paramount in their minds, and their products necessarily and purposely incorporate relationship-enhancing components to help the specific interventions to work as intended (e.g., therapist is portrayed as active collaborator or coach, clarifying expectations and responsibilities for therapist and patient, talking about concerns or thoughts about procedures, homework assignments, getting patient input/ratings for how productive, useful, and helpful each therapy session is). Because efficacy studies show such good results, it can virtually be presumed that the protocols used necessarily *have* to include relationship enhancing variables or they could not possibly find the strong results they do.

Relationship is a necessary component of any treatment, but it can also easily be argued that it is not necessary *and* sufficient. Having a great therapeutic relationship is inherently clinically valuable, but relationship alone can be incapable of changing specific symptoms patients suffer with. Specific, concrete intervention procedures are needed to affect such change, but interventions cannot be delivered in a relationship vacuum. Because of the field's professional investment in facilitating maximal or optimal outcomes in patients, some have indeed argued that practitioners should ask themselves whether they have *both* relationship and effective, targeted interventions—the necessary and sufficient combination for successful outcomes (Nezu, 1996). It is also clear that patients rate practitioners who are directive and use concrete, specifically targeted interventions as more caring, empathic, and professional than nondirective therapists; indeed, as is evidenced in the patient accounts in chapter 1, perhaps protocols and procedures really serve to enhance relationship, not detract from it, and thereby also encourage strongly positive outcomes. At least, let it be clearly stated that being directive *and* warm are not mutually exclusive skills; thus, the suggestion that the practitioner who delivers protocol-driven products is a "technician," void of feeling and caring, simply does not pass the test of both scientific logic and more subjective commonsense.

Second, the argument is also often made that manual-based or *standardized* (i.e., nomothetic) products ignore individual or idiosyncratic (i.e., ideographic) differences. In essence, the accusation is that manuals view all patients and problems as being the same or that manuals are cookbooks that are indiscriminately used to treat every single patient using the same recipe over and over again in a "cookie cutter" fashion. If this were true, then the patient would be forced to fit the mold of the manual, instead of the manual materials modularly being fitted to match patient concerns.

Because many, if not most, manuals are cognitive behavioral in their base, this simply is not realistically possible. Cognitive-behavioral theory is predicated on the view that people are made up of interdependent feelings, thoughts, and behaviors, often also integrating the person's interdependent interactions with various social systems surrounding them. The treatment components found within protocols inevitably address these various areas of personal functioning, and therefore cannot ignore what a person feels, thinks, does, and what systems within which the person struggles. What a person feels, thinks, and does is inherently personal, and can vary both broadly and narrowly from one patient to the next. Addis, Wade, and Hatgis (1999) accurately report that there is no evidence to support the idea that individual, idiosyncratic needs are unmet by standardized treatments. I would go a step further to suggest that because of cognitive-behavioral theory's view of human functioning, CBT will by default look at idiosyncratic areas of functioning; indeed, cognitive-behavioral therapy, and by default manual-based treatment, is by fundamental design going to address individual differences, not ignore them.

A variation on the argument that manuals do not address individual needs is that manuals do not meet the needs of comorbidity. That is, the argument goes, manuals and protocols cannot address the complex needs of real patients in everyday treatment settings who do not present with clean, single diagnoses. Because in everyday practice, manuals tend to be used in a modular fashion (i.e., apropos modules from various manuals are drawn together as idiosyncratically indicated by individual patients' treatment needs), this concern appears on initial inspection to be somewhat moot. However, when the evidence is also carefully examined about whether or not multiple problems negatively affect outcome, Addis et al. (1999) further reported that comorbidity does not predict treatment response and results of applying manualized treatments to comorbid conditions are comparable to results found in studies carefully screening out comorbidity. Comorbidity seems to be less of an issue than the critics may fear, and there is indeed mounting evidence (e.g., Borkovec, Abel, & Newman, 1995; Lehman, Brown, & Barlow, 1998; Wade, Treat, & Stuart, 1998) that standardized treatment outcome effects generalize to other, not specifically treated issues.

Third, and perhaps more understandable than the previous two arguments, some practitioners may fear and be intimidated by manual-based treatments. After all, no helping professional, whether researcher or practitioner, wants to feel ineffective or incompetent. Because empirically supported approaches frequently produce such strong, positive changes (i.e., frequently in excess of effect size = 1.00), it can logically be reasoned that a common fear pertains to how an individual therapist will measure up with his or her own patients against intimidatingly strong efficacy results. In today's environment, in which reimbursement by third-party payers and managed care may also be tied to performance and outcome, appearing not as adept compared with strong findings prevalent in the literature can easily be experienced as extremely threatening. After all, most practitioners are unlikely to have chosen their field of work simply because they like the work. Pragmatically, most practitioners are also overwhelmingly likely to be trying to make a living. Indeed, if income becomes tied to adopting and using empirically supported approaches, then there is a much greater pressure to be at least proficient if not outright good at it. To date, unfortunately, there are very few strong training programs that provide systematic training in evidence-based procedures. Additionally, since the dissemination of research findings from academic and efficacy research settings have largely failed to adequately reach the average practitioner, many are left with only tertiary insights and experience with such methods.

Is it any mystery, given what is potentially at stake (e.g., self-efficacy, livelihoods), especially in light of the general lack of available training opportunities, that the empirical approaches are often seen as the school yard bully or big brother? Given the current health care climate, empirically oriented treatments are becoming further politicized by showing up in practice guidelines and expert consensus, which collectively can have the air of suggesting practitioners who choose to not adopt and regularly use such methods are equivalent to rogue elements. The assertion there is a civil war raging within psychotherapy is not far from the truth. From limited work examining therapist satisfaction with these approaches, when adequately trained and supervised in their proper use, emerges the knowledge that practitioners do *not* find them uncreative, constraining, boring, or unfulfilling (Addis et al., 1999). This is further supported by my own anecdotal experience in training many predoctoral and postdoctoral psychologists and psychiatrists in evidence-based and manual-based approaches. Overwhelmingly, I have found that practitioners who have adopted these methods find the work to be the most satisfying work they have done, because patients often positively change in profound ways. There is commonly a great deal of excitement about learning how to *properly* use manuals and protocols in everyday practice, and the vast majority of practitioners I have trained have no significant difficulty adopting and correctly using the strategies.

Fourth, some practitioners do not feel manuals and protocols are credible. Indeed, the field is roughly split between those practitioners who believe manual-based treatment will positively influence outcome and those who believe it will negatively shape results. Practitioner attitudes about whether empirical approaches will help or hurt seem to be more a product of what individual practitioners believe a manual is. Some see it as an imposed evil, as something that will suck the life out of the art they are delivering, and something that will stifle creativity in this privileged work. Such antiempirical practitioners may never see eye to eye with those who, instead, see manual-based treatment as a solid foundation for individualized case formulation and idiographic, flexible treatment. Ultimately, practitioners are the end-users of manuals, and as such there may be both pragmatic and philosophical concerns about adaptation and utilization of such systems for operation.

Fifth, some practitioners have concerns about being supplanted by technicians, or that restrictions in clinical innovations (i.e., rigidity) will result. As reported earlier, human therapists do better than computerized treatment, suggesting that a technician could never fully replace the many sophisticated functions a well-trained and seasoned helping professional brings to treatment. There may be some minimal aspects or functions that could be performed by someone less trained and experienced, but for the everyday patients seen on the front lines of community-level care it is highly unlikely that a technician can adequately and fully take over.

It is clear, at least from a non-antiempirical perspective, that manual-based approaches do not employ rigidity in treatment. Nor is it a requirement to deliver such methods in a lock-step, unempathic fashion; in fact, there are many safeguards built into such protocols to facilitate human connection and trust. Although protocols are science-based, there is no lack of art in them and in their application. In fact, such approaches can even enhance innovations. Consider just for a moment all of what has become known about the mechanism of psychopathology and its change through the development and testing of empirical interventions. Through empiricism, new answers have been discovered, effective help has been delivered to millions of sufferers worldwide, and new ideas for better preparing the health care field for the demands of an ever-growing population have been developed and implemented. At least from the perspective of science, innovation and progress have been enhanced and fueled by these kinds of approaches, not the opposite. Then again, fear is often not rational!

Also, there are at times questions on the topic of feasibility. These are important questions because they address such issues of training in—and implementation of—evidence-based treatments. This is what the push for dissemination has focused on and has proportionately failed at producing; such a lack of transportation of the approaches and their use point to this area as a centrally important topic. Within this topic is also imbedded the question about how well patients view and accept these treatments.

In terms of training, these approaches present a bit of an enigma in that there are not that many programs that provide strong foundation training in these types of methods. Most doctor of philosophy, doctor of psychology, masters of science, and masters of arts programs are generalist programs that focus more exclusively in providing training in the basics of psychotherapy (e.g., relationship). Few provide, as a standard, the opportunity for learning how to use manuals and protocols properly in everyday settings (and in research, for that matter). Collectively, the most common experience is that many practitioners have to obtain this specialized knowledge and experience after earning their degree. This presents a unique challenge within health care in which many practitioners' workdays are already filled with various activities, leaving little room for consuming research findings or reading treatment manuals. Yet, the political and social environment is such that there is an increasing push for asking such practitioners to use the very methods they have not been trained in. Inadvertently, this complex circumstance of "socio-politico-medico" need is fueling many of these fears. Knowing the existing demands, I have begun strongly recommending that my graduate students read, study, and practice with one manual every semester, above and beyond what they will learn about in my courses already. When they finish I know they will not have as much free time to devote to additional training.

From a training perspective, still, I am also teaching graduate students an important if not pivotal clinical skill that is failure analysis. Many practitioners exhibit concerns, if not outright fears, that they will not do well using a protocol treatment. Sometimes, especially when the practitioner expects to not do well, this becomes a self-fulfilling prophecy and he or she actually does not do well delivering manual-based help. The patient appears to worsen, when he or she should not. For skeptics of manuals, this might be enough to make them quickly abandon manuals; after all, their fears were confirmed. In such a position, when treatment is not going as well as anticipated, practitioners would do well to not throw out the baby (i.e., prospective progress and strong positive change) with the bathwater (i.e., the manual). Instead, it would serve them and their patients well if they carefully examined and analyzed why the intervention did not work as anticipated. If practitioners always threw out something that did not work with a particular patient, they would be left with no remaining strategies in the end to help anyone with.

Rather than focus on failing per se, it becomes more important to pick one's pride off of the floor and look at what might have contributed to the "failure." In training graduate students and preparing them to use these methods, I remind them that it is not so much whether they will encounter failure but rather when that will happen; therefore, I teach them the willingness to critically examine treatments that "go wrong" for the hints that explain the controlling variables that produced such an outcome. In this close evaluation of the contingencies that produced the outcome can the answers often be discovered for what would turn the progress from unexpectedly negative to back on a normally antici- pated (positive) trajectory of progress. Of course, this can only happen when the practitioner does not abandon the method wholesale at the first sign of weakness or failure. In training various professionals on the topic, I work hard at instilling the ideal that mistakes are not to be feared because there really are none. A mistake, a failure, or any other descrip- tion of less than expected progress should not be a threat automatically, but should instead be seen as an opportunity to further understand the individual aspects that make the patients who they are. "Failures" are opportunities for strengthening bonds and greater understanding and appreciation. Working from a manual or protocol requires a willingness to investigate causes for questionable performance. Following a proto- col does not equate to a lack of panache; if practitioners do not readily abandon their own favored ways of intervening with human suffering, why think that stopping the use of manuals makes any more sense. I would like to preserve the belief that practitioners generally are not so bigoted as to not explore that which feels different from their own modus operandi. Nonetheless, people tend to fear and reject what is different. This happens most frequently under two polar opposites, either when people are unaware or when people are very clear that they do not see the merit. Most who approach something new with balance and openness will grow and learn from the willingness to do so, much like diversity is inherently good for the well-being of any group.

Last, on the topic of whether empirically oriented treatments will be acceptable to patients, there are typical concerns that manual-based approaches will seem less than credible, will seem too artificial or hokey, and patients ultimately will not return. Although these are common fears, studies conducted both nationally and internationally suggest that these approaches transport and generalize well to private practice setting and a range of everyday treatment settings and are in many cases preferable to treatment as usual (e.g., Warren, 1995; Wilson, 1996, 1998). Without the adequate dissemination and thorough use of these kinds of approaches, however, practitioners cannot have their faulty beliefs corrected through the experience of not seeing patients treated in this manner disproportionately fleeing services. Without the use of these methods, the best of critics are really acting in the absence of evidence that would elucidate their concerns. Many who get an adequate orientation to and training in these methods find them quite useful and welcome new skill sets into their repertoire of therapy tools. Some overconfident and antiempirical practitioners will likely never see the bona fide utility of these ways, and will consequently be unlikely to employ them. For good or bad, the current health care system has made practitioners take a closer look at these approaches, and most are now viewing them favorably. In the end, the patient is the beneficiary who ultimately will show everyone, through his or her progress and functioning, what works, for whom, and when.

FUTURE DIRECTIONS AND RECOMMENDATIONS

Eleanor Roosevelt once said, "You must do the thing you think you cannot do." She was obviously a wise woman, and clinical and counseling psychology would do well to earnestly take on this admonition in shifting increasingly toward using empirical evidence to inform and guide psychotherapy practice. For good or bad, this shift is happening, and this is a psychological reality for increasing numbers of practitioners, making dissemination and transportation of evidence-based approaches crucial. Even when a practitioner honestly believes that a manual-based approach is wrong, for all of the stated concerns and reasons, I would go even further to exhort them to at least give empirical treatments a fair trial and see what the outcomes can be. They should at least *try* to do the things they think they cannot. I cannot make them use exposure treatments, but I will ask them to investigate, properly, what could be discovered, learned, and used.

Exposure Treatments for Anxiety Disorders may go a little further in planting the seeds of curiosity and willingness to put controversy aside and *try* exposure interventions with patients who clearly would stand to benefit from their use. Exposure techniques have a long and strongly established history. True, they have not been without controversy, but in movement toward increasingly using supported treatments, they are likely to see more of the light of day. However, to not be a Professor Gallagher, it will be important to train practitioners in the correct and humane use of these powerful methods.

I became what I am today the day I found myself curious with wonderment. That miraculous day happened long before my own discovery of behavioral learning theory and what could be realized through its systematic application to anxiety disorders. It began a long time ago when as a child, I was seeking to know and understand just how the world and all in it work. Unfortunately, I lost touch with that sense of wonder and questioning for some time. Then, learning how to conduct behavior therapy allowed me to rediscover that sense of wonder and natural curiosity again. The best surveys (e.g., Addis & Krasnow, 2000) suggest practitioners' attitudes may stand in their way of rediscovering science-based and manual-based practice, the pathways to wonderment and curiosity. I suspect these attitudes are reflective of subjective practitioner fears, but my sense of it is that our fears have led us astray. In this realization, I am reminded of a passage from Dante's Inferno (from *The Divine Comedy*): "In the midway of this our mortal life, I find me in a gloomy wood, astray gone from the *path direct*" (Dante, 1909, p. 1). Behavior therapy, and more explicitly exposure therapy, is conceptually that path direct from which practitioners have strayed. We must reacquaint ourselves with direct paths to human well-being, and stop straying far and wide from what can be supported as ameliorating suffering. We may have to go out on a limb; after all, if we do not, how can we reach the fruit?

Fears are just that: fears. If practitioners fear using exposure, then it would suggest this fear would be best treated by using this methodology with patients. There is no better way than exposure to test our subjective beliefs. For some, this may require a shift toward empiricism and measurement. This, I am arguing, may not be so bad, because it will promote further fascination and intrigue through compelling findings. Training in how to conduct evidence-based practice comes both through education and practice; therefore, practitioners should seek out both to gain familiarity with empirical methods.

In closing, I am reminded of one of my former patients who insightfully offered that she was so grateful for having expanded her life to its fullest after undergoing treatment and that she felt exposure therapy was the only therapy that "worked." Profound statements like this remind me every day that exposure works (it is efficacious), it works for lots of different kinds of problems in everyday treatment settings (it is effective), and it works relatively quickly (it is efficient). Her happiness and newfound well being suggest that exposure treatments deserve more attention and use. Practitioners need more training and experience with these potent ways of changing pathological anxiety and fear. Start early. Start now. There is much work to be done. Martin Luther King is quoted as saying, "The time is always right to do what is right." Consider what time it is ... (see Figure 7.2).

FIGURE 7.2 A call to action.

Manuals and
Other Resources

Anger

Deffenbacher, J. L., & McKay, M. (2000). *Overcoming situational and general anger: A protocol for the treatment of anger based on relaxation, cognitive restructuring, and coping skills training (therapist protocol).* Oakland, CA: New Harbinger.

Deffenbacher, J. L., & McKay, M. (2000). *Overcoming situational and general anger: A protocol for the treatment of anger based on relaxation, cognitive restructuring, and coping skills training (client manual).* Oakland, CA: New Harbinger.

McKay, M., & Rogers, P. (2000). *The anger control workbook.* Oakland, CA: New Harbinger.

Depression

Emery, G. (2000). *Overcoming depression: A cognitive-behavior protocol for the treatment of depression (therapist protocol).* Oakland, CA: New Harbinger.

Emery, G. (2000). *Overcoming depression: A cognitive-behavior protocol for the treatment of depression (client manual).* Oakland, CA: New Harbinger.

Gilson, M., & Freeman, A. (1999). *Overcoming depression: A cognitive therapy approach to taming the depression BEAST (client workbook).* San Antonio, TX: Psychological Corporation.

Greenberger, D., & Padesky, C. A. (1995). *Mind over mood: A cognitive therapy treatment manual for clients.* New York: Guilford.

Martell, C. R., Addis, M. E., & Jacobson, N. S. (2001). *Depression in context: Strategies for guided action.* New York: Norton.

Padesky, C. A., & Greenberger, D. (1995). *Clinician's guide to mind over mood.* New York: Guilford.

Paterson, R .J. (2002). *Your depression map.* Oakland, CA: New Harbinger.
Persons, J. B., Davidson, J., & Tompkins, M. A. (2001). *Essential components of cognitive-behavioral therapy for depression.* Washington, DC: American Psychological Association.
Schiraldi, G. R. (2001). *The self-esteem workbook.* Oakland, CA: New Harbinger.
Segal, Z. V., Williams, J. M. G., & Teasdale, J. D. (2002). *Mindfulness-based cognitive therapy for depression: A new approach to preventing relapse.* New York: Guilford.
Weissman, M. M. (1995). *Mastering depression through interpersonal psychotherapy (client workbook).* San Antonio, TX: Psychological Corporation.
Weissman, M. M. (1995). *Mastering depression through interpersonal psychotherapy (monitoring forms booklet).* San Antonio, TX: Psychological Corporation.

Generalized Anxiety

Craske, M. G., Barlow, D. H., & O'Leary, T. A. (1992). *Mastery of your anxiety and worry (client workbook).* San Antonio, TX: Psychological Corporation.
Rugh, J. L., & Sanderson, W. C. (2004). *Treating generalized anxiety disorder: Evidence-based strategies, tools, and techniques.* New York: Guilford Press.
White, J. (1999). *Overcoming generalized anxiety disorder: A relaxation, cognitive restructuring, and exposure-based protocol for the treatment of GAD (therapist protocol).* Oakland, CA: New Harbinger.
White, J. (1999). *Overcoming generalized anxiety disorder: A relaxation, cognitive restructuring, and exposure-based protocol for the treatment of GAD (client manual).* Oakland, CA: New Harbinger.
Zinbarg, R. E., Craske, M. G., & Barlow, D. H. (1993). *Mastery of your anxiety and worry (therapist guide).* San Antonio, TX: Psychological Corporation.

Obsessive-Compulsive Disorder

Foa, E. B., & Kozak, M. J. (1997). *Mastery of obsessive-compulsive disorder (client workbook).* San Antonio, TX: Psychological Corporation.
Hyman, B. M., & Pedrick, C. (1999). *The OCD workbook: Your guide to breaking free from obsessive-compulsive disorder.* Oakland, CA: New Harbinger.

Steketee, G. (1999). *Overcoming obsessive-compulsive disorder: A behavioral and cognitive protocol for the treatment of OCD (therapist protocol)*. Oakland, CA: New Harbinger.

Steketee, G. (1999). *Overcoming obsessive-compulsive disorder: A behavioral and cognitive protocol for the treatment of OCD (client manual)*. Oakland, CA: New Harbinger.

Panic and Agoraphobia

Barlow, D. H., & Craske, M. G. (2000). *Mastery of your anxiety and panic (MAP-3): Client workbook for anxiety and panic:* (3rd ed.). San Antonio, TX: Graywind/Psychological Corporation.

Craske, M. G., & Barlow, D. H. (2000). *Mastery of your anxiety and panic: Client workbook for agoraphobia (MAP-3)* (3rd ed.). San Antonio, TX: Psychological Corporation.

Craske, M. G., Barlow, D. H., & Meadows, E. A. (2000). *Mastery of your anxiety and panic: Therapist guide for anxiety, panic, and agoraphobia (MAP-3)* (3rd ed.). San Antonio, TX: Psychological Corporation.

Otto, M. W., Jones, J. C., Craske, M. G., & Barlow, D. H. (1996). *Stopping anxiety medication: Panic control therapy for benzodiazepine discontinuation (therapist guide)*. San Antonio, TX: Psychological Corporation.

Otto, M. W., Pollack, M. H., & Barlow, D. H. (1995). *Stopping anxiety medication: Panic control therapy for benzodiazepine discontinuation (patient workbook)*. San Antonio, TX: Psychological Corporation.

Zuercher-White, E. (1999). *Overcoming panic disorder and agoraphobia: A cognitive restructuring and exposure-based protocol for the treatment of panic and agoraphobia (therapist protocol)*. Oakland, CA: New Harbinger.

Zuercher-White, E. (1999). *Overcoming panic disorder and agoraphobia: A cognitive restructuring and exposure-based protocol for the treatment of panic and agoraphobia (client manual)*. Oakland, CA: New Harbinger.

Zuercher-White, E. (1999). *Treating panic disorder and agoraphobia: A step-by-step clinical guide*. Oakland, CA: New Harbinger.

Posttraumatic Stress Disorder

Rothbaum, B. O., & Foa, E. B. (1999). *Reclaiming your life after rape: Cognitive-behavioral therapy for posttraumatic stress disorder (client workbook)*. San Antonio, TX: Psychological Corporation.

Smyth, L. (1999). *Overcoming post-traumatic stress disorder: A cognitive-behavioral exposure-based protocol for the treatment of PTSD and the other anxiety disorders (therapist protocol)*. Oakland, CA: New Harbinger.

Smyth, L. (1999). *Overcoming post-traumatic stress disorder: A cognitive-behavioral exposure-based protocol for the treatment of PTSD and the other anxiety disorders (client manual)*. Oakland, CA: New Harbinger.

Williams, M. B., & Poijula, S. (2002). *The PTSD workbook: Simple, effective techniques for overcoming traumatic stress symptoms*. Oakland, CA: New Harbinger.

Social Anxiety

Heimburg, R. G., & Becker, R. E. (2002). *Cognitive-behavioral group therapy for social phobia: Basic mechanisms and clinical strategies*. New York: Guilford.

Hope, D. A., Heimburg, R. G., Juster, H. R., & Turk, C. L. (2000). *Managing social anxiety: A cognitive-behavioral therapy approach*. San Antonio, TX: Psychological Corporation.

Specific Phobia

Bourne, E. J. (1998). *Overcoming specific phobia: A hierarchy and exposure-based protocol for the treatment of all specific phobias (therapist protocol)*. Oakland, CA: New Harbinger Press.

Bourne, E. J. (1998). *Overcoming specific phobia: A hierarchy and exposure-based protocol for the treatment of all specific phobias (client manual)*. Oakland, CA: New Harbinger Press.

Substance Use

Daley, D. C., & Marlatt, G. A. (1997). *Managing your drug or alcohol problem (therapist guide)*. San Antonio, TX: Psychological Corporation.

Daley, D. C., & Marlatt, G. A. (1997). *Managing your drug or alcohol problem (client workbook)*. San Antonio, TX: Psychological Corporation.

Generic/General

Antony, M. M., & Swinson, R. P. (2000). *Phobic disorders and panic in adults: A guide to assessment and treatment*. Washington, DC: American Psychological Association.

Claiborn, J., & Pedrick, C. (2001). *The habit change workbook*. Oakland, CA: New Harbinger.

Hasselt, V. B. Van & Hersen, M. (Eds.) (1996). *Sourcebook of psychological treatment manuals for adult disorders*. New York: Plenum.

Leahy, R. L. (2000). *Treatment plans and interventions for depression and anxiety disorders*. New York: Guilford Press.

Narrow-Band Instruments Commonly Used in Cognitive-Behavioral Practice

1. Panic and Agoraphobia

   Agoraphobic Cognitions Questionnaire (ACQ)
   Anxiety Sensitivity Index (ASI)
   Body Sensations Interpretation Questionnaire (BSIQ)
   Body Sensations Questionnaire (BSQ)
   Mobility Inventory for agoraphobia (MI)
   Panic and Agoraphobia Scale (PAS)
   Panic Diary (PD)
   Panic Disorder Severity Scale (PDSS)

2. Specific Phobia

   Acrophobia Questionnaire (AQ)
   Blood-Injection Symptom Scale (BISS)
   Claustrophobia General Cognitions Questionnaire (CGCQ)
   Claustrophobia Situations Questionnaire (CSQ)
   Claustrophobia Questionnaire (CLQ)
   Dental Anxiety Inventory (DAI)
   Dental Cognitions Questionnaire (DCQ)
   Dental Fear Survey (DFS)
   Dog Phobia Questionnaire (DPQ)
   Fear of Flying Scale (FFS)
   Fear of Spiders Questionnaire (FSQ)
   Medical Fear Survey (MFS)
   Snake Questionnaire (SNAQ)

Spider Phobia Beliefs Questionnaire (SBQ)
Spider Questionnaire (SPQ)

3. Social Anxiety Disorder

Liebowitz Social Anxiety Scale (LSAS)
Self-Statements during Public Speaking scale (SSPS)
Social Phobia and Anxiety Inventory (SPAI)
Social Phobia Inventory (SPIN)
Social Phobia Scale (SPS)
Social Interaction Anxiety Scale (SIAS)

4. Obsessive-Compulsive Disorder

Interpretations of Intrusions scale (III)
Maudsley Obsessional Compulsive Inventory (MOCI)
Obsessive Beliefs Questionnaire (OBQ)
Obsessive Compulsive Inventory (OCI)
Overvalued Ideation Scale (OVIS)
Responsibility Attitude Scale (RAS)
Responsibility Interpretations Questionnaire (RIQ)
Symmetry, Ordering, and Arranging Questionnaire (SOAQ)
Thought-Action Fusion scale (TAF scale)
Yale-Brown Obsessive-Compulsive Scale (Y-BOCS)

5. Posttraumatic Stress Disorder

Accident Fear Questionnaire (AFQ)
Dissociative Experiences Scale (DES)
Distressing Event Questionnaire (DEQ)
Impact of Event Scale (IES)
Posttraumatic Cognitions Inventory (PTCI)
Trauma-Related Guilt inventory (TRGI)
Trauma Symptom Inventory (TSI)
Traumatic Life Events Questionnaire (TLEQ)

6. Generalized Anxiety Disorder

Anxious Thoughts Inventory (AnTI)
Intolerance for Uncertainty Scale (IUS)
Meta Cognitions Questionnaire (MCQ)
Penn State Worry Questionnaire (PSWQ)
Why Worry scale (WW)
Worry and Anxiety Questionnaire (WAQ)

COMPLETE REFERENCES, NORMATIVE INFORMATION, AND ADMINISTRATION FACTS

Antony, M. M, Orsillo, S. M., & Roemer, L. (Eds.). (2001). *Practitioner's guide to empirically based measures of anxiety.* New York: Kluwer/Plenum.

A REFERENCE TEXT FOR DEPRESSION

Nezu, A. M., Ronan, G. F., Meadows, E. A., & McClure, K. S. (2000). *Practitioner's guide to empirically based measures of depression.* New York: Kluwer/Plenum.

Data Necessary From a Narrow-Band Instrument to Assess Meaningful Change in Therapy

SYMBOL	DEFINITION
M_0	Clinical mean on narrow-band instrument of choice
M_1	Normal population mean on narrow-band instrument
S_0	Clinical standard deviation on instrument
S_1	Normal population deviation on instrument
r_{xx}	Test-retest reliability of the instrument in question
X_1	Patient pretreatment score on instrument
X_2	Patient posttreatment score on instrument
S_{Diff}	Standard error of difference between prescores and postscores
S_E	Standard error of measurement

Steps required to gauge meaningful clinical significance:

1. Clinical cutoff "c" formula: Threshold point between clinical and normal distributions

$$c = [(S_0 \times M_1) + (S_1 \times M_0)/S_0 + S_1]$$

2. Reliable change index (RCI) formula: Is change large enough not to be treatment effect?

$$RCI = [(X_2 - X_1)/S_{Diff}], \text{ where } S_{Diff} = \sqrt{2(S_E)^2}, \text{ and } S_E = S_1\sqrt{1 - r_{xx}}$$

3. Recovered status: Points a, b, c must all be satisfied (yes answers to a, b, and c).
   a. Did patient start in clinical distribution and finish in normal distribution?
   b. Did patient cross the clinical cutoff "c"?
   c. Did patient achieve reliable change?

Example of Calculating Clinical Significance

Instrument in question: Commonly used for:

Intolerance for uncertainty (IUS)   Generalized anxiety and most anxiety disorders

Reference

Freeston, M. H., Rheaume, J., Letarte, H., Dugas, M. J., & Ladouceur, R. (1994). Why do people worry? *Personality and Individual Differences, 17*, 791–802.

REQUIRED DATA

M_0 73.36 (clinical mean)

M_1 54.38 (normal population mean)

S_0 17.17 (clinical standard deviation)

S_1 19.07 (normal population standard)

r_{xx} 0.74 (test-retest reliability)

X_1 103 (pretreatment/baseline score)

X_2 54 (posttreatment score)

S_{Diff} 13.76 (standard error of difference between prescores and postscores)

S_E 9.73 (standard error of measurement)

$$C = \frac{(17.17 \times 73.36) + (19.07 \times 54.38)}{17.17 + 19.07}$$

$$C = \frac{S_O M_1 + S_1 M_O}{S_O + S_1}$$

Therefore:

$$C = (1259.59 + 1037.03)/36.24 = 2296.62/36.24 = 63.37$$

and:

$$RC = \frac{X_2 - X_1}{S_{diff}}$$

$$RC = (103 - 54)/13.76 = 49/13.76 = 3.56$$

and:

$$S_E = 19.07\sqrt{1 - 0.74}$$

$$S_{diff} = \sqrt{2(S_E)^2}$$

$$SE = 19.07 \times 0.51 = 9.73$$

S_{Diff} = square root of (2×94.68) = square root $189.36 = 13.76$

Summary

Patient X started in the clinical distribution, crossed the clinical cutoff point, finished in the normal distribution, and realized reliable change. Taken together, this means Patient X can be called "recovered," which is clinical language for saying he "looks" more like a functional person than a dysfunctional person (as measured by the IUS). That is, he is *indistinguishable* (on the IUS) from a person belonging to the "normals."

References

Abelson, J. L., & Curtis, G. C. (1989). Cardiac and neuroendocrine responses to exposure therapy in height phobics: Desynchrony with the physiological response system. *Behaviour Research and Therapy, 27*, 556–561.

Abrahamson, D. J. (1999). Outcomes, guidelines, and manuals: On leading horses to water. *Clinical Psychology: Science and Practice, 6*, 467–471.

Abramowitz, J. S. (2001). Treatment of scrupulous obsessions and compulsions using exposure and response prevention: A case report. *Cognitive and Behavioral Practice, 8*, 79–85.

Abramowitz, J. S. (2002). Treatment of obsessive thoughts and cognitive rituals using exposure and response prevention. *Clinical Case Studies, 1*, 6–24.

Ackerman, S. J., & Hilsenroth, M. J. (2003). A review of therapist characteristics and techniques positively impacting the therapeutic alliance. *Clinical Psychology Review, 23*, 1–33.

Addis, M. E. (1997). Evaluating the treatment manual as a means of disseminating empirically validated psychotherapies. *Clinical Psychology: Science and Practice, 4*, 1–11.

Addis, M. E. (2002). Methods for disseminating research products and increasing evidence-based practice: Promises, obstacles, and future directions. *Clinical Psychology: Science and Practice, 9*, 367–378.

Addis, M. E., Hatgis, C., Soysa, C. K., Zaslavsky, I., & Bourne, L. S. (1999). The dialectics of manual-based treatment. *The Behavior Therapist, 22*, 130–132.

Addis, M. E., & Krasnow, A. D. (2000). A national survey of practicing psychologists' attitudes towards psychotherapy treatment manuals. *Journal of Consulting and Clinical Psychology, 68*, 331–339.

Addis, M. E., Wade, W., & Hatgis, C. (1999). Barriers to dissemination of evidence-based practices: Addressing practitioners' concerns about manual-based psychotherapies. *Clinical Psychology: Science and Practice, 6*, 430–441.

Agras, W. S. (1965). An investigation of decrements of anxiety responses during systematic desensitization. *Behaviour Research and Therapy, 2*, 267–270.

Agras, W. S., Chapin, H. N., & Oliveau, D. C. (1972). The natural history of phobia. *Archives of General Psychiatry, 26*, 315–317.

American Psychiatric Association (1980). *Diagnostic and statistical manual of mental disorders* (3rd ed.). Washington, DC: Author.

American Psychiatric Association (2000). *Diagnostic and statistical manual of mental disorders* (4th ed., text revision). Washington, DC: Author.

American Psychological Association (2002). Ethical principles of psychologists and code of conduct. *American Psychologist, 57*, 1060–1073.

Andrews, G., Creamer, M., Crino, R., Hunt, C., Lampe, L., & Page, A. (2003). *The treatment of anxiety disorders: Clinician guides and patient manuals* (2nd ed.). New York: Cambridge University Press.

Antony, M. A., & Swinson, R. P. (2000). Exposure-based strategies and social skills training. In M.A. Swinson & R.P. Swinson, *Phobic disorders and panic in adults: A guide to assessment and treatment* (pp. 191–238). Washington, DC: American Psychological Association.

Antony, M. M., & Barlow, D. H. (2002). Preface. In M. M. Antony & D. H. Barlow (Eds.), *Handbook of assessment and treatment planning for psychological disorders* (pp. xiii–xv). New York: Guilford Press.

Antony, M. M., Craske, M. G., & Barlow, D. H. (1995). *Mastery of your specific phobia*. Albany, NY: Graywind Publications.

Arntz, A., Rauner, M., & Van den Hout, M. (1995). "If I feel anxious, there must be danger": Ex-consequentia reasoning in inferring danger in anxiety disorders. *Behaviour Research and Therapy, 33*, 917–925.

Astin, M., & Rothbaum, B. O. (2000). Exposure therapy for the treatment of posttraumatic stress disorder. *National Center for PTSD Clinical Quarterly, 9*, 49–54.

Azrin, N. H., Nunn, R. G., & Frantz, S. E. (1980). Treatment of hair-pulling (trichotillomania): A comparative study of habit reversal and negative practice training. *Behavior Therapy and Experimental Psychiatry, 11*, 13–20.

Baer, L. (1993). Behavior therapy for obsessive compulsive disorder in the office-based practice. *Journal of Clinical Psychiatry, 54(6 Suppl)*, 10–15.

Baer, L., & Minichiello, W. E. (1998). Behavior therapy for obsessive-compulsive disorder. In M. A. Jenike, L. Baer, & W. E. Minichiello (Eds.), *Obsessive-compulsive disorders: Practical management* (3rd ed.) (pp. 337–367). Boston: Mosby.

Ballenger, J. C. (1998). Treatment of panic disorder in the general medical setting. *Journal of Psychosomatic Research, 44*, 5–15.

Bandler, R., & Grinder, J. (1979). *Frogs into princes: Neuro-linguistic programming*. Moab, UT: Real People Press.

Barlow, D. H. (1991a). Disorders of emotion. *Psychological Inquiry, 2*, 58–71.

Barlow, D. H. (1991b). Disorders of emotions: Clarification, elaboration, and future directions. *Psychological Inquiry, 2,* 97–105.

Barlow, D. H. (2002). *Anxiety and its disorders: The nature and treatment of anxiety and panic* (2nd ed.). New York: Guilford Press.

Barlow, D. H., Cohen, A. S., Waddell, M., Vermilyea, J. A., Klosko, J. S., Blanchard, E., & DiNardo, P. A. (1984). Panic and generalized anxiety disorders: Nature and treatment. *Behavior Therapy, 15,* 431–449.

Barlow, D. H., & Craske, M. G. (1989). *Mastery of your anxiety and panic.* Albany, NY: Graywind.

Barlow, D. H., & Craske, M. G. (2000). *Mastery of your anxiety and panic (MAP-3): Client workbook for anxiety and panic* (3rd ed.). San Antonio, TX: Graywind/Psychological Corporation.

Barlow, D. H., Craske, M. G., Cerny, J. A., & Klosko, J. S. (1989). Behavioral treatment of panic disorder. *Behavior Therapy, 20,* 261–282.

Barlow, D. H., & Durand, V. M. (1999). *Abnormal psychology* (2nd ed.). Pacific Grove, CA: Brooks/Cole Publishing.

Barlow, D. H., Gorman, J. M., Shear, M. K., & Woods, S. W. (2000). Cognitive-behavioral therapy, imipramine, or their combination for panic disorder: A randomized controlled study. *Journal of the American Medical Association, 283,* 2529–2536.

Barlow, D. H., & Hersen, M. (1984). *Single case experimental designs: Strategies for studying behavior change* (2nd ed.). Boston: Allyn & Bacon.

Barlow, D. H., Moscovitch, D. A., & Micco, J. A. (2004). Psychotherapeutic interventions for phobias: A review. In M. Maj, H. S. Akiskal, J. J. Lopez-lbor, & A. Okasha (Eds.), *Phobias* (pp. 179–210). Chichester, England: John Wiley.

Bear, G. (1999). Proving the dream. In J. L. Casti & A. Karlqvist (Eds.), *Mission to Abisko: Stories and myths in the creation of scientific "truth"* (pp. 7–16). Reading, MA: Perseus Books.

Beck, A. T., & Emery, G. (1985). *Anxiety disorders and phobias: A cognitive perspective.* New York: Basic Books.

Beck, A. T., Freeman, A., Davis, A., & Associates (2004). *Cognitive therapy of personality disorders* (2nd ed). New York: Guilford Press.

Beck, A. T., Steer, R. A., & Brown, G. K. (1996). *Manual for the BDI-II.* San Antonio, TX: Psychological Corporation.

Beck, A. T., Ward, C. H., Mendelson, M., Mock, J., & Erbaugh, J. (1961). An inventory for measuring depression. *Archives of General Psychiatry, 41,* 561–571.

Beck, A. T., Ward, C. H., Mendelson, M., Mock, J. E., & Erbaugh, J. K (1962). Reliability of psychiatric diagnoses: 2. A study of consistency of clinical judgments and ratings. *American Journal of Psychiatry, 119,* 351–357.

Becker, C.B., & Zayfert, C. (2001). Integrating DBT-based techniques and concepts to facilitate exposure treatment for PTSD. *Cognitive and Behavioral Practice, 8,* 107–122.

Becker, C.B., Zayfert, C., & Anderson, E. (2004). A survey of psychologists' attitudes towards and utilization of exposure therapy for PTSD. *Behaviour Research and Therapy, 42,* 277–292.

Bejerot, S. (1998). *Vem var det du sa var normal?* [Who did you say was normal?] Stockholm: Bokförlaget Cura AB.

Bejerot, S. (1999). *Att förstå tvångssyndrom.* [To understand obsessive-compulsive disorder.] Täby, Sweden: Pfizer AB.

Bennett, M. J. (1992). The managed care setting as a framework for clinical practice. In J. L. Feldman & R. J. Fitzpatrick (Eds.), *Managed mental healthcare: Administrative and clinical issues* (pp. 203–218). Washington, DC: American Psychiatric Association Press.

Berman, P. S. (1997). *Case conceptualization and treatment planning: Exercises for integrating theory with clinical practice.* Thousand Oaks, CA: Sage Publications.

Beutler, L. E. (1991). Have all won and must all have prizes? Revisiting Luborsky et al.'s research. In A. Bellack, M. Hersen, & A. Kazdin (Eds.), *International handbook of behavior modification and therapy* (pp. 139–165). New York: Plenum Press.

Beutler, L. E. (2002). It isn't the size, but the fit. *Clinical Psychology: Science and Practice, 9,* 434–438.

Bland, R. C., Orn, H., & Newman, S. C. (1988). Lifetime prevalence of psychiatric disorders in Edmonton. *Acta Psychiatrica Scandinavica, 77(Suppl. 338),* 24–32.

Boersma, K., den Hengst, S., Dekker, J., & Emmelkamp, P. M. G. (1976). Exposure and response prevention in the natural environment: A comparison with obsessive-compulsive patients. *Behaviour Research and Therapy, 14,* 19–24.

Bohart, A. C., O'Hara, M., & Leitner, L. M. (1998). Empirically violated treatments: Disenfranchisement of humanistic and other psychotherapies. *Psychotherapy Research, 8,* 141–157.

Boone, M. L., McNeil, D. W., Masia, C. L., Turk, C. L., Carter, L. E., Ries, B. J., et al. (1999). Multimodal comparisons of social phobia subtypes and avoidance personality disorder. *Journal of Anxiety Disorders, 13,* 271–292.

Borkovec, T. D. (1994). The nature, functions, and origins of worry. In G. C. L. Davey & F. Tallis (Eds.), *Worrying: Perspectives on theory, assessment, and treatment.* New York: John Wiley.

Borkovec, T. D., Abel, J L., & Newman, H. (1995). Effects of psychotherapy on comorbid conditions in generalized anxiety disorder. *Journal of Consulting and Clinical Psychology, 63,* 479–483.

Borkovec, T. D., & Castonguay, L. G. (1998). What is the scientific meaning of empirically supported therapy? *Journal of Consulting and Clinical Psychology, 66,* 136–142.

Borkovec, T. D., & Costello, E. (1993). Efficacy of applied relaxation and cognitive-behavioral therapy in the treatment of generalized anxiety disorder. *Journal of Consulting and Clinical Psychology, 61,* 611–619.

Borkovec, T. D., & O'Brien, G. T. (1976). Methodological and target behavior issues in analogue therapy outcome research. *Progress in Behavior Modification, 3,* 133–172.

Borkovec, T. D., & Sides, J. K. (1979). The contribution of relaxation and expectancy to fear reduction via graded, imaginal exposure to feared stimuli. *Behaviour Research and Therapy, 17,* 529–540.

Botella, C., Banos, R. M., Guillen, V., Perpina, C., Alcaniz, M., & Pons, A. (2000). Telepsychology: Public speaking feat treatment in Internet. *Cyberpsychology and Behavior: The Impact of the Internet, Multimedia and Virtual Reality on Behavior and Society, 3,* 959–968.

Botella, C., Banos, R. M., Perpina, C., Villa, H., Alcaniz, M., & Rey, A. (1998). Virtual reality treatment of claustrophobia: A case report. *Behaviour Research and Therapy, 36,* 239–246.

Botella, C., Villa, H., Banos, R. M., Perpina, C., & Garcia-Palacious, A. (1999). The treatment of claustrophobia with virtual reality: Changes in other phobic behaviors not specifically treated. *Cyberpsychology and Behavior: The Impact of the Internet, Multimedia and Virtual Reality on Behavior and Society, 2,* 135–141.

Bourdon, K. H., Boyd, J. H., Rae, D. S., Burns, B. J., Thomas, J. W., & Locke, B. Z. (1988). Gender differences in phobias: Results of the ECA community study. *Journal of Anxiety Disorders, 2,* 227–241.

Bourne, E. J. (1998a). *Overcoming specific phobia: A hierarchy and exposure-based protocol for the treatment of all specific phobias (client manual).* Oakland, CA: New Harbinger Press.

Bourne, E. J. (1998b). *Overcoming specific phobia: A hierarchy and exposure-based protocol for the treatment of all specific phobias (therapist protocol).* Oakland, CA: New Harbinger Press.

Brawman-Mintzer, O., Lydiard, R. B., Emmanuel, N., Payeur, R., Johnson, M., Roberts, J., et al. (1993). Psychiatric comorbidity with generalized anxiety disorder. *American Journal of Psychiatry, 150,* 1216–1218.

Brown, T. A., & Barlow, D. H. (1992). Comorbidity among anxiety disorders: Implications for treatment and DSM-IV. *Journal of Consulting and Clinical Psychology, 60,* 835–844.

Brown, T. A., Di Nardo, P. A., & Barlow, D. H. (1994). *Anxiety disorders interview schedule for DSM-IV (ADIS-IV).* San Antonio, TX: Psychological Corporation.

Bruch, M., & Bond, F. W. (1998). *Beyond diagnosis: Case formulation approaches in CBT.* Chichester, England: John Wiley.

Bullinger, A. H., Roessler, A., & Mueller-Spahn, F. (1998). 3D VR as a tool in cognitive-behavioral therapy of claustrophobic patients. *Cyberpsychology and Behavior: The Impact of the Internet, Multimedia and Virtual Reality on Behavior and Society, 1,* 139–146.

Burkett, B. G., & Whitley, G. (1998). *Stolen valor: How the Vietnam generation was robbed of its heroes and its history.* Dallas, TX: Verity.

Callahan, R. (1995, August). *A thought field therapy (TFT) algorithm for trauma: A reproducible experiment in psychotherapy.* Paper presented at the 105th Annual Convention of the American Psychological Association, New York, NY.

Calvocoressi, L., McDougle, C. I., Wasylink, S., Goodman, W. K., Trufan, S. J., & Price, L. H. (1993). Inpatient treatment of patients with severe obsessive-compulsive disorder. *Hospital and Community Psychiatry, 44,* 1150–1154.

Campbell, J. M. (2004). Statistical comparison of four effect sizes for single-subject designs. *Behavior Modification, 28,* 234–246.

Canter, M. B., Bennett, B. E., Jones, S. E., & Nagy, T. F. (1994). *Ethics for psychologists: A commentary on the APA ethics code.* Washington, DC: American Psychological Association.

Carlin, A. S., Hoffman, H. G., Weghorst, S. (1997). Virtual reality and tactile augmentation in the treatment of spider phobia: A case report. *Behaviour Research and Therapy, 35,* 153–158.

Castonguay, L. G., Schut, A. J., Constantino, M. J., & Halperin, G. S. (1999). Assessing the role of treatment manuals: Have they become necessary but nonsufficient ingredients of change? *Clinical Psychology: Science and Practice, 6,* 449–455.

Chambless, D. L. (1996). In defense of dissemination of empirically supported psychological interventions. *Clinical Psychology: Science and Practice, 3,* 230–235.

Chambless, D. L., Baker, M. J., Baucom, D. H., Beutler, L. E., Calhoun, K. S., Crits-Christoph, P., et al. (1998). Update on empirically validated therapies, II. *The Clinical Psychologist, 51,* 3–16.

Chambless, D. L., Caputo, G. C., Bright, P., & Gallagher, R. (1984). The assessment of fear in agoraphobics: The body sensations questionnaire and the agoraphobic cognitions questionnaire. *Journal of Consulting and Clinical Psychology, 52,* 1090–1097.

Chambless, D. L., Caputo, G. C., Jasin, S. E., Gracely, E. J., & Williams, C. (1985). The mobility inventory for agoraphobia. *Behaviour Research and Therapy, 23,* 35–44.

Chambless, D. L., & Ollendick, T. H. (2001). Empirically supported psychological interventions: Controversies and evidence. *Annual Review of Psychology, 52*, 685–716.

Clark, D. M. (2001). A cognitive perspective on social phobia. In W.R. Crozier & L.E. Alden (Eds.), *International handbook of social anxiety: Concepts, research and interventions relating to the self and shyness* (pp. 405–430). Chichester, England: John Wiley.

Clark, D. M. (2004). *Cognitive-behavioral therapy for OCD*. New York: Guilford Press.

Clark, D. M., & Wells, A. (1995). A cognitive model of social phobia. In R. Heimburg, M. Liebowitz, D. A. Hope, & F. R. Schneier (Eds.), *Social phobia: Diagnosis, assessment and treatment* (pp. 69–93). New York: Guilford Press.

Clement, P. (1996). Evaluation in private practice. *Clinical Psychology: Science and Practice, 3*, 146–159.

Clum, G. A., & Pendrey, D. (1987). Depression symptomatology as a non-requisite for successful treatment of panic with antidepressant medications. *Journal of Anxiety Disorder, 1(4)*, 337–344.

Cohen, D. C. (1977). Comparison of self-report and behavioral procedures for assessing acrophobia. *Behavior Therapy, 8*, 17–23.

Coryell, W., Noyes, R., & House, J. D. (1986). Mortality rates amongst outpatients with anxiety disorders. *American Journal of Psychiatry, 143*, 508–510.

Craig, G. (Producer). (1997). *Six days at the VA: Using emotional freedom therapy* [Videotape]. (Available from Gary Craig, 1102 Redwood Boulevard, Novato, CA 94947).

Craighead, W. E., & Craighead, L. W. (1998). Manual-based treatments: Suggestions for improving their clinical utility and acceptability. *Clinical Psychology: Science and Practice, 5*, 403–407.

Craske, M. G. (1999). *Anxiety disorders: Psychological approaches to theory and treatment*. Boulder, CO: Westview Press.

Craske, M. G., & Barlow, D. H. (2000). *Mastery of your anxiety and panic: Client workbook for agoraphobia (MAP-3)* (3rd ed.). San Antonio, TX: Psychological Corporation.

Craske, M. G., & Barlow, D. H. (2001). Panic disorder and agoraphobia. In D.H. Barlow (Ed.), *Clinical handbook of psychological disorders: A step-by-step treatment manual* (3rd ed., pp. 1–59). New York: Guilford Press.

Craske, M. G., Barlow, D. H., & Meadows, E. A. (2000). *Mastery of your anxiety and panic: Therapist guide for anxiety, panic, and agoraphobia (MAP-3)* (3rd ed.). San Antonio, TX: Psychological Corporation.

Crits-Christoph, P., Baranackie, K., Kurcias, J. S., Beck, A. T., Carroll, K., Perry, K., et al. (1991). Meta-analysis of therapist effects in psychotherapy outcome studies. *Psychotherapy Research, 1,* 81–91.

Dante, A. (1909). *The divine comedy.* Boston: Harvard Classics.

Darwin, C. (1965). *Expression of the emotions in man and animal.* Chicago: University of Chicago Press. (Original work published 1872).

Davidson, J. R. T. (1996). Quality of life and costs in panic disorder. *Bulletin of the Menninger Clinic, 60(Suppl. A),* A5–A11.

Davidson, P. R., & Parker, K. C. H. (2001). Eye movement desensitization and reprocessing (EMDR): A meta-analysis. *Journal of Consulting and Clinical Psychology, 69,* 305–316.

DeBell, C., & Jones, D. R. (1997). As good as it seems? A review of EMDR experimental research. *Professional Psychology: Research and Practice, 28,* 153–163.

Depression Guideline Panel (1993). *Depression in primary care: Volume 2. Treatment of Major Depression, Clinical Practice Guidelines, Number 5* (AHCPR Publication No. 93-0551). Washington, DC: U.S. Government Printing Office.

Devilly, G. J., & Spence, S. H. (1999). The relative efficacy and treatment of EMDR and a cognitive-behavior trauma protocol in the amelioration of posttraumatic stress disorder. *Journal of Anxiety Disorders, 13,* 131–157.

Di Nardo, P. A., Brown, T. A., & Barlow, D. H. (1994). *Anxiety disorders interview schedule for DSM-IV: Lifetime version.* San Antonio, TX: Psychological Corporation.

Drummond, L. M. (1993). The treatment of severe, chronic, resistant obsessive-compulsive disorder: An evaluation of an in-patient programme using behavioural psychotherapy in combination with other treatments. *British Journal of Psychiatry, 163,* 223–229.

Dugas, M. J., Gagnon, F., Ladouceur, R., & Freeston, M. H. (1998). Generalized anxiety disorder: A preliminary test of a conceptual model. *Behaviour Research and Therapy, 36,* 215–226.

Dugas, M. J., & Ladouceur, R. (2000). Treatment of GAD: Targeting intolerance of uncertainty in two types of worry. *Behavior Modification, 24,* 635–657.

Dugas, M. J., Ladouceur, R., Léger, E., Freeston, M. H., Langlois, F., Provencher, M. D., & Boisvert, J.-M. (2003). Group cognitive-behavioral therapy for generalized anxiety disorder: Treatment outcome and long-term follow-up. *Journal of Consulting and Clinical Psychology, 71,* 821–825.

Eels, T. D. (1997). *Handbook of psychotherapy case formulation.* New York: Guilford Press.

Eels, T. D., Kendjelic, E. M., & Lucas, C. P. (1998). What's in a case formulation? Development and use of a content coding manual. *The Journal of Psychotherapy Practice and Research, 7,* 144–153.

Ekman, P. (1992). Are there basic emotions? *Psychological Review, 99,* 550–553.

Ekman, P. (1994). All emotions are basic. In P. Ekman & R. J. Davidson (Eds.), *The nature of emotion: Fundamental questions* (pp. 15–19). New York: Oxford University Press.

Elliott, R. E. (1998). The empirically supported treatments controversy. *Psychotherapy Research, 8,* 115–170.

EMDR Institute, Inc. (1995). *International EMDR conference: Research and clinical applications.* Pacific Grove, CA: Author.

EMDR Institute, Inc. (1997). Promotional advertisement. *Monitor, 28,* 49.

Emmelkamp, P .M. G. (1982). *Phobic and obsessive-compulsive disorders: Theory, research, and practice.* New York: Plenum Press.

Emmelkamp, P. M. G. (1994). Behavior therapy with adults. In A. E. Bergin & S. L. Garfield (Eds.), *Handbook of psychotherapy and behavior change* (4th ed.) (pp. 379–427). New York: John Wiley.

Emmelkamp, P. M. G., Bouman, T. K., & Scholing, A. (1992). *Anxiety disorders: A practitioner's guide.* Chichester, England: John Wiley & Sons.

Emmelkamp, P. M. G., Kloek, J., & Blaauw, E. (1992). Obsessive-compulsive disorder. In P.H. Wilson (Ed.), *Principles and practice of relapse prevention* (pp. 213–234). New York: Guilford Press.

Emmelkamp, P. M. G., van Linden-van den Heuvell, C., Rüphan, M., & Sanderman, R. (1988). De thuisbehandeling van dwangstoornis [Home-based treatment of obsessive-compulsive disorder]. *Gedragstherapie, 21,* 235–245.

Emmelkamp, P. M. G., van Linden-van den Heuvell, C., Rüphan, M., & Sanderman, R. (1989). Home-based treatment of obsessive-compulsive patients: Intersession interval and therapist involvement. *Behaviour Therapy and Research, 27,* 89–93.

Fanselow, M. S. (1984). Shock-induced analgesia on the formalin test: Effects of shock severity, naloxone, hypophysectomy, and associate variables. *Behavioral Neuroscience, 98,* 269–277.

Feeny, N. C., Hembree, E. A., & Zoellner, L. A. (2003). Myths regarding exposure therapy for PTSD. *Cognitive and Behavioral Practice, 10,* 85–90.

Fensterheim, H. (1996). Eye movement desensitization and reprocessing with complex personality pathology: An integrative therapy. *Journal of Psychotherapy Integration, 6,* 27–38.

First, M. B., Spitzer, R. L., Gibbon, M., & Williams, J. B. W. (1996). *Structured clinical interview for DSM-IV axis I disorders research version—Patient edition (SCID-I/P, ver. 2.0).* New York: New York State Psychiatric Institute, Biometrics Research Department.

First, M. B., Spitzer, R. L., Gibbon, M., & Williams, J. B. W. (1997). *Structured clinical interview for DSM-IV axis I disorders (SCID-I)— Clinician version*. Washington, DC: Psychiatric Press.

Flint, A. J. (1994). Epidemiology and comorbidity of anxiety disorders in the elderly. *American Journal of Psychiatry, 151,* 640–649.

Foa, E. B. (2000). Psychosocial treatment of posttraumatic stress disorder. *Journal of Clinical Psychiatry, 61,* 43–48.

Foa, E. B., Abramowitz, J. S., Franklin, M. E., & Kozak, M. J. (1999). Feared consequences, fixity of belief, and treatment outcome in patients with obsessive-compulsive disorder. *Behavior Therapy, 30,* 717–724.

Foa, E. B., Ehlers, A., Clark, D. M., Tolin, D. F., & Orsillo, S. M. (1999). The posttraumatic cognitions inventory (PTCI): Development and validation. *Psychological Assessment, 11,* 303–314.

Foa, E. B., & Emmelkamp, P. M. G. (1983). *Failures in behavior therapy.* Chichester, England: John Wiley.

Foa, E. B., & Franklin, M. E. (2001). Obsessive-compulsive disorder. In D.H. Barlow (Ed.), *Clinical handbook of psychological disorders: A step-by-step treatment manual* (3rd ed.) (pp. 209–263). New York: Guilford Press.

Foa, E. B., & Kozak, M. J. (1985). Treatment of anxiety disorders: Implications for psychopathology. In A. H. Tuma & J. D. Maser (Eds.), *Anxiety and the anxiety disorders* (pp. 421–452). Hillsdale, NJ: Erlbaum.

Foa, E. B., & Kozak, M. J. (1986). Emotional processing of fear: Exposure to corrective information. *Psychological Bulletin, 99,* 20–35.

Foa, E. B., & Rothbaum, B. O. (1998). *Treating the trauma of rape: Cognitive-behavioral therapy for PTSD.* New York: Guilford Press.

Foertsch, C., Manning, S. Y., & Dimeff, L. (2003). Difficult-to-treat patients: The approach from dialectical behavior therapy. In R. L. Leahy (Ed.), *Roadblocks in cognitive-behavioral therapy: Transforming challenges into opportunities for change* (pp. 255–273). New York: Guilford Press.

Fonagy, P. (1999). Achieving evidence-based psychotherapy practice: A psychodynamic perspective on the general acceptance of treatment manuals. *Clinical Psychology: Science and Practice, 6,* 442–444.

Fonagy, P., & Target, M. (1996). Should we allow psychotherapy research to determine clinical practice? *Clinical Psychology: Science and Practice, 3,* 245–250.

Fox, R. E. (1996). Charlatanism, scientism, and psychology's social contract. *American Psychologist, 51,* 777–784.

Franklin, M. E., Abramowitz, J. S., Kozak, M. J., Levitt, J., & Foa, E. B. (2000). Effectiveness of exposure and ritual prevention for obsessive compulsive disorder: Randomized compared to non-randomized samples. *Journal of Consulting and Clinical Psychology, 68,* 594–602.

Freeman, A., & McCloskey, R. D. (2003). Impediments to effective psychotherapy. In R. L. Leahy (Ed.), *Roadblocks in cognitive-behavioral therapy: Transforming challenges into opportunities for change* (pp. 24–48). New York: Guilford Press.

Fritzler, B. K., Hecker, J. E., & Losee, M. C. (1997). Self-directed treatment with minimal therapist contact: Preliminary findings for obsessive-compulsive disorder. *Behaviour Research and Therapy, 35,* 627–631.

Frost, R. O., & Gross, R. C. (1993). The hoarding of possessions. *Behaviour Research and Therapy, 31,* 367–381.

Frost, R. O., & Hartl, T. (1996). A cognitive-behavioral model of compulsive hoarding. *Behaviour Research and Therapy, 34,* 341–350.

Frost, R. O., Krause, M., & Steketee, G. (1996). Hoarding and obsessive compulsive symptoms. *Behavior Modification, 20,* 116–132.

Furer, P., Walker, J. R., & Freeston, M. H. (2001). Approach to integrated cognitive-behavior therapy for intense illness worries. In G. J. G. Asmundson, S. Taylor, & B. J. Cox (Eds.), *Health anxiety: Clinical and research perspectives on hypochondriasis and related conditions* (pp. 161–192). Chichester, England: John Wiley.

Furer, P., Walker, J. R., & Vincent, N. (1999, November). *Cognitive behavioral group treatment for hypochondriasis.* Poster session presented at the meeting of the Association for Advancement of Behavior Therapy, Toronto, Canada.

Gallo, F. P. (1995, March 23). Reflections on active ingredients in efficient treatments of PTSD, Part 1. *Electronic Journal of Traumatology, 2(1).* Retrieved March 19, 2005, from http://www.fsu.edu/~trauma/art2v2i1.html

Garfield, S. L. (1996). Some problems with "validated" forms of psychotherapy. *Clinical Psychology: Science and Practice, 3,* 218–229.

Gerbode, F. (1985). *Beyond psychology: An introduction to metapsychology.* Palo Alto, CA: IRM Press.

Gerbode, F. (1995, May). *Presentation on traumatic incident reduction.* Paper presented at the Active Ingredients in Efficient Treatments of PTSD Conference, Florida State University, Tallahassee, FL.

Goldfried, M. R., & Wolfe, B. E. (1998). Toward a more clinically valid approach to therapy research. *Journal of Consulting and Clinical Psychology, 66,* 143–150.

Goldstein, A. J., deBeurs, E., Chambless, D. L., & Wilson, K. A. (2000). EMDR for panic disorder with agoraphobia: Comparison with wait-list and credible attention-placebo control conditions. *Journal of Consulting and Clinical Psychology, 68,* 947–956.

Goodman, W. K., Price, L. H., Rasmussen, S. A., Mazure, C., Fleischmann, R. L., Hill, C. L., et al. (1989a). The Yale-Brown obsessive compulsive scale: Part I. Development, use and reliability. *Archives of General Psychiatry, 46,* 1006–1011.

Goodman, W. K., Price, L.H., Rasmussen, S.A., Mazure, C., Fleischmann, R L., Hill, C. L., et al. (1989b). The Yale-Brown obsessive compulsive scale: Part II. Validity. *Archives of General Psychiatry, 46,* 1012–1016.

Gottlieb, B. H. (1997). *Coping with chronic stress.* New York: Plenum Press.

Gray, M. J., & Acierno, R. (2002). Posttraumatic stress disorder. In M. Hersen (Ed.), *Clinical behavior therapy: Adults and children* (pp. 106–124). New York: John Wiley.

Greenberg, P. E., Sisitsky, T., Kessler, R. C., Finkelstein, S. N., Berndt, E. R., Davidson, J. R. T., et al. (1999). The economic burden of anxiety disorders in the 1990s. *Journal of Clinical Psychiatry, 60,* 427–435.

Hafner, R. J., & Marks, I. M. (1976). Exposure in vivo in agoraphobics: Contributions of diazepam, group exposure, and anxiety evocation. *Psychological Medicine, 6,* 71–88.

Hamilton, M. (1959). The assessment of anxiety states by rating. *British Journal of Medical Psychology, 32,* 50–55.

Hamilton, M. (1960). A rating scale for depression. *Journal of Neurology, Neurosurgery, and Psychiatry, 23,* 56–62.

Hammen, C. (1991). Generation of stress in the course of unipolar depression. *Journal of Abnormal Psychology, 100,* 555–561.

Hasselt, V. B. van, & Hersen, M. (Eds.). (1996). *Sourcebook of psychological treatment manuals for adult disorders.* New York: Plenum Press.

Hayes, S. N., Kaholokula, J. K., & Nelson, K. (1999). The idiographic application of nomothetic, empirically based treatments. *Clinical Psychology: Science and Practice, 6,* 456–461.

Hays, P. A. (1996). Addressing the complexities of culture and gender in counseling. *Journal of Counseling and Development, 74,* 332–338.

Hays, P. A. (2001). *Addressing cultural complexities in practice: A framework for clinicians and counselors.* Washington, DC: American Psychological Association.

Hazlett-Stevens, H., & Craske, M. G. (2003). Live (in vivo) exposure. In W. O'Donohue, J. E. Fisher, & S. C. Hayes (Eds.), *Cognitive behavior therapy: Applying empirically supported techniques in your practice* (pp. 223–228). Hoboken, NJ: John Wiley & Sons.

Hebert, J. D. (2003). The science and practice of empirically supported treatments. *Behavior Modification, 27,* 412–430.

Heimburg, R. G., & Becker, R. E. (2002). *Cognitive-behavioral group therapy for social phobia: Basic mechanisms and clinical practice.* New York: Guilford Press.

Heimburg, R. G., Dodge, C. S., Hope, D. A., Kennedy, C. R., Zolla, L. J., & Becker, R. E. (1990). Cognitive behavioral group treatment for social phobia: Comparison with a credible placebo control. *Cognitive Therapy and Research, 14,* 1–23.

Heimburg, R. G., Turk, C. L., & Mennin, D. S. (Eds.). (2004). *Generalized anxiety disorder: Advances in research and practice.* New York: Guilford Press.

Heinrichs, N., Hofmann, S. G., & Spiegel, D. A. (in press). Panic disorder with agoraphobia. In F. Bond & W. Dryden (Eds.), *Handbook of brief cognitive-behavioral therapy.* Chichester, UK: John Wiley.

Hembree, E. A., Rauch, S. A. M., & Foa, E. B. (2003). Beyond the manual: The insider's guide to prolonged exposure therapy for PTSD. *Cognitive and Behavioral Practice, 10,* 22–30.

Henggeler, S. W., & Schoenwald, S. K. (2002). Treatment manuals: Necessary, but far from sufficient. *Clinical Psychology: Science and Practice, 9,* 419–420.

Henry, W. P. (1998). Science, politics, and the politics of science: The use and misuse of empirically validated treatment research. *Psychotherapy Research, 8,* 126–140.

Herbert, J. D. (2003). Introduction to the special series on empirically supported treatments. *Behavior Modification, 27,* 287–289.

Herbert, J. D., Lilienfeld, S. O., Lohr, J. M., Montgomery, R. W., O'Donohue, W. T., Rosen, G. M., et al. (2000). Science and pseudoscience in the development of eye movement desensitization and reprocessing: Implications for clinical psychology. *Clinical Psychology Review, 20,* 945–971.

Hersen, M. (1982). Single-case experimental designs. In A. S. Bellack, M. Hersen, & A. E. Kazdin (Eds.), *International handbook of behavior modification and therapy* (pp. 175–210). New York: Plenum Press.

Hersen, M. (Ed.). (2002). *Clinical behavior therapy: Adults and children.* New York: John Wiley.

Hersen, M., & Bellack, A. S. (1999). *Handbook of comparative interventions for adult disorders.* New York: Wiley

Hersen, M., & Biaggio, M. (Eds.). (2000). *Effective brief therapies: A clinician's guide.* New York: Academic Press.

Hoogduin, C. A. L., & Hoogduin, W. A. (1984). The out-patient treatment of patients with an obsessional-compulsive disorder. *Behaviour Therapy and Research, 22,* 455–459.

Horvath, A. O., & Symonds, B. D. (1991). Relationship between working alliance and outcome in psychotherapy: A meta-analysis. *Journal of Counseling Psychology, 38,* 139–149.

Hout, M. van den, Emmelkamp, P., Kraaykamp, H., & Griez, E. (1988). Behavioral treatment of obsessive-compulsives: Inpatient vs outpatient. *Behaviour Therapy and Research, 26,* 331–332.

Insel, T. R., & Akiskal, H. S. (1986). Obsessive-compulsive disorder with psychotic features: A phenomenological analysis. *American Journal of Psychiatry, 143,* 1527–1533.

Izard, C. E. (1992). Basic emotions, relations among emotions, and emotion-cognition relations. *Psychological Review, 99,* 561–565.

Jacobson, N. S., Follette, W. C., & Revenstorf, D. (1984). Psychotherapy outcome research: Methods for reporting variability and evaluating clinical significance. *Behavior Therapy, 15,* 336–352.

Jacobson, N. S., & Truax, P. (1991). Clinical significance: A statistical approach to defining meaningful change in psychotherapy research. *Journal of Consulting and Clinical Psychology, 59,* 12–19.

Jang, D. P., Ku, J. H., Shin, M. B., Choi, Y. H., & Kim, S. I. (2000). Objective validation of the effectiveness of virtual reality psychotherapy. *Cyberpsychology and Behavior: The Impact of the Internet, Multimedia and Virtual Reality on Behavior and Society, 3,* 321–326.

Jenike, M.A. (2000). Neurosurgical treatment of obsessive-compulsive disorder. In W. K. Goodman, M. V. Rudorfer, & J. D. Maser (Eds.), *Obsessive-compulsive disorder: Contemporary issues in treatment* (pp. 457–482). Mahwah, NJ: Lawrence Erlbaum Associates.

Jenike, M. A., Baer, L., Ballantine, H. T., Martuza, R. L., Tynes, S., Giriunas, I., et al. (1991). Cingulotomy for refractory obsessive-compulsive disorder: A long-term follow-up of 33 patients. *Archives of General Psychiatry, 48,* 548–555.

Jenike, M.A., Baer, L., & Minichiello, W. E. (1998). An overview of obsessive-compulsive disorder. In M. A. Jenike, L. Baer, & W. E. Minichiello (Eds.), *Obsessive-compulsive disorders: Practical management* (3rd ed.) (pp. 3–11). Boston: Mosby.

Johnson, J., Weissman, M. M., & Klerman, G. L. (1990). Panic disorder, comorbidity, and suicide attempts. *Archives of General Psychiatry, 47,* 805–808.

Johnstone, K. A., & Page, A. C. (2004). Attention to phobic stimuli during exposure: The effect of distraction on anxiety reduction, self-efficacy and perceived control. *Behaviour Research and Therapy, 42,* 249–275.

Kamphuis, J. H., Emmelkamp, P. M. G., & Krijn, M. (2002). Specific phobia. In M. Hersen (Ed.), *Clinical behavior therapy: Adults and children* (pp. 75–89). New York: John Wiley.

Kaplan, H. I., & Saddock, B. J. (1993). *Synopsis of psychiatry* (6th ed., revised). Baltimore: Williams & Wilkins.

Katsching, H., & Amering, M. (1994). The long-term course of panic disorder. In B. E. Wolf & J. D. Maser (Eds.), *Treatment of panic disorder: A consensus development conference.* Washington, DC: American Psychiatric Press.

Keller, M. B., & Baker, L. (1992). The clinical course of panic disorder and depression. *Journal of Clinical Psychiatry, 53,* 5–8.

Kendall, P. C. (1998a). Empirically supported psychological therapies. *Journal of Consulting and Clinical Psychology, 66,* 3–6.

Kendall, P. (1998b). Directing misperceptions: Researching the issues facing manual-based treatments. *Clinical Psychology: Science and Practice, 5,* 396–399.

Kendall, P. C., Chu, B., Gifford, A., Hayes, C., & Nauta, M. (1998). Breathing life into a manual: Flexibility and creativity with manual-based treatments. *Cognitive and Behavioral Practice, 5,* 177–198.

Kessler, R. C., McGonagle, K. A., Zhao, S., Nelson, C. B., Hughes, M., Eshleman, S., et al. (1994). Lifetime and 12-month prevalence of DSM-III-R psychiatric disorders in the United States: Results from the National Comorbidity Survey. *Archives of General Psychiatry, 51,* 8–19.

Kessler, R., Sonnega, A., Bromet, E., Hughes, M., & Nelson, C. (1995). Posttraumatic stress disorder in the national comorbidity survey. *Archives of General Psychiatry, 52,* 1048–1060.

Kettlewell, P. W. (2004). Development, dissemination, and implementation of evidence- based treatments: Commentary. *Clinical Psychology: Science and Practice, 11,* 190–195.

Kilpatrick, D., Acierno, R., Resnick, H., Saunders, B., & Best, C. (1997). A 2-year longitudinal analysis of the relationship between violent assault and substance use in women. *Journal of Consulting and Clinical Psychology, 65,* 834–847.

Koocher, G. P., & Keith-Spiegel, P. (1998). *Ethics in psychology: Professional standards and cases* (2nd ed.). New York: Oxford University Press.

Koran, L. M. (1999). *Obsessive-compulsive and related disorders in adults: A comprehensive clinical guide.* Cambridge, England: Cambridge University Press.

Kosslyn, S. M., Brunn, J., Cave, K. R., & Wallach, R. W. (1984). Individual differences in mental imagery ability: A computational analysis. *Cognition, 18,* 195–243.

Kozak, M. J., & Foa, E. B. (1994). Obsessions, overvalued ideas, and delusions in obsessive-compulsive disorder. *Behaviour Research and Therapy, 32,* 343–353.

Kozak, M. J., Liebowitz, M. R., & Foa, E. B. (2000). Cognitive behavior therapy and pharmacotherapy for obsessive-compulsive disorder: The NIMH-sponsored collaborative study. In W. K. Goodman, M. V. Rudorfer, & J. D. Maser (Eds.), *Obsessive-compulsive disorder: Contemporary issues in treatment* (pp. 501–530). Mahwah, NJ: Lawrence Erlbaum Associates.

Krug-Porzelius, L. (2002). Overview. In M. Hersen & L. Krug-Porzelius (Eds.), *Diagnosis, conceptualization, and treatment planning for adults: A step-by-step guide* (pp. 3–12). Mahwah, NJ: Erlbaum.

Laberge, B., Gauthier, J. G., Cote, G., Plamondon, J., & Cormier, H. J. (1993). Cognitive-behavioral therapy of panic disorder with secondary depression: A preliminary investigation. *Journal of Consulting and Clinical Psychology, 61,* 1028–1037.

Lambert, M. J. (1992). *The handbook of psychology integration.* New York: Basic Books.

Lambert, M. J. (1998). Manual-based treatment and clinical practice: Hangman of life or promising development. *Clinical Psychology: Science and Practice, 5,* 391–395.

Lazarus, A. A. (1971). *Behavior therapy and beyond.* New York: McGraw-Hill.

Lazarus, A. A., Beutler, L. E., & Norcross, J. C. (1992). The future of technical eclecticism. *Psychotherapy, 29,* 11–20.

Leckman, J. F., Walker, D. E., & Cohen, D. J. (1993). Premonitory urges in Tourette's syndrome. *American Journal of Psychiatry, 150,* 98–102.

Lehman, C. L., Brown, T. A., & Barlow, D. H. (1998). Effects of cognitive-behavioral treatment for panic disorder with agoraphobia on concurrent alcohol abuse. *Behavior Therapy, 29,* 423–434.

Leitenburg, H., & Callahan, E. J. (1973). Reinforced practice and reduction of different kinds of fears in adults and children. *Behaviour Research and Therapy, 11,* 19–30.

Levendusky, P. G., Willis, B. S., & Ghinassi, F. A. (1994). The therapeutic contracting program: A comprehensive continuum of care model. *Psychiatric Quarterly, 65,* 189–208.

Levin, R. B., & Gross, A. M. (1985). The role of relaxation in systematic desensitization. *Behaviour Research and Therapy, 23,* 187–196.

Lindkvist, K. (1999). *Bättre lite skit i hörnet än ett rent helvete.* [Better a little dirt in the corner, than a clean hell.] Täby, Sweden: Pfizer AB.

Lindsay, M., Crino, R., & Andrews, G. (1997). Controlled trial of exposure and response prevention in obsessive-compulsive disorder. *British Journal of Psychiatry, 171,* 135–139.

Lohr, J. M. (1996). Analysis by analogy for the mental health clinician [review of F. Shapiro, 1995]. *Contemporary Psychology, 41,* 879–880.

Lohr, J. M., Tolin, D. F., & Lilienfeld, S. O. (1998). Efficacy of eye movement desensitization and reprocessing: Implications for behavior therapy. *Behavior Therapy, 29,* 123–156.

Lteif, G. N., & Mavissakalian, M. R. (1995). Life events and panic disorder/agoraphobia. *Comprehensive Psychiatry, 36,* 118–122.

Luborsky, L., Singer, B., & Luborsky, L. (1975). Comparative studies of psychotherapies: Is it true that "Everyone has won and everyone must have process?" *Archives of General Psychiatry, 32,* 995–1008.

Maj, M., Akiskal, H. S., Lopez-Ibor, J. J., & Okasha, A. (Eds.). (2004). *Phobias.* Chichester, England: John Wiley.

Makatura, T. J., Lam, C. S., Leahy, B. J., Castillo, M. T., & Kalpakjian, C. Z. (1999). Standardized memory tests and the appraisal of everyday memory. *Brain Injury, 13,* 355–367.

Mansueto, C. (1991). Trichotillomania in focus. *OCD Newsletter, 5,* 10–11.

Marcks, B. A., Woods, D. W., Teng, E. J., Twohig, M. P. (2004). What do those who know, know? Investigating providers' knowledge about tourette syndrome and its treatment. *Cognitive and Behavioral Practice, 11,* 298–305.

Marks, I. M., & Lader, M. (1973). Anxiety states (anxiety neurosis): A review. *Journal of Nervous and Mental Disease, 156,* 3–18.

Marks, I. M., & Mathews, A. M. (1979). Brief standard self-rating for phobic patients. *Behaviour Research and Therapy, 17,* 263–267.

Marlatt, G. A., & Gordon, J. R. (Eds.). (1985). *Relapse prevention: Maintenance strategies in the treatment of addictive disorders.* New York: Guilford Press.

Mattick, R. P., & Clarke, J. C. (1998). Development and validation of measures of social phobia scrutiny and social interaction anxiety. *Behaviour Research and Therapy, 31,* 305–313.

McClelland, J. L., & Rumelhart, D. E. (1987). *Parallel distributed processing: Explorations in the microstructure of cognition. Psychological and biological models* (Vol. 2). Cambridge, MA: MIT Press.

McGrath, J. M., & Frueh, B. C. (2002). Fraudulent claims of combat heroics within the VA? *Psychiatric Services, 53,* 345.

McLean, P. D., Whittal, M. L., Thordarson, D. S., Taylor, S., Söchting, I., Koch, W.J., et al. (2001). Cognitive versus behavior therapy in the group treatment of obsessive-compulsive disorder. *Journal of Consulting and Clinical Psychology, 69,* 205–214.

McLean, P. D., & Woody, S. R. (2001). *Anxiety disorders in adults: An evidence-based approach to psychological treatment.* New York: Oxford University Press.

McNally, R. J. (1999). On eye movement and animal magnetism: A reply to Greenwald's defense of EMDR. *Journal of Anxiety Disorder, 13,* 617–620.

McNally, R. J. (2003). Progress and controversy in the study of posttraumatic stress disorder. *Annual Review of Psychology, 54,* 229–252.

McNeil, D. W. (2000). Terminology and evolution of constructs in social anxiety and social phobia. In S. G. Hofmann & P. M. DiBartolo (Eds.), *Social phobia and social anxiety: An integration* (pp. 8–19). Needham Heights, MA: Allyn & Bacon.

McNeil, D. W., Ries, B. J., Taylor, L., Boone, M. L., Carter, L. E., Turk, C. L., et al. (1995). Comparison of social phobia subtypes using Stroop tests. *Journal of Anxiety Disorders, 9,* 47–57.

Meichenbaum, D. (1977). *Cognitive-behavior modification: An integrative approach.* New York: Plenum Press.

Meichenbaum, D., & Novaco, R. (1977). Stress inoculation: A preventive approach. In C. Speilberger & I. Sarason (Eds.), *Stress and anxiety* (Vol. 5). New York: Halstead Press.

Meier, S.T. (1999). Training the practitioner-scientist: Bridging case conceptualization, assessment, and intervention. *The Counseling Psychologist, 27,* 846–869.

Mesh, S. & Loeb, J. (2002). Practical issues in conducting home-based early interventions. In L. Vandecreek & T.L. Jackson (Eds.), *Innovations in clinical practice: A source book* (pp. 399–409). Sarasota, FL: Professional Resource Press.

Meyer, V. (1966). Modification of expectations in cases with obsessional rituals. *Behaviour Research and Therapy, 4,* 273–280.

Meyer, V., & Chesser, E. S. (1970). *Behavior therapy in clinical psychiatry.* New York: Science House.

Michael, J. (1982). Distinguishing between the discriminative and motivational functions of stimuli. *Journal of the Experimental Analysis of Behavior, 37,* 149–158.

Miklowitz, D. J. (2001). Bipolar disorder. In D. H. Barlow (Ed.), *Clinical handbook of psychological disorders* (3rd ed.) (pp. 523–561). New York: Guilford Press.

Miller, C. (2005). Informed consent to treatment. In M. Hersen & J. Rosqvist (Eds.), *Encyclopedia of Behavior Modification and Cognitive Behavior Therapy* (Vol. 1) (pp. 337-339). Thousand Oaks, CA: Sage Publishers.

Miller, W. R., & Rollnick, S. (2002). *Motivational interviewing: Preparing people to change addictive behavior.* New York: Guilford Press.

Moras, K. (1993). The use of treatment manuals to train psychotherapists: Observations and recommendations. *Psychotherapy, 30,* 581–586.

Mossman, D. (1994). At the VA, it pays to be sick. *Public Interest, 114,* 35–47.

Mowrer, O. H. (1939). Stimulus response theory of anxiety. *Psychological Review, 46,* 553–565.

Mowrer, O. H. (1947). On the dual nature of learning: A reinterpretation of "conditioning" and "problem solving." *Harvard Educational Review, 17,* 102–148.

Mowrer, O. H. (1960). *Learning theory and behavior.* New York: John Wiley.

Muris, P., & Merckelbach, H. (1999). Traumatic memories, eye movements, phobia, and panic: A critical note on the proliferation of EMDR. *Journal of Anxiety Disorders, 13,* 209–223.

Muris, P., Merckelbach, H., Holdrinet, I., & Sigsenaar, M. (1998). Treating phobic children: Effects of EMDR versus exposure. *Journal of Consulting and Clinical Psychology, 66,* 193–198.

Najavits, L. M., Weiss, R. D., Shaw, S. R., & Dierberger, A. E. (2000). Psychotherapists' views of treatment manuals. *Professional Psychology: Research and Practice, 31,* 404–408.

Needleman, L. D. (1999). *Cognitive case conceptualization: A guidebook for practitioners.* Mahwah, NJ: Erlbaum.

Newman, C. (August, 2004). Why are we so fat? *National Geographic,* 46–61.

Newman, F. (1999). *The whole lesbian sex book: A passionate guide for all of us.* San Francisco: Cleis Press.

Newman, S. C., & Bland, R. C. (1994). Life events and the 1-year prevalence of major depressive episode, generalized anxiety disorder, and panic disorder in a community sample. *Comprehensive Psychiatry, 35,* 76–82.

Neziroglu, F., & Stevens, K. P. (2002). Insight: Its conceptualization and assessment. In R. O. Frost & G. Steketee (Eds.), *Cognitive approaches to obsessions and compulsions: Theory, assessment, and treatment.* (pp. 183–193). Amsterdam: Pergamon Press.

Nezu, A. M. (1996). What are we doing to our patients and should we care if anyone else knows? *Clinical Psychology: Science and Practice, 3,* 160–163.

Nezu, A. M., Nezu, C. M., & Lombardo, E. (2004). *Cognitive-behavioral case formulation and treatment design: A problem-solving approach.* New York: Springer Publishing.

Norcross, J. C. (2002). Empirically supported therapy relationships. In J. C. Norcross (Ed.), *Psychotherapy relationships that work* (pp. 3–16). New York: Oxford University Press.

Norris, F. H. (1992). Epidemiology of trauma: Frequency and impact of different potentially traumatic events on different demographic groups. *Journal of Consulting and Clinical Psychology, 60,* 409–418.

North, M. M., North, S. M., & Coble, J. R. (1998). VR therapy: An effective treatment for the fear of public speaking. *International Journal of Virtual Reality, 3,* 2–7.

Noyes, R., Clancy, J., Hoenk, P. R., & Slymen, D. J. (1980). The prognosis of anxiety neurosis. *Archives of General Psychiatry, 37,* 173–178.

O'Donohue, W. T., & Thorpe, S. (1996). EMDR as marginal science [Review of F. Shapiro, 1995]. *The Scientist Practitioner, 5,* 17–19.

Oppen, P. van, & Arntz, A. (1994). Cognitive therapy for obsessive-compulsive disorder. *Behaviour research and therapy, 32,* 79–87.

Oppen, P. van, & Emmelkamp, P. M. G. (2000). Issues in cognitive treatment of obsessive-compulsive disorder. In W.K. Goodman, M.V. Rudorfer, & J.D. Maser (Eds.), *Obsessive compulsive disorder: Contemporary issues in treatment* (pp. 117–132). Mahwah, NJ: Erlbaum.

Öst, L.-G. (1987). Applied relaxation: Description of a coping technique and review of controlled studies. *Behaviour Research and Therapy, 25,* 397–409.

Öst, L.-G. (1988a). Applied relaxation vs. progressive relaxation in the treatment of panic disorder. *Behaviour Research and Therapy, 25,* 13–22.

Öst, L.-G. (1988b). Applied relaxation: Description of an effective coping technique. *Scandinavian Journal of Behavioural Therapy, 17,* 83–96.

Öst, L.-G. (1989a). A maintenance program for behavioral treatment of anxiety disorders. *Behaviour Research and Therapy, 27,* 123–130.

Öst, L.-G. (1989b).One-session treatment for specific phobias. *Behaviour Research and Therapy, 27,* 1–7.

Öst, L.-G. (1996). Long-term effects of behavior therapy for specific phobia. In M. R. Mavissakalian & R. F. Prien (Eds.), *Long-term treatments of anxiety disorders* (pp. 171–199). Washington, DC: American Psychiatric Press.

Öst, L.-G. (1997). *Manual for the 1-session treatment of specific phobias.* Stockholm: Stockholm University.

Öst, L.-G., Brandberg, M., & Alm, T. (1997). One vs. five sessions of exposure in the treatment of flying phobia. *Behaviour Research and Therapy, 35,* 987–996.

Öst, L.-G. Fellenius, J., & Sterner, U. (1991). Applied tension, exposure in vivo, and tension-only in the treatment of blood phobia. *Behaviour Research and Therapy, 29,* 561–574.

Öst, L.-G., Lindahl, I. L., Sterner, U., & Jerremalm, A. (1984). Exposure in vivo vs. applied relaxation in the treatment of blood phobia. *Behaviour Research and Therapy, 22,* 205–216.

Öst, L.-G., & Sterner, U. (1987). Applied tension: A specific behavioral method for treatment of blood phobia. *Behaviour Research and Therapy, 25,* 25–29.

Öst, L.-G., Westling, B. E., & Hellström, K. (1995). Applied tension, exposure in vivo and cognitive methods in the treatment of panic disorder with agoraphobia. *Behaviour Research and Therapy, 33,* 145–158.

Otto, M. W. (2000). Stories and metaphors in cognitive-behavior therapy. *Cognitive and Behavior Practice, 7,* 166–172.

Otto, M. W., Jones, J. C., Craske, M. G., & Barlow, D. H. (1996). *Stopping anxiety medication: Panic control therapy for benzodiazepine discontinuation* (therapist guide). San Antonio, TX: Psychological Corporation.

Otto, M. W., Pollack, M. H., & Barlow, D. H. (1995). *Stopping anxiety medication: Panic control therapy for benzodiazepine discontinuation* (client workbook). San Antonio, TX: Psychological Corporation.

Overcoming obesity in America. (2004, June 7). *Time*, pp. 57–113.

Panksepp, J. (1992). A critical role for "affective neuroscience" in resolving what is basic about basic emotions. *Psychological Review, 99,* 554–560.

Parker, R., & Brossart, D. F. (2003). Evaluating single-case research data: A comparison of seven statistical methods. *Behavior Therapy, 34,* 189–211.

Parnell, L. (1996). Eye movement desensitization and reprocessing (EMDR) and spiritual unfolding. *Journal of Transpersonal Psychology, 28,* 129–153.

Paterson, R. (1997a). *The changeways core programme trainer's manual.* Vancouver, BC, Canada: Changeways.

Paterson, R. (1997b). *Relaxation programme trainer's manual.* Vancouver, BC, Canada: Changeways.

Patrek, J. (2002). The psychological impact of sexual assault. In J. Patrek & B. Hedge (Eds.), *The trauma of sexual assault: Treatment, prevention, and practice* (pp. 19–43). Chichester, England: John Wiley.

Persons, J. B. (1989). *Cognitive therapy in practice: A case formulation approach.* New York: Norton.

Persons, J. B., & Silberschatz, G. (1998). Are results of randomized controlled trials useful to psychotherapists? *Journal of Consulting and Clinical Psychology, 66,* 126–135.

Petermann, F., & Müller, J. (2001). *Clinical psychology and single-case evidence: A practical approach to treatment, planning and evaluation.* Chichester, England: John Wiley.

Petroski, H. (1992). *To engineer is human: The role of failure in successful design.* New York: St. Martin's Press.

Pitman, R. K., Orr, S. P., Altman, B., Longpre, R. E., Poire, R. E., & Macklin, M. L. (1996). Emotional processing during eye movement desensitization and reprocessing therapy of Vietnam veterans with chronic posttraumatic stress disorder. *Comprehensive Psychiatry, 37,* 419–429.

Pollack, M. H., Otto, M. W., Rosenbaum, J. F., Sachs, G., O'Neil, C., Ascher, R., et al. (1990). Longitudinal course of panic disorder: Findings from the Massachusetts General Hospital naturalistic study. *Journal of Clinical Psychiatry, 51,* 12–16.

Pollard, C. A. (2000). Inpatient treatment of refractory obsessive-compulsive disorder. In W. K. Goodman, M. V. Rudorfer, & J. D. Maser (Eds.), *Obsessive-compulsive disorder: Contemporary issues in treatment,* (pp. 223–231). Mahwah, NJ: Lawrence Erlbaum Associates.

Powers, M. B., Smits, J. A. J., & Telch, M. J. (2004). Disentangling the effects of safety-behavior utilization and safety-behavior availability during exposure-based treatment: A placebo-controlled trial. *Journal of Consulting and Clinical Psychology, 72,* 448–454.

Prochaska, J. O. (2000). Change at differing stages. In R. E. Ingram & C. R. Snyder (Eds.), *Handbook of psychological change: Psychotherapy processes and practices in the 21st century* (pp. 109–127). New York: John Wiley.

Proctor, R. W., & Capaldi, E. J. (2001). Empirical evaluation and justification of methodologies in psychological science. *Psychological Bulletin, 127,* 759–772.

Quality Assurance Project (1982). A treatment outline for agoraphobia. *Australian and New Zealand Journal of Psychiatry, 19,* 25–33.

Rachman, S. (1979). The return of fear. *Behaviour Research and Therapy, 17,* 164–166.

Rachman, S. (1989). The return of fear: Review and prospect. *Clinical Psychology Review, 9,* 147–168.

Rachman S., & Hodgson, G. T. (1980a). *The effects of psychological therapy.* Oxford, England: Pergamon Press.

Rachman S., & Hodgson, G. T. (1980b). *Obsessions and compulsions.* Englewood Cliffs, NJ: Prentice-Hall.

Raue, P. J., Goldfried, M. R., & Barkham, M. (1997). The therapeutic alliance in psychodynamic-interpersonal and cognitive-behavioral therapy. *Journal of Consulting and Clinical Psychology, 65,* 582–587.

Reason, J. (1990). *Human error.* Cambridge, England: Cambridge University Press.

Reich, J. (2000). The relationship of social phobia to avoidant personality disorder. In S. G. Hofmann & P. M. DiBartolo (Eds.), *Social phobia and social anxiety: An integration* (pp. 148–161). Needham Heights, MA: Allyn & Bacon.

Reitzel, L. R., Burns, A. B., Repper, K. K., Wingate, K. K., & Joiner Jr., T. E. (2004). The effects of therapist availability on the frequency of patient-initiated between-session contact. *Professional Psychology: Research and Practice, 35,* 291–296.

Rosen, G. M. (1995). The Aleutian enterprise sinking and posttraumatic stress disorder: Misdiagnosis in clinical and forensic settings. *Professional Psychology: Research and Practice, 26,* 82–87.

Rosen, G. M. (1999). Treatment fidelity and research in eye movement desensitization and reprocessing (EMDR). *Journal of Anxiety Disorders, 13,* 173–184.

Rosen, G. M., & Davison, G. C. (2003). Psychology should list empirically supported principles of change (ESPs) and not credential trademarked therapies or other treatment packages. *Behavior Modification, 27,* 300–312.

Rosqvist, J. (2002). *A current meta-analysis on the treatment of obsessive-compulsive disorder: An updated comparison of cognitive and behavior therapy.* Unpublished doctoral dissertation, Pacific University, Forest Grove, OR.

Rosqvist, J., Egan, D., Manzo, P., Baer, L., Jenike, M., & Willis, B. S. (2001). Home-based behavior therapy for obsessive-compulsive disorder: A case-series with data. *Journal of Anxiety Disorders, 15*, 395–400.

Rosqvist, J., Sundsmo, A., MacLane, C., Cullen, K., & Cartinella, J. (in press). Outside the office walls: Ecological relevance in the treatment of refractory obsessive-compulsive disorder. In F. Columbus (Ed.), *Progress in obsessive compulsive disorder research.* Hauppauge, NY: Nova Science Publishers.

Rosqvist, J., Sundsmo, A., MacLane, C., Cullen, K., Clothier Norling, D., Davies, M., et al. (in press). Analogue and virtual reality assessment. In M. Hersen (Ed.), *Clinical handbook of behavioral assessment (CHOBA), Volume 1: Adult assessment.* New York: Academic Press.

Rosqvist, J., Thomas, J. C., & Egan, D. (2002). Home-based cognitive-behavioral treatment of chronic, refractory obsessive-compulsive disorder can be effective: Single case analysis of four patients. *Behavior Modification, 26,* 205–222.

Rosqvist, J., Thomas, J. C., Egan, D., & Haney, B. J. (2002). Home-based cognitive-behavioral therapy successfully treats severe, chronic, and refractory obsessive-compulsive disorder. *Clinical Case Studies, 1,* 95–121.

Rothbaum, B. O. (1997). A controlled study of eye movement desensitization and reprocessing in the treatment of posttraumatic stress disordered sexual assault victims. *Bulletin of the Menninger Clinic, 61,* 317–334.

Rothbaum, B. O. (2004). Technology and manual-based therapies. *Clinical Psychology: Science and Practice, 11,* 339–341.

Rumelhart, D. E., & McClelland, J. L. (1986). *Parallel distributed processing: Explorations in the microstructure of cognition. Foundations* (Vol. 1.). Cambridge, MA: MIT Press.

Russell, J. A. (1980). A circumplex model of affect. *Journal of Personality and Social Psychology, 39,* 1161–1178.

Russell, J. A., & Mehrabian, A. (1977). Evidence for a three-factor theory of emotions. *Journal of Research in Personality, 11,* 273–294.

Rygh, J. L., & Sanderson, W. C. (2004). *Treating generalized anxiety disorder: Evidence-based strategies, tools, and techniques.* New York: Guilford Press.

Sacco, W. P., & Beck, A. T. (1995). Cognitive theory and therapy. In E. E. Beckham & W. R. Leber (Eds.), *Handbook of depression* (2nd ed.) (pp. 329–351). New York Guilford Press.

Salkovskis, P. M., Richards, C., & Forrester, E. (2000). Psychological treatment of refractory obsessive-compulsive disorder and related problems. In W. K. Goodman, M. V. Rudorfer, & J. D. Maser (Eds.), *Obsessive-compulsive disorder: Contemporary issues in treatment* (pp. 201–221). Mahwah, NJ: Lawrence Erlbaum Associates.

Salter, A. (1949). *Conditioned reflex therapy.* New York: Creative Age.

Sanderson, W. C. (2003). Why empirically supported psychological treatments are important. *Behavior Modification, 27,* 290–299.

Sanderson, W. C., & Carpenter, R. (1992). Eye movement desensitization versus image confrontation: A single-session crossover study of 58 phobic subjects. *Journal of Behavior Therapy and Experimental Psychiatry, 23,* 269–275.

Sanderson, W. C., & Woody, S. (1995). Manuals for empirically validated treatments: A project of the Division of Clinical Psychology, American Psychological Association Task Force on Psychological Interventions. *The Clinical Psychologist, 48,* 7–11.

Schneier, F. R. (1999). Extreme fear, shyness, and social phobia. In L. A. Schmidt & J. Schulkin (Eds.), *Extreme fear, shyness, and social phobia: Origins, biological mechanisms, and clinical outcomes* (pp. 273–293). New York: Oxford University Press.

Shapiro, D. A. (1995). Finding out how psychotherapies help people change. *Psychotherapy Research, 5,* 1–21.

Shapiro, F. (1995). *Eye movement desensitization and reprocessing: Basic principles, protocols, and procedures.* New York: Guilford.

Shapiro, F. (1998). *From the desk of Francine Shapiro.* (Available from the Eye Movement Desensitization and Reprocessing International Association, P.O. Box 141925, Austin, TX 78714-1925).

Silverman, W. H. (1996). Cookbooks, manuals, and paint-by-numbers: Psychotherapy in the 90s. *Psychotherapy, 33,* 207–215.

Silverman, W. K., & Albano, A. M. (1996). *Anxiety disorders interview schedule for children.* San Antonio, TX: Psychological Corporation.

Silverstein, C., & Picano, F. (1992). *The new joy of gay sex.* New York: Harper Collins.

Skinner, B. F. (1963). Selection by consequence. *Science, 7,* 477–481.

Sloan, T., & Telch, M. J. (2002). The effects of safety-seeking behavior and guided threat reappraisal on fear reduction during exposure: An experimental investigation. *Behaviour Research and Therapy, 40,* 235–251.

Smith, E. W. L. (1995). A passionate, rational response to the "manualization" of psychotherapy. *Psychotherapy Bulletin, 30,* 36–40.

Spitzer, R. L., & Fleiss, J. L. (1974). A re-analysis of the reliability of psychiatric diagnosis. *British Journal of Psychiatry, 125,* 341–347.

Stampfl, T. G., & Levis, D. J. (1967). Essentials of implosive therapy. *Journal of Abnormal Psychology, 72,* 496–503.

Stanley, M. A., Borden, J. W., Bell, G. E., & Wagner, A. L. (1994). Nonclinical hair-pulling: Phenomenology and related psychopathology. *Journal of Anxiety Disorders, 8,* 119–130.

Stanley, M. A., & Mouton, S. G. (1996). Trichotillomania treatment manual. In V. B. Van Hasselt & M. Hersen (Eds.), *Sourcebook of psychological treatment manuals for adult disorders* (pp. 657–687). New York: Plenum Press.

Stanley, M. A., Swann, A. C., Bowers, T. C., Davis, M. L., & Taylor, D. J. (1992). A comparison of clinical features in trichotillomania and obsessive-compulsive disorder. *Behaviour Research and Therapy, 30,* 39–44.

Steketee, G. S. (1993). *Treatment of obsessive compulsive disorder.* New York: Guilford Press.

Steketee, G., Frost, R. O., & Kyrios, M. (2003). Beliefs about possessions among compulsive hoarders. *Cognitive Therapy and Research, 27,* 463–479.

Steketee, G., Frost, R. O., Wincze, J., Greene, K., & Douglass, H. (2000). Group and individual treatment of compulsive hoarding: A pilot study. *Behavioural and Cognitive Psychotherapy, 28,* 259–268.

Steketee, G., & Tynes L. L. (1991). Behavioral treatment of obsessive-compulsive disorder. In M. T. Pato & J. Zohar (Eds.), *Current treatments of obsessive compulsive disorder* (pp. 61–86). Washington, DC: American Psychiatric Press.

Steketee, G. S., & Pruyn, N. A. (1998). Families of individuals with obsessive-compulsive disorder. In R. P. Swinson, M. M. Antony, S. Rachman, & M. A. Richter (Eds.), *Obsessive-compulsive disorder: Theory, research, and treatment* (pp. 120–140). New York: Guilford Press.

Stricker, G., & Trierweiler, S. J. (1995). The local clinical scientist: A bridge between science and practice. *American Psychologist, 50,* 995–1002.

Sturmey, P. (1996). *Functional analysis in clinical psychology.* Chichester, England: John Wiley.

Suinn, R. M. (1990). *Anxiety management training: A behavior therapy.* New York: Plenum Press.

Summerfeldt, L. J., & Antony, M. M. (2002). Structured and semistructured diagnostic interviews. In M. M. Antony & D. H. Barlow (Eds.), *Handbook of assessment and treatment planning for psychological disorders* (pp. 3–37). New York: Guilford Press.

Swedo, S. E., & Leonard, H. L. (1992). Trichotillomania: An obsessive-compulsive spectrum disorder? *Psychiatric Clinics of North America, 15,* 777–790.

Swendsen, J. D., Merikangas, K. R., Canino, G. J., Rubio-Stipec, M., & Angst, J. (1998). The comorbidity of alcoholism with anxiety and depressive disorders in four geographic communities. *Comprehensive Psychiatry, 39,* 176–184.

Task Force on Promotion and Dissemination of Psychological Procedures (1993). Training in and dissemination of empirically-validated psychological treatments. *The Clinical Psychologist, 48,* 3–23.

Taylor, S. (2000). *Understanding and treating panic disorder: Cognitive-behavioural approaches.* Chichester, England: John Wiley.

Taylor, S., & Asmundson, G. J. G. (2004). *Treating health anxiety: A cognitive-behavioral approach.* New York: Guilford Press.

Tharp, R. G., & Wetzel, R. J. (1969). *Behavior modification in the natural environment.* New York: Academic Press.

Tomkins, M. A. (1999). Using a case formulation to manage treatment nonresponse. *Journal of Cognitive Psychotherapy, 13,* 317–330.

Tryon, W. W. (1999). A bi-directional associate memory explanation of post-traumatic stress disorder. *Clinical Psychology Review, 19,* 789–818.

Tryon, W. W. (2000). Behavior therapy as applied learning theory. *The Behavior Therapist, 23,* 131–134.

Tryon, W. W. (2002). Neural networks learning theory: Unifying radical behaviorism and cognitive neuroscience. *The Behavior Therapist, 25,* 53–57.

Tryon, W. W. (2005). Possible mechanisms for why desensitization and exposure therapy work. *Clinical Psychology Review, 25,* 67–95.

Turkat, I. (1985). *Behavioral case formulation.* New York: Plenum Press.

U.S. Environmental Protection Agency (n.d.). Retrieved April 10, 2005, from http://www.erg.com/portfolio/elearn/ecorisk/html/resource/glossary.html

Veale, D. (2002). Overvalued ideas: A conceptual analysis. *Behaviour Research and Therapy, 40,* 383–400.

Wade, W. A., Treat, T. A., & Stuart, G. L. (1998). Transporting an empirically supported treatment for panic disorder to a service clinic setting: A benchmarking strategy. *Journal of Consulting and Clinical Psychology, 66,* 231–239.

Wadström, O. (1998). *Tvångssyndrom: Orsaker och behandling i beteendeterapeutiskt Perspektiv* [Obsessive-compulsive disorder: Causes and treatment in a behavior therapy perspective.]. Linköping: Psykologinsats.

Warren, R. (1995). Panic control treatment of panic disorder with agoraphobia and comorbid major depression: A private practice case. *Journal of Cognitive Psychotherapy: An International Quarterly, 9,* 123–134.

Warren, R., & Thomas, J. C. (2003). Research in private practice. In J. C. Thomas and M. Hersen (Eds.), *Understanding research in clinical and counseling psychology* (pp. 379–396). Mahwah, NJ: Erlbaum.

Warren, R., Zgourides, G., & Jones, A. (1989). Cognitive bias and irrational belief as predictors of avoidance. *Behaviour Research and Therapy, 27,* 181–188.

Weerasekera, P. (1996). *Multiperspective case formulation: A step towards treatment integration.* Malabar, FL: Krieger Publishing.

Weissman, M. M., Klerman, G. L., Markowitz, J. S., & Ouellette, R. (1989). Suicidal ideation and suicide attempts in panic disorder and attacks. *New England Journal of Medicine, 321,* 1209–1214.

Wells, A. (1997). *Cognitive therapy of anxiety disorders: A practice manual and conceptual guide.* Chichester, England: John Wiley & Sons.

Wells, A. (2004). Foreword. In S. Taylor & G. J. G. Asmundson, *Treating health anxiety: A cognitive-behavioral approach* (pp. ix–xi). New York: Guilford Press.

Wells, A., & Carter, K. (1999). Preliminary tests of a cognitive model of generalized anxiety disorder. *Behaviour Research and Therapy, 37,* 585–594.

Wells, A., Clark, D. M., Salkovskis, P., Ludgate, J., Hackmann, A., & Gelder, M. G. (1995). Social phobia: The role of in-situation safety behaviors in maintaining anxiety and negative beliefs. *Behavior Therapy, 26,* 153–161.

Westra, H. A., & Phoenix, E. (2003). Motivational enhancement therapy in two cases of anxiety disorders: New responses to treatment refractoriness. *Clinical Case Studies, 2,* 306–322.

Widiger, T. A. (2001). Social anxiety, social phobia, and avoidant personality disorder. In W. R. Crozier & L. E. Alden (Eds.), *International handbook of social anxiety: Concepts, research and interventions related to the self and shyness* (pp. 335–356). Chichester, England: John Wiley.

Wiederhold, B. K., Gevirtz, R. N., & Spira, J. L. (2001). Virtual reality exposure therapy vs. imagery desensitization therapy in the treatment of flying phobia. In G. Riva & C. Galimberti (Eds.), *Towards cyberpsychology: Mind, cognitions and society in the internet age* (pp. 253–272). Amsterdam: IOS Press.

Wiederhold, B. K., & Wiederhold, M. D. (1999). Clinical observations during virtual reality therapy for specific phobia. *Cyberpsychology and Behavior: The Impact of the Internet, Multimedia and Virtual Reality on Behavior and Society, 2,* 161–168.

Willis, B. S. (1994). Delivery systems for the in-home treatment of obsessive-compulsive disorder. *OCD Newsletter, 8,* 3–4.

Willis, B. S., Rosqvist, J., Egan, D., & Baney, D. (1998). Inpatient and home-based treatment of OCD. In M. A. Jenike, L. Baer, & W. E. Minichiello (Eds.), *Obsessive-compulsive disorder: Practical management* (3rd ed.) (pp. 570–591). Boston: Mosby Year Book.

Wilson, E. O. (1998). *Consilience: The unity of knowledge.* New York: Knopf.

Wilson, G. T. (1996). Manual-based treatments: Clinical application of research findings. *Behaviour Research and Therapy, 34,* 295–314.

Wilson, G. T. (1998). Manual-based treatment and clinical practice. *Clinical Psychology: Science and Practice, 5*, 363–375.

Wilson, K. A., & Chambless, D. L. (1999). Inflated perceptions of responsibility and obsessive-compulsive symptoms. *Behaviour Research and Therapy, 37*, 325–335.

Wilson, S. A., Becker, L. A., & Tinker, R. H. (1995). Eye movement desensitization and reprocessing (EMDR) treatment for psychologically traumatized individuals. *Journal of Consulting and Clinical Psychology, 63*, 928–937.

Wolfe, B. E., & Maser, J. D. (Eds.). (1994). *Treatment for panic disorder: A consensus statement.* Washington, DC: American Psychiatric Association Press.

Wolpe, J. (1958). *Psychotherapy by reciprocal inhibition.* Stanford, CA: Stanford University Press.

Wolpe, J. (1961). The systematic desensitization treatment of neuroses. *Journal of Nervous and Mental Disease, 132*, 189–203.

Woody, S. R., Detweiler-Bedell, J., Teachman, B. A., & O'Hearn, T. (2003). *Treatment planning in psychotherapy: Taking the guesswork out of clinical care.* New York: Guilford Press.

Woody, S. R., & Sanderson, W. C. (1998). Manuals for empirically supported treatments: 1998 update from the task force on psychological interventions. *The Clinical Psychologist, 51*, 17–21.

Yerkes, R. M., & Dodson, J. D. (1908). The relation of strength of stimulus rapidity of habit formation. *Journal of Comparative and Neurological Psychology, 18*, 459–482.

Yonkers, K. A., Warshaw, M. G., Massion, A. O., & Keller, M. B. (1996). Phenomenology and course of generalized anxiety disorder. *British Journal of Psychiatry, 168*, 308–313.

Zayfert, C., Becker, C. B., & Gillock, K. L. (2002). Managing obstacles to the utilization of exposure therapy with PTSD patients. In L. Van de Creek (Ed.), *Innovations in clinical practice: A source book* (Vol. 20) (pp. 201–222). Sarasota, FL: Professional Resources Press.

Zuercher-White, E. (1997). *Treating panic disorder and agoraphobia: A step by step clinical guide.* Oakland, CA: New Harbinger Press.

Zuercher-White, E. (1999a). *Overcoming panic disorder and agoraphobia: A cognitive restructuring and exposure-based protocol for the treatment of panic and agoraphobia (therapist protocol).* Oakland, CA: New Harbinger Press.

Zuercher-White, E. (1999b). *Overcoming panic disorder and agoraphobia: A cognitive restructuring and exposure-based protocol for the treatment of panic and agoraphobia (client manual).* Oakland, CA: New Harbinger Press.

Index

learning within, 51
long-term maintenance of gains
    made in, 185
low treatment credibility of, 187
parody in Professor Gallagher
    cartoons, 183–184
paucity of training programs for,
    191
practitioner fear of using, 196
reputation of, 179–182, 187
role of fear hierarchy in, 47
severity of, 47
themes of resistance to, 187–195
Exposure and response prevention
    (ERP), 75
autonomous therapy in, 15, 17
efficacy of, 28
as fire shelter, 38
OCD case study, 14–15, 18–19
Exposure methods
attack on escape and avoidance
    behaviors in, xiii
direct access through, 38
four factors influencing
    effectiveness of, 46–47
habituation and extinction in, 42
importance of understanding
    mechanisms of, xii
initial symptom worsening with, 180
Exposure treatment
controversy over, 179
defined, 27–28
dropout rates, 75–76
efficacy of, xii
empirical basis with anxiety
    disorders, 81–85
expected recovery curve for, 181
future directions and
    recommendations for,
    195–197
hedonism as obstacle to, 182–186
importance of sensual engagement
    in, 57–58
poor reputation of, xiv
professional and public
    perceptions of, 179–182

reducing anxiety responses
    through, 40–41
research bases for, xiii
research-practice gap in, 186–195
scientific explanations for efficacy
    of, 49–53
single-session, 74–75
for specific phobias, 115
Exposure types, 53
artificial settings, 75–79
disaster scripts, 59–61
and ecological relevance, 75–79
flooding, 73–74
hierarchical, 73–74
in vivo, 53–57
in-imagination, 57–58
interoceptive, 66–68
loop-tape, 59–61
naturalistic settings, 66–68
partner-assisted, 68–73
script examples, 62–66
self-directed, 68–73
single-session treatment, 74–75
therapist-directed, 68–73
virtual reality, 57–58
Extinction, xiii, 74
dependence on habituation, 46,
    54–55, 71, 114
ending inaccurate anxiety
    responses through, 41–49
interference by overvalued
    ideation, 159
learning theories and early
    regressive patterns, 181
re-emergence of anxiety and fear
    after, 172
Eye movement desensitization and
    reprocessing (EMDR)
    therapy, lack of evidence-
    based support for, 90–94

F
Fading treatment, 169–170
Failure analysis, 166–167, 193, 194
Fainting reactions, 35–36, 55
Falsifiable approaches, 96
Family accommodation, 71